OECD Skills Studies

Strengthening the Governance of Skills Systems

LESSONS FROM SIX OECD COUNTRIES

OECD
BETTER POLICIES FOR BETTER LIVES

Please cite this publication as:
OECD (2020), *Strengthening the Governance of Skills Systems: Lessons from Six OECD Countries*, OECD Skills Studies, OECD Publishing, Paris, *https://doi.org/10.1787/3a4bb6ea-en*.

ISBN 978-92-64-93734-5 (print)
ISBN 978-92-64-75180-4 (pdf)

OECD Skills Studies
ISSN 2307-8723 (print)
ISSN 2307-8731 (online)

Photo credits: Cover © Studio Foltzer, Shutterstock.com/Lightspring

Corrigenda to publications may be found on line at: *www.oecd.org/about/publishing/corrigenda.htm*.

Foreword

The governance of skills systems is complex and poses many challenges for governments. Located at the intersection of education, labour market, industrial and other policies, skills policies require the co-ordinated involvement and commitment of governments, employers, trade unions, workers, teachers, students and others to be successful.

The complexity of governance arrangements of skills systems is likely to continue. Megatrends such as globalisation, technological progress and demographic change are putting pressure on skills systems to ensure that all members of society are equipped with the skills necessary to thrive in an interconnected world. This is taking place in the context of a general decentralisation trend among governments, which has the potential to further increase the number of actors involved.

Strengthening the governance of skills systems, developing relevant skills over the life course and using skills effectively in work and society were the three broad components of the updated *OECD Skills Strategy 2019*. The strategy identified four main challenges to strengthening the governance dimension of skills systems: 1) promoting co-ordination, co-operation and collaboration across the whole of government; 2) engaging with stakeholders throughout the policy cycle; 3) building integrated information systems; and 4) aligning and co-ordinating financing arrangements.

This report, *Strengthening the Governance of Skills Systems: Lessons from Six OECD Countries*, presents concrete examples of how governments with different welfare state and labour market regimes, as well as different political institutions and cultures, have addressed one or several of these challenges. It details six case studies in selected OECD countries: Estonia, Germany, Korea, Norway, Portugal, and the United States, each focusing on a particular policy or sector within the domestic skills system. Based on the evidence, the report presents a number of general policy recommendations for strengthening the governance of skills systems, together with a practical self-assessment tool for policy makers and stakeholders.

Collecting and sharing evidence of the different ways in which governments have approached the challenges of governing their skills systems holds potential for further improvement and collaborative peer learning. The OECD will continue to work with countries to design, develop and deliver better skills policies for better lives in a rapidly changing world.

Acknowledgements

The preparation of this report was led by the OECD Centre for Skills (SKC) in collaboration with a team of primary authors.

- Chapter 1 - Introduction and theoretical framework, Chapter 3 - Case study: The Alliance for Initial and Further Training in Germany and Chapter 8 - Conclusion and general policy recommendations were written by Marius R. Busemeyer, Professor of Political Science and a Speaker of the Excellence Cluster "The Politics of Inequality" at the University of Konstanz in Germany. His work centres on the comparative political economy of education and training in OECD countries, the role of public opinion in education reforms and the politics of inequality.
- Chapter 2 - Case study: The Estonian Education Information System (EHIS) and Chapter 4 - Case study: Lifelong learning in Korea were written by Gina Di Maio, Junior Researcher at the International Research Cluster "Governance in Vocational and Professional Education and Training" (GOVPET). She is based at the University of St. Gallen in Switzerland. Her research focuses on further training and the institutionalisation of social equality and economic efficiency in training.
- Chapter 6 - Case study: Portugal's National Agency for Qualification and Vocational Education and Training (ANQEP) and Chapter 7 - Case study: Massachusetts' (United States) Early Warning Indicator System (EWIS) were written by Lina Seitzl. She is a Junior Researcher at the Political Science Department of the University of St. Gallen. She works at the International Research Cluster "GOVPET". Her work focuses on employer co-ordination in education systems and the effect of digitisation on skills demands.
- Chapter 5 - Case study: Norway's Skills Policy Council and Future Skills Needs Committee was written by Daniel Unterweger, Junior Researcher at the International Research Cluster "GOVPET". He is based at the University of St. Gallen in Switzerland. His current research projects examine the integration of multinational companies and the role of the state in dual vocational and education training (VET).

Andrew Bell, Ricardo Espinoza, Ben Game and Sam Kim (SKC) shaped the research design and scope, and provided guidance and comments to the research team. Laura Reznikova (SKC) contributed analysis, drafting, and editing and co-ordinated the production process. Cuauhtémoc Rebolledo-Gómez (International Service for Remunerations and Pensions) and Serli Abrahamoglu (SKC) provided statistical support. Written contributions and comments were provided by Najung Kim, Dami Seo and Sunhwa Kim (SKC). Andrew Bell (SKC) provided analytical guidance and supervision.

Montserrat Gomendio, Head of the OECD Centre for Skills (SKC), supervised the project and provided comments, while Stefano Scarpetta (Director for Employment, Labour and Social Affairs, OECD) (ELS) and Mark Pearson (Deputy Director for Employment, Labour and Social Affairs, OECD) provided strategic oversight and comments.

Véronique Quénehen and Jennifer Cannon (SKC), Lauren Thwaites (Public Governance) and Lucy Hulett (ELS) provided invaluable support for mission organisation, report layout and design, and publication planning. Elizabeth Zachary provided proofreading and editorial support. Bohyun Kim supported missions to Korea by providing ad hoc interpretation and translation into Korean.

The OECD is grateful to the Directorate-General for Employment, Social Affairs and Inclusion and the Directorate-General for Education and Culture of the European Commission for contributing both financial support and expertise throughout the project. We are especially grateful to Alison Crabb, Head of Unit, Skills and Qualifications, Directorate-General for Employment, Social Affairs and Inclusion and Michael Horgan, Policy Officer, Skills and Qualifications, Directorate-General for Employment, Social Affairs and Inclusion.

Many government representatives and stakeholders from all the countries included in the report generously shared their insights and provided comments. Our warm thanks go to, in alphabetical order: Jonas Frister from the Federal Ministry of Education and Research (Germany), Sven Rahner from the Federal Ministry of Labour and Social Affairs (Germany) as well as Thomass Sondermann and Ute von Oertzen Becker from the Ministry for Economic Affairs and Energy (Germany). We are equally grateful to Jaak Anton and Tatjana Kiilo from the Ministry of Education and Research (Estonia). We also wish to thank Pedro Abrantes from the Ministry of Education (Portugal) as well as Alexandra Teixeira and Ana Cláudia Valente from the National Agency for Qualification and Vocational Education and Training - ANQEP (Portugal). Our many thanks also go to Siv Hilde Lindstrøm from the Permanent Delegation of Norway to the OECD and Annette Skalde from the Ministry of Education and Research (Norway). We would also like to thank Yoon-Jo Lee and Jae Young Chang from the Gyeonggi Do Provincial Institute for Lifelong Learning and Tae Hee Kim from Suwon City (Korea). We are equally grateful to Jennifer Appleyard, Nyal Fuentes and Kathryn Sandel from the Massachusetts Department of Elementary and Secondary Education (United States).

Participants at the Expert Workshop on the Governance of Skills Systems, held on 5-6 April 2018 in Paris, France, also provided valuable insights integral to the development of the report. These participants were: Jonathan Barr (OECD Centre for Entrepreneurship, SMEs, Regions and Cities), Bert Brys (OECD Centre for Tax Policy and Administration), Claire Charbit (OECD Centre for Entrepreneurship, SMEs, Regions and Cities), Donata Cutuli (Fondimpresa, Italy), Emma Duchini (University of Warwick, United Kingdom), Alessia Forti (OECD Directorate for Employment, Labour and Social Affairs), Michael Horgan (Directorate General for Employment, Social Affairs and Inclusion, European Commission), Florina Koester (OECD Directorate for Education and Skills), Marco Leonardi (University of Milan, Italy), Fabio Manca (OECD Centre for Skills), Luca Marcolin (OECD Directorate for Employment, Labour and Social Affairs), Elvio Mauri (Fondimpresa, Italy), Marco Mira D'Ercole (OECD Statistics and Data Directorate), Konstantinos Pouliakas (European Centre for the Development of Vocational Training), Marinus Rouw (OECD Directorate for Education and Skills), Micheline Scheys (National Union of Socialist Health Insurance and Promotion Services), Mariagrazia Squicciarini (OECD Directorate for Science, Technology and Innovation), Siria Taurelli (European Training Foundation), Sergio Urzua (University of Maryland, United States) and Bryan Wilson (Workforce Data Quality Campaign, United States).

Table of contents

FIGURES

TABLES

Abbreviations and acronyms

The main abbreviations and acronyms used in the report are listed below.

AIR	American Institutes for Research
ANQ	National Agency for Qualification (Agência Nacional para a Qualificação),
ANQEP	National Agency of Qualification and Vocational Education and Training (Agência Nacional para a Qualificação e o Ensino Profissional)
BA	Federal Employment Agency (Bundesagentur für Arbeit)
BBiG	Federal Law for Vocational Education and Training (Berufsbildungsgesetzes)
BDA	Federal Association of German Employers' Associations (Bundesvereinigung der Deutschen Arbeitgeberverbände)
BDI	Federal Association of German Industry (Bundesverband der Deutschen Industrie)
BfB	Federal Association of Free Vocations (Bundesverband Freier Berufe)
BIBB	Federal Institute for Vocational Education and Training (Bundesinstitut für Berufsbildung)
BMAS	Federal Ministry for Labour and Social Affairs (Bundesministerium für Arbeit und Soziales)
BMBF	Federal Ministry for Education and Research (Bundesministerium für Bildung und Forschung)
BMWi	Federal Ministry for Economic Affairs and Energy (Bundesministerium für Wirtschaft und Energie)
CDU	Christian Democratic Union (Christlich Demokratische Union Deutschlands)
CSU	Christian Social Union in Bavaria (Christlich-Soziale Union in Bayern)
Cedefop	European Centre for the Development of Vocational Training
CMEs	Co-ordinated market economies
CNQ	National Catalogue of Qualifications (Catálogo Nacional de Qualificações)
DEEC	Department of Early Education and Care
DESE	Department of Elementary and Secondary Education
DGB	German Trade Union Confederation (Deutscher Gewerkschaftsbund)
DIHK	Association of German Chambers of Commerce and Industry (Deutscher Industrie- und Handelskammertag)
ECTS	European Credit Transfer and Accumulation System
ECVET	European Credit System for Vocational Education and Training
EHIS	Estonian Education Information System (Eesti hariduse infosüsteem)
EIS	Examination Information System (Eksamite infosüsteem)
ELA	English Language Arts
EQ	Preparatory traineeship (Einstiegsqualifizierung)
ESSA	Every Student Succeeds Act
ETIS	Estonian Research Portal
EWII	Early Warning Indicator Index
EWIS	Early Warning Indicator System
FDP	Free Democratic Party (Freie Demokratische Partei)
GILL	Gyeonggi Provincial Institute for Lifelong Learning (경기도평생교육진흥원)
GNLC	Global Network of Learning Cities
HITSA	Information Technology Foundation for Education (Hariduse Infotehnoloogia Sihtasutus)

HRD	Human Resource Development Service of Korea (한국산업인력공단)
HRK	Conference of University Rectors (Hochschulrektorenkonferenz)
HwO	Trade and Crafts Code (Handwerksordnung)
IAB	Institute for Employment Research (Institut für Arbeitsmarkt und Berufsforschung)
ICT	Information and communications technology
IEFP	Institute for Employment and Vocational Training (Instituto do Emprego e Formação Profissional)
IG	Industrial Union (Industriegewerkschaft)
KEDI	Korean Educational Development Institute (한국교육개발원)
KLI	Korean Labour Institute (한국노동연구원)
KMK	Standing Conference of the Ministers of Education and Cultural Affairs of the Länder (Kultusministerkonferenz)
KORCHAM	Korean Chamber of Commerce (대한상공회의소)
KRIVET	Korean Research Institute for Vocational Education and Training (한국직업능력개발원)
KSQA	Korean Skills Quality Authority (직업심사능력평가원)
LMEs	Liberal Market Economies
LO	Norwegian Confederation of Trade Unions (Landsorganisasjonen i Norge)
MASCA	Massachusetts School Counsellors Association
MCAS	Massachusetts Comprehensive Assessment System
MERA	Massachusetts Education Reform Act
NAEP	National Assessment of Educational Progress
NAV	Norwegian Labour and Welfare Administration (Nye arbeids- og velferdsetaten)
NCLB	No Child Left Behind Act
NEET	Not in Education, Employment or Training
NGO	Non-governmental organisation
NHO	Confederation of Norwegian Enterprises (Norwegian Næringslivets Hovedorganisasjon)
NILE	National Institute for Lifelong Education (국가평생교육진흥원)
NPM	New public management
ÕIS	Study Information System (Õppeinfosüsteem)
PIAAC	Programme for the International Assessment of Adult Competences
PISA	Programme for International Student Assessment
POCH	Human Capital Operational Programme (Programa Operacional Capital Humano)
POISE	Operational Programme for Social Inclusion and Employment (Programa Operacional Inclusão Social e Emprego)
QNQ	National Qualifications Framework (Quadro Nacional de Qualificações)
RTK	State Support Service Center (Riigi Tugiteenuste Keskus)
SAIS	Admission Information System (SisseAstumise InfoSüsteem)
SANQ	Qualification Needs Anticipation System (Sistema de Antecipação de Necessidades de Qualificações)
SCS	Student course schedule
SER	Socio-Economic Council
SIMS	Student Information Management System
SLDS	Statewide Longitudinal Data Systems
SNQ	National Qualifications System (Sistema Nacional de Qualificações)
SPD	Social Democratic Party (Sozialdemokratische Partei Deutschlands)
SSDR	School Safety Discipline Report
TBU	Norwegian Technical Calculation Committee for Wage Settlements (Teknisk beregningsutvalg for inntektsoppgjørene)
UNIO	Confederation of Unions for Professionals (Utdanningsgruppenes Hovedorganisasjon)
VET	Vocational education and training
Virke	Enterprise Federation of Norway
VoC	Varieties of capitalism

VOFO	Norwegian Association for Adult Learning (Voksenopplæringsforbundet)
VOX	Norwegian Agency for Lifelong Learning (Nasjonalt senter for læring i arbeidslivet)
YS	Confederation of Vocational Unions (Yrkesorganisasjonenes Sentralforbund)
ZDH	Central Association of the German Confederation of Skilled Crafts (Zentralverband des Deutschen Handwerks)

Executive summary

Building on the *OECD Skills Strategy 2019*, this report provides a comprehensive analysis of how the governance of skills systems can be strengthened. Broadly speaking, it finds that successful skills strategies depend on the continued collaboration between ministerial departments, agencies, non-governmental stakeholders and local actors across different levels of government. More specifically, it identifies four challenges that need to be met in order to strengthen skills systems:

- Promote co-ordination, co-operation and collaboration across the whole of government.
- Engage with stakeholders throughout the policy cycle.
- Build integrated information systems.
- Align and co-ordinate financing arrangements.

The bulk of the report is devoted to a series of case studies that showcase how different countries have responded to these challenges by promoting innovative solutions and new approaches in the governance of skills policies. Each case study focuses on a particular example of innovation rather than the skills system of the country as a whole. The cases are selected as representatives of different welfare state regimes and political economy models across the OECD.

Overview of chapters

Chapter 1. Introduction and theoretical framework introduces the overall framework of the report, focusing on the four main challenges identified above. It also provides some background on the selection process of the case studies.

Chapter 2. Case Study: The Estonian Education Information System (EHIS) studies EHIS as an example of building integrated information systems. EHIS combines data on student achievement with information on teachers and school contexts. The data can be connected to information on labour market outcomes, allowing a fine-grained analysis of educational and employment trajectories.

Chapter 3. Case Study: The Alliance for Initial and Further Training in Germany highlights the benefits and challenges of policy co-ordination according to a “whole-of-government approach”. The Alliance for Initial and Further Training in its current form was established in 2014 and brings together a broad range of stakeholders such as ministerial departments, employer associations, trade unions and representatives of subnational (*Länder*) governments.

Chapter 4. Case Study: Lifelong learning in Korea introduces the local governance structure of lifelong learning in the Korean city of Suwon. The chapter documents how multiple stakeholders contribute and are involved in this system and how it is embedded in a multi-level governance structure of lifelong learning institutions that stretch to the provincial and national levels.

Chapter 5. Case Study: Norway's Skills Policy Council and Future Skills Needs Committee demonstrates how in the Norwegian case, the Skills Policy Council, supported by the Future Skills Needs Committee, helps the government to develop a comprehensive skills strategy that builds on research of current skills needs. The Skills Policy Council shows how stakeholder involvement can be combined with building integrated information systems.

Chapter 6. Case Study: Portugal's National Agency for Qualification and Vocational Education and Training (ANQEP) highlights successful institutional innovation against the background of significant fiscal constraints following the economic and fiscal crisis. Representing another example of stakeholder involvement, Portugal's National Agency of Qualification and Vocational Education and Training brings together actors from different governmental ministries and non-governmental stakeholders. This case study reveals the importance of aligning and co-ordinating financing arrangements in a context of continued austerity.

Chapter 7. Case Study: Massachusetts' (United States) Early Warning Indicator System (EWIS) complements the Estonian case study as a further example of how integrated information systems can be built up in the domain of educational governance. EWIS provides teachers, administrators and stakeholders with immediate feedback about potential students at risk of failing, allowing for swift remedial action.

Chapter 8. Conclusion and general policy recommendations provides a short summary of the main insights from the report, as well as general policy recommendations.

Overall recommendations

Reflecting on the insights from the individual case studies, the concluding section provides a number of general policy recommendations for strengthening the governance of skills systems. More specifically, policy makers are advised to:

- Establish co-ordinating committees with a meaningful mandate and clear internal governance structures in order to avoid overlap between the competing mandates of committees and agencies.
- Promote the involvement and commitment of non-governmental stakeholders, but pay attention to the risk of undue influence of special interests. This will require careful and balanced decision making about which stakeholders to involve in joint decisions, and about how to build trust among the actors involved.
- Support the establishment of information management systems, but ensure that they provide usable and relevant information to stakeholders and policy makers. This is more likely when stakeholders are allowed to provide input into the design of systems, and when systems rely on multiple sources of data, both quantitative and qualitative.
- Invest and commit the diversified resources needed to strengthen skills policies in order to avoid underfunding newly established institutions and governance structures. Tap into multiple sources of public and private funding if available.

These recommendations are transformed into a practical self-assessment tool that allows policy makers and stakeholders to evaluate the overall potential of their country and strengthen the governance of its skills policy regime.

1 Introduction and theoretical framework

Strengthening the governance of skills system is a central policy challenge across many OECD countries. This introductory chapter develops an analytical framework that informs the following case studies of skills policy in Estonia, Germany, Korea, Norway, Portugal and the United States. The framework identifies four main challenges in governing skills systems: promoting co-ordination, co-operation and collaboration across the whole of government; engaging with stakeholders throughout the policy cycle; building integrated information systems; and aligning and co-ordinating financing arrangements. The chapter discusses each of these challenges in greater detail. It also includes a short discussion of the methodological approach of this study, in particular the reasoning behind selecting cases for this study and the conduct of semi-structured interviews with experts and stakeholders in the country cases.

Background and motivation

The governance of skills systems is complex. On the one hand, the development of skills and their effective use in labour markets follows the logic of the "life course", where individuals acquire and make use of skills as they move through the different stages of their educational and employment careers. On the other hand, each of these different stages may be governed by different rules and regulations. Therefore, the governance of skills policy does not necessarily follow the life-course logic, and remains fragmented across different levels of government, as well as different public ministries and agencies.

This report tackles the fundamental challenge of strengthening and improving the governance of skills systems. Issues related to the development and effective use of skills remain at the forefront of debates about the transformation of industrial economies to post-industrial knowledge economies. Investing in skills and ensuring access to different forms of learning is crucial to prevent the social exclusion of disadvantaged students, learners and workers, as well as to effectively mobilise existing skills in the economy.

For the purposes of this report, a skills system can be broadly defined as covering all institutions and individuals, as well as policies, laws and regulations, concerned with the development and use of skills in the economy. Therefore, skills policies are at the intersection between various sectors of the education system, including early childhood education and care (ECEC); schools; vocational education and training (VET); adult learning and higher education; labour market policies, especially those that aim to make use of existing skills such as active labour market and training policies; policies that support the adoption of high performance workplace practices; and certain immigration policies.

The core challenge in governing complex skills systems is that policy-making responsibilities for the various policies are usually widely distributed across levels of government, as well as ministries and public agencies. Furthermore, there is often little active co-ordination between these institutions, which hampers the effectiveness of strategies to mobilise the use of skills. The guiding question of this report is therefore: as OECD countries transform into post-industrial knowledge economies, how can the governance of skills systems be strengthened and improved in order to promote the development and effective use of skills?

This question is related to and motivated by the *OECD Skills Strategy 2019* (OECD, 2019[1]). The skills strategy framework has three dimensions: 1) developing relevant skills over the life course; 2) using skills effectively in work and society; and 3) strengthening the governance of skills systems. While this report focuses on the third of these dimensions, it also contributes and refers to the other two key dimensions as they are inherently related. The first dimension centres on lifelong learning, for example by promoting policies that make lifelong learning visible, rewarding, affordable, accessible and relevant. The second dimension focuses on the use of skills in the economy, for instance via policies that reduce skill imbalances, stimulate the demand for high-level skills, expand the pool of available talent, or promote social and labour market participation.

Strengthening the governance dimension of these and related policies raises four main challenges:

1. Promoting co-ordination, co-operation and collaboration across the whole of government.
2. Engaging stakeholders throughout the policy cycle.
3. Building integrated information systems.
4. Aligning and co-ordinating financing arrangements.

The goal of this report is to derive concrete policy recommendations about how governments can tackle these challenges. It presents findings from six case studies in selected OECD countries: Estonia (Chapter 2), Germany (Chapter 3), Korea (Chapter 4), Norway (Chapter 5), Portugal (Chapter 6) and the United States (Chapter 7). These countries are selected to cover a broad range of cases with different welfare state and labour market regimes, as well as different political institutions and cultures. Each case study focuses on a particular policy or sector in the country's skills system, the study of which holds important lessons for other countries.

It is important to emphasise that country case studies are not simply highlighting "best-practice" examples, since there is rarely a case which performs "best" on all dimensions under consideration. Rather, each case study contributes insights regarding how policy makers have responded to one or (usually) several of the four challenges mentioned above. In the final chapter of the report, these different insights are integrated into a comprehensive set of policy recommendations on how to strengthen the governance of skills systems in a broad range of cases. The different policy recommendations are subsequently translated into a practical self-assessment tool for policy makers and stakeholders (see Annex A). Based on a number of "yes/no" questions, the tool allows all interested parties to assess the strength of their own country's arrangements for governing skills policies.

In developing policy recommendations, either for a particular country or for a larger set of cases, it is important to recognise both the idiosyncratic characteristics of the case as well as more broadly held characteristics that are – under certain conditions – generalizable to a larger set of cases. At times, policy reports veer between the two extremes of arguing that "every country is different" or implying that "one size fits all". This report aims to tread a middle ground between these two extremes by devising policy recommendations that are applicable and relevant for more than one country case, but at the same time identifying the conditions under which these recommendations can be transferred to other cases.

Adopting an "institutionalist" perspective is helpful in this regard. This perspective argues that countries can be classified and grouped into different kinds of institutional regimes, for example welfare state regimes (Esping-Andersen, 1990[2]), varieties of capitalism (VoC) (Hall and Soskice, 2001[3]) or – more relevant for this report – skill formation regimes (Busemeyer and Trampusch, 2012[4]). Institutional regimes are (more or less) coherent configurations of institutions covering different spheres of the economy that incentivise and shape the behaviour of actors in a particular system or country. Hence, rather than devising recommendations for individual countries, this report aims to identify governance practices that can be transferable to a larger set of cases, although not necessarily all cases in the OECD.

The remainder of this introductory chapter is structured as follows: the next section provides additional background on the four main challenges; this is followed by a description of how the cases were selected; and finally there are remarks on methodological aspects.

Core challenges in the governance of skills systems

Policy makers are confronted with a range of issues regarding skills policies that can be considered under four main challenges: 1) promoting co-ordination, co-operation and collaboration across the whole of government; 2) engaging with stakeholders throughout the policy cycle; 3) building integrated information systems; and 4) aligning and co-ordinating financing arrangements. The following section discusses each of the four challenges in greater detail. Corresponding policy recommendations on how to deal with these challenges are presented in the final chapter of this report, following the case studies.

Promoting co-ordination, co-operation and collaboration across the whole of government

Legal competencies and decision-making powers in skills policy are often widely distributed in both the vertical and horizontal dimensions of policy making. The vertical dimension concerns different levels of government, from local governments to regional and other subnational governments to the federal level. OECD countries differ widely regarding how exactly competencies are distributed along the vertical dimension, but broadly speaking, centralised countries, such as France or Japan, can be distinguished from decentralised countries, which delegate significant decision-making powers to lower levels of government. Among decentralised countries, there is a further distinction between countries with a formally federalist constitution (e.g. Australia, Belgium, Canada, Germany and the United States) and those without (e.g. the Netherlands, Scandinavian countries and the United Kingdom). In both groups, the involvement of the national government in skills policies is more limited than in purely centralised systems. However, among countries with systems that are formally unitary, but de facto decentralised, local governments and authorities may have a considerably higher degree of autonomy than in formally federalist countries, in which decision-making powers are often concentrated at the intermediate level of subnational governments (such as Canadian provinces, or German *Länder*).

Regarding the horizontal dimension of co-ordination, skills policies often require collaboration between different governmental departments. According to the conventional division of labour, education ministries and agencies are in charge of policies related to skills development, whereas labour market ministries and agencies are more concerned with policies that maximise the effective use of these policies by promoting further training opportunities and labour market activation measures. Ministries of economy and/or industry may also play a key role in skills policy by developing and promoting policies and strategies for regional, sectoral or general economic development, in which skills often occupy a central place. Ministries of finance are responsible for ensuring that policy and governance decisions are backed up with the required financial resources, and for aligning financial incentives to maximise the effectiveness of skills policies.

This seemingly neat division of labour, however, underestimates the real-world complexities of educational and employment careers, which are increasingly characterised by intermittent employment and non-linear trajectories, and where the movement between phases of skill development and usage becomes a permanent condition rather than a one-time event in the early stages of the life course. Disregarding these complexities risks promoting the social exclusion of disadvantaged workers and learners who fall between the gaps at the transitory edges of the various subsystems.

The dimension of horizontal co-ordination stretches beyond the scope of government In a narrow sense as the two dimensions of promoting co-ordination across the whole of government and stakeholder involvement are strongly connected. Societal stakeholders such as trade unions, employers' associations, individual businesses and workers, as well as training providers, research institutes and non-profit organisations, are all deeply involved and engaged in the governance of skills systems. In OECD countries, decisions on the allocation of labour are ultimately market decisions, in which employer's demand for certain types of labour is somehow matched by the supply of workers with particular skills. The role of government policy in this area is to set and further develop the regulatory framework that ensures an effective match between skills demand and supply, while also preventing the emergence of market failures, such as the systematic exclusion of disadvantaged groups and individuals. Where exactly to draw the line between government regulation and market autonomy, and how to balance the potentially competing interests of actors involved, is a matter of political decision and political majorities. For the purpose of this report, it is important to acknowledge that societal stakeholders are regularly involved in governance decisions and therefore need to be taken into account in efforts to improve the co-ordination of decision-making processes in skills policy (there is more on the issue of stakeholder involvement in the next section).

In addressing the issue of co-ordination and collaboration along the vertical and horizontal dimensions, this report subscribes to the whole-of-government approach (Christensen and Laegreid, 2007[5]; UNESCO and ILO, 2018[6]). This approach is based on the idea that the adoption of administrative practices according to the new public management (NPM) model, which has been influential in many OECD countries and beyond, contributes to fragmentation in the development and implementation of policies. This is because the NPM approach recommends the adoption of market-oriented steering modes to the world of public administration, which promotes competition rather than collaboration between actors and institutions. The whole-of-government approach, instead, adopts a holistic perspective that aims to maximise the payoffs of collaborative decision making, while maintaining the autonomy of the actors involved. As observed by Christensen and Laegreid (2007[5]): "WG [whole-of-government] activities may span any or all levels of government and involve groups outside government. It is about joining up at the top, but also about joining up at the base, enhancing local level integration, and involving public-private partnerships."

Thus, in an ideal setting, the whole-of-government approach amounts to a collective and well-co-ordinated policy response to pressing problems. In a more realistic setting, the implementation of policies according to the whole-of-government model alone is challenging. Given the multitude of actors with different interests, achieving a consensus between a broad range of stakeholders within and outside government is difficult, maybe impossible if distributive conflicts ("who gets what from whom?") are dominant. Furthermore, implementing the whole-of-government approach requires actors to adopt a certain kind of "interaction orientation" (Scharpf, 1997[7]), i.e. they would need to participate in collective decision making with a motivation to contribute to joint problem solving rather than particularistic bargaining. This kind of interaction orientation needs to be present in most, if not all actors in the system, as there is a danger that even actors motivated by problem solving may resort to particularistic bargaining if they realise that others are doing so. Finally, there is a danger that the whole-of-government approach may deteriorate into some form of centralised super-bureaucracy, in which the autonomy of stakeholders outside of government are compromised. Hence, the involvement of non-governmental stakeholders in governance decisions is crucial (see next section for more on this point).

The broader challenge of policy co-ordination along the horizontal and vertical dimensions can be summarised in three main challenges:

1. **Putting skills policies at the top of the government agenda:** Maximising the potential of skills policies to contribute to economic well-being and social inclusion implies that these policies have to be put at (or close to) the top of the government's policy-making agenda. As legal competencies and decision-making powers are distributed across levels of government and governmental departments (see above), prioritising skills policies is more challenging compared to other policies, since there is no single agency or actor that is fully responsible – besides the government as a whole. Skills policies therefore compete with a multitude of other policy priorities for the top spot in the government agenda. Some of these competing policies may be better placed to occupy the central place in the government agenda as they promise concrete benefits to policy makers (and their voters) in the present, whereas skills policies often require policy makers to adopt a long-term oriented perspective. Furthermore, even though policies that support skills investment are broadly popular among citizens, they are still often politically contested and debated (Busemeyer et al., 2018[8]). Citizens (and political parties representing their interests) may disagree regarding the relative distribution of fiscal resources across different policy areas, or on the relative emphasis to be put on concerns related to social inclusion or economic growth. Furthermore, citizens may, and often do, disagree regarding the design of skills policies, for instance, the role of the state versus private providers. For policy makers, the challenge is to integrate these competing interests into a coherent whole that can serve as a guiding model for policy reforms, while keeping skills policy at the top of the agenda.

2. **Identifying and engaging with relevant stakeholders:** As argued above, adopting a whole-of-government approach entails the notion of pursuing collaborative partnerships between state and non-state actors. A first challenge to overcome in this regard is to identify who the relevant stakeholders actually are. Depending on the complexity and size of a particular skills system, policy makers at the central level may simply not be aware of the multitude of non-state actors involved in governance decisions at different levels of government. Related to this is how to distinguish between relevant and non-relevant actors and stakeholders, even when all of them are known. There are clearly strong incentives for non-state actors to get involved in governmental decision making; at the same time, not all of those who could potentially be involved should necessarily be involved, not least because some might pursue a particularistic or idiosyncratic agenda. Ideally, governmental actors should have at their disposal a general rule, recognised as legitimate and effective by those concerned, that helps them to distinguish between relevant and non-relevant actors. Ultimately, decisions about which stakeholders to involve and how strongly depends on the prevailing political context. Once stakeholders are properly identified, governmental actors still need to find ways to effectively engage and communicate with them, which will be discussed in greater detail in the next section. The central challenge for stakeholder engagement with the whole-of-government approach is how to create commitment among stakeholders to adopt a joint orientation towards problem solving, rather than particularistic bargaining, and to follow and take seriously a strategic agenda at the same time.
3. **Encouraging co-ordination between central and subnational authorities:** Achieving collaboration and co-ordination across levels of government (vertical dimension of co-ordination) is at least as challenging as engaging with non-state stakeholders (horizontal dimension of co-ordination). Compared with other policy areas, subnational governments usually have more competencies and decision-making powers in skills policies, which makes subnational governments particularly sensitive regarding efforts to re-balance or challenge the existing division of labour between central and lower levels of government. Furthermore, depending on the country context, competencies for different parts of the skills system are distributed unevenly across levels of government. For instance, labour market or lifelong learning policies are often in the hands of central ministries or agencies as they are directly related to national labour markets, whereas responsibility for the provision and financing of education, in particular schooling but also higher education, is delegated to subnational governments. In some cases, local governments are strongly involved in education and labour market policies, whereas in others, these responsibilities are divided between local authorities and local representatives of national agencies. To sum up, the distribution of governance competencies across levels of government is likely to vary significantly across different parts of the skills system, which is a challenge, and debates about re-organising the co-ordination between central and subnational authorities are likely to accompany political conflicts about the proper division of labour.

Engaging stakeholders throughout the policy cycle

Engaging with non-state stakeholders can be an effective instrument to support policy makers in dealing with the inherent complexities of skills policies. However, the process of engagement needs to be well-balanced and grounded in sound strategy to avoid the involvement of a multitude of stakeholders contributing to, rather than mitigating, further complexity.

There are various benefits of stakeholder engagement from the perspective of policy makers. First, stakeholders contribute valuable information to the policy-making process that is difficult for policy makers to access themselves. For instance, non-state stakeholders have experience regarding the real-world effects of policies and regulations, which might be quite different from the steering effects that governmental policy makers initially intended. This is also because non-state stakeholders have a certain leeway to influence the implementation of policies themselves. Information from non-state stakeholders is a valuable resource as it provides governmental decision makers with a sense of "what works and what doesn't".

Informational input is particularly helpful for the implementation phase of policies, but also during the phase of policy formulation and design. The notion of the "policy cycle", which is commonly used as a point of reference in policy studies, implies that there is a constant feedback process between the phases of policy implementation and (re-)design as policies are revised according to implementation experiences and, ideally, based on input from research. Implementation experiences from stakeholders are therefore a valuable input into governmental decision making not only during the implementation phase, when governments try to improve the implementation of existing policies, but also during the policy design phase, when they attempt to design "better" policies for the next loop of the policy cycle.

The second benefit to stakeholder engagement is that the involvement of non-state stakeholders generates political legitimacy, which can itself be an important resource during the implementation phase. In order to be fully accepted and supported by those concerned, governance decisions should ideally be based on a broad consensus between involved actors. This will increase the likelihood that policy decisions will be implemented according to the initial intentions of decision makers, and thus improve the overall effectiveness of the decision-making process.

However, this ideal setting depends on a number of preconditions, some of which may be difficult to achieve. If the issue in question does not have significant distributional implications (i.e. if it is not immediately related to the distribution or redistribution of resources), and if stakeholders in principle share similar goals, then consensus among stakeholders is easier to achieve. Furthermore, the quality of decisions taken is more likely to surpass the low threshold of "least common denominator policies" if different stakeholders contribute their particular informational inputs to jointly solving a commonly perceived problem. In contrast, if the policy issue under debate is related to distributional conflicts and if the actors involved do not share similar goals, the decision-making process is likely to be more contentious. This can lead to either gridlock, when no decisions are taken, or low-quality decisions ("lowest common denominator") where contentious, but probably important issues are systematically excluded from the agenda.

To some extent, government decision makers can mitigate some of these problems. For instance, they can attempt to promote a shared understanding of the underlying problems and goals of policy making. They could also make available additional resources to lessen distributional conflicts, i.e. to transform them from re-distributional conflicts ("who gets what from whom?") into merely distributional conflicts ("who gets what from the central government's budget?"), but these efforts have inherent limitations. Thus, a first precondition for stakeholder engagement to work is that the policy issue under debate is not too contentious and burdened with distributional implications.

A second important precondition is that actors involved in governance decisions adopt a constructive interaction orientation (Scharpf, 1997[7]) that values joint problem solving rather than particularistic bargaining and "strategising". Independent of the nature of the issue under debate (see previous point), actors involved in the process of decision making need to be open to joint efforts of problem solving and not regard their involvement in the process as merely another opportunity to extract resources from the central government or other stakeholders. To some extent actors always weigh the costs and benefits of involvement based on their individual assessment, and joint problem-solving actions need to create some tangible pay-offs for the actors involved in order to be sustainable and legitimate in the long run. However, joint problem solving only works if the actors involved at least partly adopt a problem-solving interaction orientation. Otherwise, stakeholder engagement boils down to "pork barrel politics"[1] in the worst case, which would eventually undermine the overall legitimacy of engagement with non-state stakeholders. Joint problem solving also implies that involved stakeholders need to share a certain understanding about the distribution of authority and decision-making powers within the group, in particular, which actors have the capacity and legitimacy to set the overall strategy.

A third precondition for stakeholder involvement to create political legitimacy is that stakeholders represent the diversity of positions within society, rather than particular segments, in order to prevent the "capture" of decision-making processes by special interests. This may be the most challenging precondition to be met as it is directly connected to the contested role of the state (or government) in mediating, channelling and influencing the distribution of power and influence across societal stakeholders and interest groups. As a consequence, there are widely different practices and philosophies across countries, which need to be taken into account when developing concrete policy recommendations.

It is possible to distinguish between a "pluralist" and a "corporatist" perspective regarding the legitimacy of stakeholder involvement and the role of the state (Lehmbruch, 1979[9]; Schmitter, 1979[10]; Streeck and Schmitter, 1985[11]). According to the pluralist view, the diversity of interests in society is best represented by associations and when the state refrains from intervening in the free competition of associations for members and influence. Similar to the notion of free competition in the marketplace, competition between associations and interest groups will eventually ensure that the prevailing groups are those that enjoy the largest degree of support and legitimacy among citizens. The pluralist view implies a more distant "at arms' length" relationship between the state and interest groups in order to prevent the state from tilting the scales in favour one particular group. Pluralist practices of stakeholder engagement are commonly applied in the "liberal" welfare states, market economies and skills formation regimes of Anglo-Saxon countries.

Critics of the pluralist view say that the supposedly free competition between interest groups leads to power asymmetries and inequalities, as some types of interest are easier to mobilise and organise than others (Olson, 1965[12]; Offe and Wiesenthal, 1980[13]). Olson's theory of collective action, for instance, highlights the fact that the broad, diffuse interests that often go along with collective concerns are more difficult to organise and mobilise than particularistic "special interests". Thus, in the worst case, the supposedly free competition of interests and interest groups may lead to the dominance of special interests as they have more resources at their disposal than interest groups representing diffuse interests and the "common good".

Corporatist practices of interest mediation try to mitigate and neutralise real or perceived imbalances of power between stakeholders by setting up decision-making bodies that put representatives of opposing interests on a level playing field that is to some extent independent of the previous real distribution of power and influence. The most common forms of corporatist decision making concern the involvement of business associations and trade unions, as these represent opposing interests in the arguably most important political cleavage in OECD countries – the conflict between business and labour interests. In countries where corporatist practices of stakeholder involvement have a long tradition, such as Austria, Belgium, Germany, the Netherlands, Scandinavian countries, Switzerland and – to a lesser extent – Southern European countries, unions and employers are regularly involved in policy decisions through established decision-making bodies, such as the Socio-Economic Council (SER) in the Netherlands or the Federal Institute for Vocational Education and Training (BIBB) in Germany.

An important advantage of corporatist decision making is that stakeholder involvement throughout the different stages of the policy cycle enhances the commitment of non-state actors to joint decisions, which facilitates the implementation of policy decisions later on. Furthermore, government actors can draw on the expertise and informational input of non-state actors during the policy design stage. However, compared to pluralism there is a higher risk that the continued involvement of the same stakeholders through the same decision-making bodies could lead to the emergence of an "insider-outsider cleavage", where newly emerging interests have a harder time accessing decision making than established stakeholders. Furthermore, corporatist decision making does not fully prevent the risk of capture of governmental decision making by special interests. On the one hand, state actors are more likely to reach out to groups that tend to be under-represented in a free competition of interests (e.g. consumer or environmental groups) due to their lack of resources in corporatist settings, but on the other hand, these kinds of groups may become particularly dependent on state support for their survival, which affects their strategic positioning.

A final precondition that needs to be fulfilled in order to mobilise the potential of stakeholder engagement to create political legitimacy is that the involvement of non-state actors has to be meaningful and consequential, and not merely "window dressing". This requires a genuine willingness on the part of policy makers to share decision-making powers, which ultimately depends on a certain degree of trust between non-state and governmental actors. Policy makers need to trust non-state actors to consider collective concerns rather than pursuing particularistic goals single-mindedly, and non-state actors need to trust the government to take their input seriously before they commit significant resources to getting involved in governance decisions.

Meaningful engagement with stakeholders is more likely when they have a formally pre-defined role in governance decisions and decision-making bodies. For instance, the government could make the passing of a particular policy reform conditional on stakeholders achieving consensus. In contrast, meaningful engagement is less likely, and commensurate claims are less credible, when stakeholder involvement happens in a more ad hoc and informal manner, such as when stakeholders are merely invited to provide input at a particular point in time during the policy process (e.g. by submitting opinions via a website or issuing position papers), but are not involved in a continuous manner throughout the whole process. In this sense, pluralist practices may be more susceptible to superficial stakeholder engagement than corporatist practices. If the goal is to maximise the number of stakeholders involved, the multitude of opinions voiced may become so large that governmental actors retain the ultimate decision-making powers. In corporatist settings, the number of actors may be smaller and limited to the most "relevant" actors, but the influence of these actors on decision making is likely to be larger, which contributes to a more significant involvement of non-state actors.

Meaningful stakeholder involvement throughout the policy cycle can be summarised in four key challenges:

1. **Building stakeholders' trust:** Building mutual trust between governmental and societal actors is crucial to ensure meaningful stakeholder involvement. Lack of trust is often a significant obstacle to expanding the role of stakeholders in governance decisions, particularly in countries without a long tradition of social partnership and stakeholder involvement through corporatist decision-making bodies. On the one hand, government actors need to develop trust in the capacity and willingness of stakeholders to contribute constructively to joint decision making rather than maximising their own self-interests. On the other hand, stakeholders need to trust governmental actors that their input is meaningful and valued in decision making. Both sides need to actively contribute to overcoming this mutual lack of trust. Trust building can and should be supported by efforts to design the process of stakeholder involvement in particular ways. For instance, stakeholder engagement should be meaningful and continuous rather than superficial and fleeting. Meaningful engagement is more likely when stakeholders are involved through pre-defined and at least partly formalised channels and bodies rather than in an ad hoc manner. Furthermore, governmental actors in charge of the overall process should be attentive to the overall balance of interests involved in the project in order to prevent the emergence of stark power asymmetries or the systematic exclusion of particular groups from the process. These efforts also increase the overall legitimacy of the engagement process.
2. **Engaging stakeholders takes time:** There are several reasons for stakeholder engagement taking a significant amount of time. First, the initial step of stakeholder engagement is to identify all relevant (as well as potentially non-relevant) actors. Depending on the size and complexity of the skills system, this may take a significant amount of time. Furthermore, the process of separating "relevant" from "non-relevant" actors could be politically contentious and therefore, also time consuming. Mapping skills systems in terms of relevant actors and institutions before a particular process of stakeholder involvement begins is helpful to save time. Second, building trust also takes

time, but is crucial to ensure the long-term sustainability and effectiveness of the governance system. Building trust is based on repeated interactions between the actors involved and cannot be created quickly. Third, the process of stakeholder involvement often goes along with the presumption that resulting decisions are based on a broad consensus between the actors involved. Organising and achieving such a consensus takes time if the underlying issues are contentious and involve distributional conflicts. Furthermore, some actors may use and abuse the process of stakeholder involvement to pressure others into supporting their particularistic goals, as consensus-oriented decision-making grants significant "hold-up" power to individual actors. In order to deal with this particular challenge, governmental actors need to retain some degree of unilateral decision-making power, which they can activate in the case of gridlock. Scharpf (1997[7]) introduced the term "shadow of hierarchy" to describe this situation. Governments need to find a way to stay responsive to demands from a general public that may demand immediate action in response to salient problems, at the same time as allowing meaningful stakeholder engagement to develop and unfold over a longer period of time.

3. **Resourcing adequately:** Meaningful stakeholder involvement depends on the availability of sufficient and adequate resources. Providing these resources is challenging for policy makers. Besides the general scarcity of fiscal resources, a particular challenge in this regard is that providing fiscal support to non-state actors may be perceived as privileging special interests in the general public. Nevertheless, it is crucial in order to achieve meaningful stakeholder engagement. Resources need to be made available to bodies and institutions in charge of organising the process of stakeholder involvement if they are formally established as independent entities. Providing adequate resources to advisory bodies of this kind puts stakeholder involvement on a more secure, long-term foundation, and could also be invested in research capacities so that non-state actors have access to information and knowledge acquired independently of governmental bodies and agencies. Expanding the research capacities of independent advisory bodies that involve stakeholders would also support the creation of mutual trust and a joint problem-solving orientation among stakeholders as they can refer to a common, yet government-independent, source of information. Providing adequate resources for stakeholder engagement could also involve supporting the organisation and mobilisation of stakeholders themselves, in particular groups that represent diffuse rather than special interests and that therefore find it more difficult to mobilise resources. Providing direct support for stakeholders and groups should be contingent on these actors meeting certain requirements, such as democratic procedures in electing key personnel.

4. **Resolving conflicts of interest:** The notion of stakeholder involvement usually goes along with the idea that governance decisions made in co-operation with stakeholders are based on a broad consensus shared by all actors involved in the process. However, in real-world settings, there are issues relating to conflicts about (re-)distribution, underlying values or power relations. If the nature of the issue under discussion falls into the latter category, the outcome of consensus-oriented processes involving a larger number of stakeholders may be unsatisfactory, amounting to "lowest common denominator" rather than encompassing policy solutions. If decision making requires the agreement of all involved then each individual actor has veto power, which means that significant departures from the status quo are less likely, particularly if some actors would have to accept losses. Hence, taking up the challenge of meaningful stakeholder involvement not only requires governments to be able to organise consensus-oriented solutions, but also to have at their disposal strategies for conflict resolution. Providing a sound evidence base to policy deliberations is one potential instrument in this regard, as it promotes interaction orientations among actors that are geared towards joint problem solving rather than particularistic bargaining and ideological in-fighting.

Building integrated information systems

Making good governance decisions depends on the availability of high-quality data and information. In recent decades, the OECD and other organisations have made available a range of data sources on educational attainment, adult skills and labour market outcomes. This wealth of data has triggered and made possible a wave of new research on the determinants of learning and employment trajectories, transition processes, social exclusion and inclusion, the influence of socio-economic background on educational performance, and many other issues of relevance for the governance of skills systems. Before data of this kind became available, political debates about skills policies were often strongly driven by ideological conflicts, with limited input from neutral and objective data sources. Political-ideological conflict is an inherent component of any political decision-making process, as actors subscribe to different values and represent different sectors of society with different material interests. However, before the rise of evidence-based policy making, ideological conflicts were also more likely to materialise in the form of differing opinions on the causal relationship between two (or more) variables.

For instance, before data became widely available, some might have argued that parental background obviously strongly shapes the educational attainment of children, whereas others might have questioned the strength of this association. As data on educational attainment and parental background became available, it became possible to determine (more or less) exactly the strength of the association between parental background and educational attainment. Individuals subscribing to different ideologies might still disagree about the policy responses that should be taken in response to this fact (i.e. more or less state involvement, more or less tracking in schools, etc.), but at least ideological debates are provided with a layer of objective knowledge that can help to defuse ideological conflicts to some extent (see previous section).

The real world of policy making is still far from an ideal governance model in which decisions are based on and informed by input from high-quality data and information management systems; however, improving the informational foundations of governance decisions could significantly contribute to strengthening and improving these decisions.

Building integrated information systems can be summarised in three concrete challenges:

1. **The multiplicity of data sources:** Existing data sources on skills outcomes and policies are often fragmented, covering only parts of the skills system. In decentralised systems, data collection may also be fragmented across levels of government, as individual regions or municipalities collect their own data that may not be immediately comparable to data from other regions. Furthermore, most large-scale assessments at the international or national level are only available in the form of cross-sectional data rather than longitudinal or panel data, which makes it difficult to trace learning and employment paths over time. Of particular importance are the transition points between different sectors of the skills system, i.e. from secondary to post-secondary education or from education to employment. Hence, a comprehensive approach to building integrated information systems could aim to generate data on how individuals proceed through the various stages of their education and employment careers, from primary to secondary and higher education to employment. This implies the importance not only of information about skills and educational outcomes, but also skills assessment and anticipation exercises, labour market conditions, and learning opportunities. Collecting data of this magnitude would likely trigger serious concerns about data protection and usage among the general public, which need to be taken seriously when developing these systems. Information systems will only be accepted and used when there is a commensurate "user culture" in a particular country context. Furthermore, quantitative data from surveys and assessments should be complemented with qualitative data from other sources such as self-assessments from educators and the outcomes of school review processes.
2. **The multiplicity of end users:** Once established, skills, learning and labour market information systems will be used by a multiplicity of users such as parents, teachers, students, researchers,

policy makers and stakeholders. Different users will pose different demands to the design of information systems. Parents and students may value accessibility and transparency, whereas researchers would put stronger emphasis on data quality and availability. Policy makers and stakeholders involved in governance decisions will likely require data to be provided in a way that makes it immediately relevant for governance decisions. Regional and local governments will expect information systems to provide data for their particular zone of influence. This multitude of users and demands poses a significant challenge to policy makers when establishing and fine-tuning information management systems. If information systems are perceived as not creating sufficient user value (while being expensive), it is unlikely that enough public support can be created for their establishment and continued maintenance.

3. **Management of complexities:** The management of large-scale information systems poses significant challenges. On the technical side, information systems need to be able to deal with the multiplicity of data sources and potentially huge amounts of data. This requires significant resources for infrastructural investments and maintenance, as well as special attention to privacy concerns among the general public related to data storage. The size of information system varies with the size of the population of a particular country. Estonia, with a population of 1.3 million, has been a pioneer in setting up a comprehensive education information system (see case study below), but scaling up these efforts to populations the size of Germany (83 million inhabitants) or even the United States (328 million inhabitants) seems challenging, if not impossible. However, if regional solutions have to be sought for larger countries, the ensuing challenge is how to harmonise them across regions. On the political side, the use value of information systems for policy making depends on their contribution to solving concrete governance problems. Hence, the output from information systems needs to be systematically connected as input to decision-making processes in the governance of skills systems. However, establishing such a connection creates new challenges as actors adopt their strategies and priorities in order to reflect the system's parameters ("teaching to the test"), which creates negative and/or unintended side effects. Establishing information systems that rely on a multitude of data sources, including both quantitative and qualitative data, might mitigate these unintended side effects, but will also increase the complexity of information management systems.

Aligning and co-ordinating financing arrangements

Decisions about the governance of skills systems (or any other policy field) are inherently linked to questions about financing. Decisions such as the expansion or retrenchment of programmes and personnel, the building up of infrastructure such as complex information management systems, or the (re-)design of the policy-making process by involving stakeholders require or affect decisions about the allocation, distribution and re-distribution of fiscal resources. Although some government policy decisions are mainly regulatory in nature, there will often be fiscal implications.

As briefly mentioned above, the central role of skills and skills policies in the socio-economic transformation of industrial to post-industrial knowledge economies is widely recognised in OECD countries. Furthermore, plans to increase investments in education and training generally receive popular support among citizens and voters (Busemeyer et al., 2018[8]). At the same time, political calls to invest in skills and skill development are constantly at risk of being superseded by more pressing and short-term oriented demands.

This is partly due to the fact that although educational investments in schools and universities may create short-term benefits for parents, students, teachers and professors, the bulk of the pay-off in terms of economic growth, employment opportunities and social inclusion will only materialise at some distant point in the future when the current beneficiaries of educational investments are in the labour market. Therefore, other more pressing concerns such as fighting unemployment, increasing pensions or expanding healthcare with clear and immediate pay-offs in the present are likely to outdo long-term concerns for investment (Streeck and Mertens, 2011[14]). Governments keen on promoting skills policies therefore must find ways to ensure a sufficient level of investment in education and skills, while also taking seriously the short-term concerns of citizens and voters.

Investments in skills may also lose out to other policy areas in terms of fiscal resources because the benefits of education and skills are shared between a multitude of stakeholders, and the incentives for investing in skills are often not well-aligned between these stakeholders. Educational investments create significant public benefits such as a well-educated citizenry that participates actively in political and societal life, which boosts employment and wage growth. At the same time, educational investments generate significant private benefits for those at the receiving end of these benefits, primarily in the form of higher wages and better employment prospects. It is very difficult to identify exactly how public and private benefits for a given amount of educational investments are distributed. The predominant incentive structure, however, is not geared at maximising the total sum of investments in education, but rather the opposite. From the private perspective, the financing contribution of the public side should be as large as possible in order to minimise individual costs, whereas from the public perspective, which is often under pressure to constrain growth in expenditure, there is significant interest in increasing the financing contribution of private actors, such as through fees or taxes, and in reducing overall costs.

The distribution of financing responsibilities across levels of government also needs to be considered. This is particularly important in formally federalist countries, but also in formally unitary, but de facto decentralised, systems. There are many examples where financing responsibilities and incentive structures are not well-aligned. For instance, when the legal competencies for raising taxes and other sources of revenue mainly lie in the hands of the central government, but the administration and implementation of policies is left to lower levels of government (as in Germany, for example), the central government does not have strong incentives to maximise potentially available fiscal resources. Furthermore, if lower levels of government do not have to worry about raising revenue, they might overspend or misallocate resources to politically salient sectors of the skills system.

Incentive structures in the private sector can also be misaligned, for example, individuals could underinvest in skills development if education aspirations compete with short-term pressing needs. This is particularly important in the case of adult learning, which remains a relatively weakly institutionalised sector of skills systems in many OECD countries. In this case, governmental policies, such as statutory rights for lifelong learning, the provision of education credits or vouchers, counselling, and the set-up of a supporting infrastructure, can help to partly shift the underlying incentives to maximise the potential of skills policies. Individual incentives can also be misaligned when individual educational choices constituting the supply of skills on the labour market do not match the needs of labour market actors (the demand side). Philosophies vary across different countries on how to deal with the problem of skills (mis-)match, for example by tying educational choices to market forces through high tuition fees, or by adjusting the number of available study places to the skills needs of the economy. Each of these has advantages and disadvantages that need to be carefully balanced and interpreted in light of country-specific political contexts.

Incentives to invest in skills may also be misaligned in the case of business actors. As Becker (1993[15]) already highlighted in his human capital theory, business actors have strong incentives to invest in the development of specific skills among their workers that have immediate pay-offs in terms of productivity, but little incentive to invest in broader, more general, transferable and multi-faceted (Streeck, 1996[16]) skills that may have the greatest overall benefit on employment and growth, as labour market demands are constantly adapting to a changing environment. Hence, government policies need to make sure that business actors overcome short-term urges to invest in specific skills by devising policies that reward or push actors into providing more general, widely usable skills.

In countries with a strong collective skills policy regime (Busemeyer and Trampusch, 2012[4]), these incentives are provided in the form of collective wage bargaining arrangements, corporatist decision-making bodies that include different and multiple stakeholders in decision making, and a regulatory policy environment that prevents (for better or worse) the fast turnover of workers in the short term. Liberal skill regimes rely on market forces to nudge employers into investing in skills, but some, such as the United Kingdom and Ireland, have experimented recently with levy-grant schemes in the domain of vocational training. These schemes can be an effective instrument to align the incentives of business actors with the needs of skills development: Firms pay a certain levy, depending on the size of their payroll, into a joint fund. The created revenue is then used to finance training measures in individual firms. This way, training firms can offset their levy payments with training subsidies received, which sets strong incentives to offer and participate in training.

The main challenges in the domain of fiscal incentives and resources can be summarised as follows:

1. **Diversifying sources of funding:** The payoffs of skills investments are distributed between the public, individuals (households) and businesses. Therefore, there is a case to be made that each of these three sectors should contribute to the financing of skills investment. However, countries are likely to differ regarding how exactly the fiscal burden should be shared, depending on political conditions, historical developments and culture. Hence, re-shifting the boundary in the financing of skills policies between public and private actors is likely to be contentious as it is associated with redistributive conflicts. Nevertheless, a certain diversification of funding sources could help maximise the potential of skills policies to impact future growth and employment, and avoid or at least mitigate misaligned incentive structures. For instance, levy-grant schemes can spur employers to invest more in skill development, whereas education credits and vouchers can help individuals avoid underinvestment in education.
2. **Finding appropriate resource allocation and budgeting mechanisms:** Besides raising and securing the required funds for skills investment, a significant challenge remains in how to distribute and allocate available fiscal resources in an efficient and fair manner across different levels of government and sectors of the skills system. The core issue is to avoid incentive structures that decrease the amount of resources available overall, and support incentive structures that maximise the amount of available resources. A first priority in this regard is to avoid financial arrangements where responsibilities for raising revenues and for spending are located at different levels of government, which is likely to lead to either under or overinvestment. A second priority is to tie fiscal strategies in the domain of skills policies to long-term goals and multi-year planning processes of the government, which should decrease the likelihood that investment priorities and goals fall prey to short-term urges and pressures. Finally, a third priority is to make sure that the use of financial resources is clearly tied to accountability mechanisms and some form of performance measurement. This helps both the effectiveness (do investments have the desired effect?) and efficiency (how much needs to be spent to achieve a particular goal?) of spending, which in turn improves the evidence base for decisions regarding the prioritisation of policy programmes and instruments.
3. **Ensuring equity in funding considerations:** Policy makers are increasingly concerned about equity-related aspects in the distribution of funding. Research has found that educational investments can contribute to mitigating inequality in the long term (Busemeyer, 2015[17]; Huber and Stephens, 2014[18]; Solga, 2014[19]). However, the contribution of skills policies to lowering inequality depends on an equitable distribution of educational resources in the first place to ensure equal chances of opportunity and low barriers of access. If left to market forces alone, decisions about the allocation of fiscal resources to different actors and sectors of the skills system may aggravate rather than mitigate inequalities, as well-performing regions or sectors usually have more resources at their disposal. Policy makers are therefore confronted with the challenge of allocating resources in a way that helps weak performers to improve, while also rewarding strong sectors and regions to maintain their incentives to perform well. Addressing this challenge can be supported by a clear and widely communicated strategy of how to balance equity with other

concerns. The exact balance between these different concerns likely depends on the political context.

4. **Providing adequate resources:** Previous work by the OECD in the context of the Skills Strategy projects has often revealed a certain imbalance between policy responsibilities and resource allocation. If policy making or implementation responsibilities are delegated from the central to the subnational level, or from government actors to semi-public or private agencies and institutions, decision makers need to make sure that the provided resources match these responsibilities. For instance, if agencies are tasked with involving stakeholders or with conducting research they need to have resources at their disposal that allow for engagement with stakeholders and researchers to be meaningful. Furthermore, the matching of resources to responsibilities needs to be undertaken in a way that enables incentive structures that support the formation of joint problem-solving perspectives, rather than encouraging particularistic bargaining. The former is more likely if public-private partnerships and stakeholder involvement are based on mutual trust rather than overly detailed and onerous accountability mechanisms.

Methodological approach

Based on the theoretical framework introduced later on in this chapter, this report provides a series of case studies from Estonia, Germany, Korea, Norway, Portugal and the United States. It is important to emphasise that the case studies do not aim to describe these countries in their entirety, but instead focus on the particular policy reforms, issues or sectors of the skills system likely to be most relevant from an international comparative perspective as they highlight successful examples of innovation in skills policies. At the same time, the country case studies should not be interpreted as "best-practice" examples that can be easily transferred to other countries. Each case has strengths and weaknesses that need to be discussed, and each skills system has idiosyncratic characteristics that affect the possibilities for policy transfer. However, taken together the six case studies show how countries have addressed the four challenges identified in this report (Table 1.1). By studying these cases in detail, it is possible to derive general statements about a broader set of OECD member and partner economies in order to identify institutional arrangements that underpin the effective governance of skills system.

Table 1.1 How the case studies correspond to skills system governance challenges

	Governance challenges			
	Promoting co-ordination across the whole of government	Engaging stakeholders throughout the policy cycle	Building integrated information systems	Aligning and co-ordinating financing arrangements
Estonia (Estonian Education Information System- EHIS)		X	X	
Germany (The Alliance for Initial and Further Training)	X	X		X
Korea (Lifelong learning)	X	X		X
Norway (Skills Policy Council and Future Skills Needs Committee)	X	X	X	
Portugal (National Agency for Qualification and Vocational Education and Training - ANQEP)	X	X		X
United States (Massachusetts' Early Warning Indicator System)	X		X	

In order to allow researchers to draw generalizable conclusions from a relatively small set of cases, the cases needed to be carefully selected based on a sound strategy (Gerring, 2006[20]). When undertaking such a task, simple comparisons ("A is different from B") can (and should) be avoided as long as the case selection is theory-driven. Thick descriptions of cases were welcome and important. However, case studies also needed to have an analytical focus to provide insights regarding their broader relevance and contribution. For the purpose of this report, a "case" is defined as a particular institution that is part of a larger skills system. As such, cases of this kind are always embedded in broader institutional arrangements of skills development and use in the particular countries. The case selection strategy used in this report follows the approach of selecting the "most diverse cases" in terms of both the dependent (skills policies) and the independent variable (prevailing institutional context) - for introductions to the case selection literature, see Gerring (2006[20]); Seawright and Gerring (2008[21]).

Regarding the diversity of institutional contexts, this report focuses on two aspects: 1) the institutional set-up of the system for skills development and use ("skills regime"), which encompasses the intersection between education and training institutions, as well as labour markets and industrial relations; and, 2) the degree of centralisation/decentralisation in skills regimes, which has implications for the co-ordination of policy-making activities across different levels of government.

Skills regimes and varieties of capitalism

The pertinent literature regarding the diversity of skills regimes distinguishes between different types depending on the public commitment to, and employer involvement in, vocational education and training (Busemeyer and Trampusch, 2012[4]), as well as different "varieties of capitalism" (Hall and Soskice, 2001[3]). The core argument of scholarship in this tradition is that decisions by businesses, students, parents and households are strongly conditioned by the prevailing institutional context. As a consequence of actors adapting their preferences and strategies to the status quo, the probability of radical policy change decreases over time, whereas the likelihood of institutional stability increases. The literature broadly distinguishes between two different types of capitalism: liberal market economies (LMEs) and co-ordinated market economies (CMEs).

In LMEs, co-ordination between and among employers occurs primarily via open market mechanisms, which contributes to confrontational relationships between employers and trade unions, and a rather distant ("arm's length") relationship between employers and state actors. Typical examples for LMEs are Australia, Canada, the United Kingdom and the United States. This report focuses on the United States.

In CMEs, in contrast, relationships between actors and stakeholders often rely on non-market forms of co-ordination, primarily via intermediate associations such as employers' associations, trade unions and local chambers of industry and commerce. Many of these institutions also exist in LMEs, but in CMEs they play a much more important role in the governance of skills regimes due to the dominance of the "corporatist" model of interest mediation in CMEs. The notion of "corporatism" (Lehmbruch, 1979[9]; Schmitter, 1979[10]) implies that stakeholders and representatives of the interests of different sections of society are continuously "incorporated" into governmental decision making, as well as during the implementation process of government policies.

The advantage of systematically incorporating societal interests into decision-making and implementation processes, which are often consensus-oriented in corporatist countries, is that decisions reflect broader societal needs rather than particular urges of the current government majority (Lijphart, 1999[22]). Furthermore, if broad consensus between the major stakeholders in society is reached during the decision-making process, there is likely to be less conflict and opposition during the implementation phase, which contributes to a more stable, sustainable and reliable institutional framework in the long term. However, corporatist decision making also has downsides. For example, since decision-making processes aim to achieve consensual solutions, they may be slow and cumbersome, particularly when the issues at hand have distributional implications. These processes are also prone to individual actors exercising veto power for individualistic, particularistic reasons. Corporatism therefore requires all participants to have a particular "interaction orientation" (Scharpf, 1997[7]), i.e. a certain willingness to forego particularistic goals in order to achieve collectively binding and welfare-improving solutions.

Although early literature on VoC only distinguished between LMEs and CMEs, more recent contributions have identified the diversity of institutional regimes within the large group of CMEs (Amable, 2003[23]; Anderson and Hassel, 2013[24]; Busemeyer, 2009[25]). For instance, researchers have identified an Asian model of capitalism (Amable, 2003[23]) in which large corporations (and their internal labour markets) play a decisive role in the development and use of skills. Rather than investing in the development of skills for broader labour market needs, employers and firms in the Asian model tend to focus on particular "segments" of the labour market, which are defined by the concrete skills needs of large, multinational corporations. As a consequence, this model has been named the "segmentalist" skills regime in the literature (Busemeyer and Trampusch, 2012[4]). In this model, employers are strongly committed to the development of skills, but trade unions and worker representatives are much less involved in the governance of the skills regime. This report studies Korea as a representative of this regime type.

A contrasting model can be found in Scandinavian countries, which have a long tradition of corporatist decision making going back to the late 19th and early 20th century (Martin and Swank, 2012[26]). In these countries, organisational representatives of employers and workers (as well as other societal interests) are regularly included in governance decisions. Due to the historical power of trade unions and social democratic government parties, the influence of worker interests is much higher than in other countries, which is also mirrored by a higher level of union density (i.e. the share of workers who are union members). The historical dominance of unions and social democrats in government has led to a partial marginalisation of employers in the provision and financing of training, as public financing and provision has crowded out the private involvement of employers (Lundahl et al., 2010[27]). In this "statist" skills regime (Busemeyer and Trampusch, 2012[4]), governmental policies need to pay particular attention to the challenge of mobilising employers (as well as workers) to engage in skills development at the workplace. This report studies the case of skills councils in Norway as an example of such a regime.

Corporatist decision making is also widespread in Continental Europe, with countries such as, Austria, Belgium, Germany, the Netherlands and Switzerland often regarded as typical representatives of consensus-oriented decision making in formal or informal "grand coalitions", with a strong involvement of interest associations that represent different sections of society. With a stronger focus on skills development and usage, the regimes within this subset of Continental European countries are commonly referred to as "collective" skills regimes (Busemeyer and Trampusch, 2012[4]). Similar to the "statist" skill regimes in Scandinavian countries, business interests and workers' groups are strongly involved in the governance of the skills regime. However, in contrast to Scandinavian countries, the influence of employer associations (and employers themselves) is stronger. In concrete terms, this implies that employers and firms have a greater leeway in setting the content of workplace training, which increases the commitment of employers to provide such training. Different from the "segmentalist" skills regime, unions and workers' representatives are stronger, which means that the leeway for individual firms to design training content and implement particular skills policies is more constrained. In short, the governance regime encourages and requires actors, stakeholders and representatives of different societal interests to work together, representing a "collective" approach to skills development and usage. The collective skills regime has many strengths, such as a strong involvement of employers and strong public commitment of governmental actors to skills policies. However, a significant downside is that decision-making processes can take a long time and lead to "lowest-common-denominator" solutions if the agreement of all actors is necessary to move forward. This report studies the case of Germany as a typical representative of a collective skills regime.

Further discussions in the literature on skills regimes and VoC centre on the question of whether Southern European countries constitute a model of their own, or whether they should be regarded as a variant of the other regime types discussed above (Amable, 2003[23]; Ferrera, 1996[28]). Although corporatist practices are also common in Southern Europe, the intermediary associations of employers and workers are less encompassing than in the Northern European cases discussed above, and therefore more prone to representing particular segments of society rather than "workers" and "employers" as a whole.

Furthermore, the reach of these intermediate associations into their respective domains, i.e. their ability to support the government in implementing policies, is much more limited than their Northern European counterparts. Therefore, in Southern European countries more effort is devoted to establishing the institutional, organisational and societal foundations for corporatist decision making, as well as the durable and lasting involvement of societal stakeholders in the governance of skills policies. This report explores the case of Portugal as an example of this regime, in particular the establishment of the National Agency of Qualification and Vocational Education and Training (ANQEP).

Similar discussions to those concerning Southern European have occurred in the literature regarding the diversity of models of capitalism (and skills policies) in Eastern European countries (Bohle and Greskovits, 2012[29]). Even though Eastern European countries have a common history, the variety of capitalist models within these countries seems to be larger than their commonalities. For instance, the Baltic countries (Estonia, Latvia, Lithuania) tend to follow a neoliberal trajectory, with some Scandinavian elements added in (Toots and Lauri, 2017[30]), whereas the Visegrad countries (the Czech Republic, Hungary, Poland and the Slovak Republic) pursue a more statist and increasingly centrally controlled approach to economic, social and skills policies. This report focuses on the case of Estonia and the newly established Estonian Education Information System. Estonia has been at the forefront of developments regarding the implementation of digitalisation strategies in the public sector (Kattel and Mergel, 2018[31]). As argued above, the establishment of information management systems can effectively contribute to promoting collaboration across levels of government, as well as across governmental departments. As few countries have undertaken significant activities regarding the digitalisation of educational governance, Estonia is particularly interesting for further study. This case study will also provide insights into other governance dimensions, such as stakeholder involvement.

Centralisation and decentralisation

The degree of centralisation/decentralisation in a particular country was important in selecting cases for further study in this report. The degree of decentralisation has important implications for the challenge of co-ordinating policies across different levels of government, as discussed above. To some extent, the degree of decentralisation depends on country size, as a country such as the United States naturally faces different challenges in co-ordinating policies across levels of government than a country such as Estonia. However, the correlation between country size and decentralisation is not deterministic, and is largely dependent on a country's historical and cultural background. There are large countries with a relatively high degree of centralisation, such as France or Italy, but others of similar size with a more decentralised structure, such as Germany. Likewise, small countries may be federalist and decentralised (i.e. Belgium) or unitary and centralised (such as the Scandinavian countries, albeit with a strong role for municipal governments).

There are different dimensions of decentralisation: administrative, fiscal and political. These dimensions often correlate with each other, but the correlation is not deterministic. Administrative decentralisation refers to the delegation of administrative tasks to lower levels of government, which may (or may not) go along with the respective fiscal capacities and political decision-making powers. Fiscal decentralisation captures the degree to which the authority to tax and spend is delegated to lower levels of government. Again, these two aspects are related, but there may be instances where the central government delegates spending authority to lower levels of government, but restricts the leeway for subnational governments to raise their own taxes (or change levels of taxation). Political decentralisation implies that formal decision- and policy-making powers are delegated from the central to lower levels of government. In formally federalist countries, such as Canada, Germany or the United States, subnational governments and entities formally retain some aspects of independent statehood and are usually represented via secondary parliamentary chambers in the federal decision-making process. However, even in formally unitary (i.e. non-federalist) countries, local levels of government may have considerable leeway in making decisions about the provision of local benefits and services.

Broadly speaking there has been a general trend towards decentralisation in the provision and financing of welfare services, in particular education, across OECD countries (Gingrich, 2011[32]; Mons, 2004[33]). This trend has been particularly strong in countries that previously had relatively centralised forms of decision making in education, such as Sweden (Arreman and Holm, 2011[34]; Lundahl, 2002[35]) or the United Kingdom (Hudson and Lidström, 2002[36]). This can be regarded as a reaction to citizen demands for a more differentiated and regionalised, and less centralised, approach to education policy. Paradoxically, the degree of decentralisation at the bottom level, for example as measured through degree of school autonomy, may be significantly lower in formally federalist countries, such as Austria and Germany, than in formally unitary (i.e. non-federalist) countries. This is because the bulk of decision-making and administrative competencies are concentrated at the mid-level of subnational governments, which are reluctant to delegate competencies to even lower levels of government. In short, the degree of centralisation and decentralisation across the three dimensions (administrative, fiscal, political) varies significantly across countries.

Considering country-specific context conditions regarding the degree of decentralisation is important in the analysis of skills regimes, and the resulting policy recommendations. On the one hand, a higher level of decentralisation may enhance the overall flexibility of the skills regime and allow subnational governments to better adjust to particular regional needs in terms of skills and local labour markets. Decentralisation may also enhance possibilities and opportunities for stakeholders to get involved in local and regional decision making.

On the other hand, a more decentralised governance structure raises the challenges of co-ordinating policy activities across different levels of government, as well as across the variety of subnational governments. For this reason, decentralisation measures are often accompanied by efforts to recentralise other aspects of decision making, or by the setting up of new governance structures that ensure the accountability of local and subnational policy makers to nationally set standards and goals. In the case of education policy, for instance, decentralisation in educational governance has been intertwined with debates about shifting from input-oriented modes of steering (i.e. focusing on the input factors to the educational process, such as the training of teachers and investments in school infrastructure) to output-oriented modes (e.g. measuring the relative performance of individual schools, teachers and pupils in the form of comparative assessments).

Developing measures and policy recommendations that strengthen the governance of skills systems – as is the goal of this report – must consider institutional context conditions such as the degree of decentralisation in individual countries. In highly centralised countries, a certain delegation of decision-making and implementation competencies to lower levels of government might be sensible in order to improve the overall flexibility of the system and its responsiveness to local needs. In contrast, highly decentralised countries might benefit from a certain degree of recentralisation and a strengthening of accountability mechanisms across levels of government and between subnational governments in order to more effectively pursue a "whole-of-government" and co-ordinated approach to skills policy.

In order to study the variety of governance challenges related to decentralisation, this report includes and selects country cases with different degrees of decentralisation along the three dimensions mentioned above (administrative, fiscal, political). Germany and the United States are both formally federalist countries, which implies that subnational governments (German *Länder* and USA states) have a high degree of autonomy in setting policies within their respective domains. This poses particular challenges for co-ordination across levels of government, as subnational governments demand strong involvement in decision-making processes at the federal level. In the German case, the Alliance for Initial and Further Training is studied. This alliance is an attempt to bring together stakeholders from different levels of government in order to devise a joint strategy on skills policies. The United States case focuses on the local and regional levels and explores the leeway that subnational governments have in devising their own governance arrangements within a framework of governance that is significantly influenced by federal regulations.

In contrast, Korea and Portugal are formally unitary (i.e. non-federalist) and relatively centralised countries. Therefore, they in particular face the challenge of how to involve local and regional stakeholders in governance decisions at the national level. If the mid-level subnational/regional level of government is absent or weakly developed, the obvious problem is how to effectively reach out and include local stakeholders, which are usually more fragmented and numerous than subnational governments at the regional level. Both case studies explore how central governments and their agencies have managed to partly deal with this challenge.

In the final two case studies from Estonia and Norway, the challenge of co-ordinating across levels of government is less daunting, either because these countries are relatively small in size, and/or because they have a long tradition of autonomous local government.

Empirical approach to case studies

The following case studies apply standards and procedures that are common in qualitative case study research in empirical social science. Each case study first provides some background information on the historical and contemporary developments in skills policy in the particular country of interest. This background analysis is based on insights from desk-based research and the careful scanning of primary source material such as government reports, policy papers and occasionally newspaper reports, complemented with insights from scholarly literature where available.

The project team visited each country for a period of five to seven working days to conduct first-hand interviews with experts, stakeholders and representatives from different institutions and organisations involved in the governance of skills policies. For each country, one particular example, such as a particular institution, organisation or policy reform, was selected to be studied in greater detail, rather than assessing the skills regime of a country as a whole. This more focused approach is better suited to highlight and identify concrete successes and challenges in policies related to skills development and usage, and leads to more concrete policy recommendations. As stated, it is important to highlight that these examples should not be understood as "best-practice" examples, but as differentiated case studies that show what does and does not work. For each case, the interviews were transcribed and analysed following the country mission and serve as background material for the analyses and the development of policy recommendations.

Each country chapter in the report contains an extensive analysis related to the four challenges identified in Table 1.1. All chapters also include a number of country-specific policy recommendations, equally connected to the four main challenges in strengthening the governance of skills systems and summarised in Table 1.2.

Table 1.2. Overview of country-specific policy recommendations

Case study	Governance challenges	Recommendations
Estonia: The Estonian Education Information System (EHIS)	• Building integrated information systems • Engaging stakeholders throughout the policy cycle	• Use questions as drivers of data collection • Support innovative data analyses • Put the data into perspective • Streamline and automate the data collection process • Promote the use of EHIS data among schools • Increase user friendliness
Germany: The Alliance for Initial and Further Training	• Promoting co-ordination acrossthe whole of government • Engaging stakeholders throughout the policy cycle • Aligning and co-ordinating financing arrangements	• Make better use of the potential of the Alliance to promote innovative skills policies • Prevent multiplication of governance bodies • Link duration of Alliance agreements with election cycles • Allow sufficient time for meaningful stakeholder engagement
Korea: Lifelong Learning in Korea	• Promoting co-ordination across the whole of government • Engaging stakeholders throughout the policy cycle • Aligning and co-ordinating financing arrangements	• Institutionalise co-operation between the Ministry of Education and the Ministry of Employment and Labour • Strengthen vertical co-ordination • Establish a comprehensive database on lifelong learning • Introduce quality control mechanisms • Engage with employers and employees in order to develop employment relevant lifelong learning • Educate employers and employees about the importance of lifelong learning
Norway: Norway's Skills Policy Council and Future Skills Needs Committee	• Promoting co-ordination across the whole of government • Engaging stakeholders throughout the policy cycle • Building integrated information systems	• Give new governance arrangements enough time • Improve format of meetings and agenda setting process within the Skills Policy Council • Improve communication and demonstrate to Skills Policy Council members the impact of their advice • Clearly define the mandate and reporting line of the Skills Policy Council in relation to other tripartite bodies • Further improve horizontal and vertical co-operation between governance bodies • Use full potential of social partners' expertise in the Future Skills Needs Committee • Refine the mandate of the Future Skills Needs Committee concerning targeting individuals
Portugal: Portugal's National Agency for Qualification and Vocational Education and Training (ANQEP)	• Promoting co-ordination across the whole of government • Engaging stakeholders throughout the policy cycle • Aligning and co-ordinating financing arrangements	• Stabilise ANQEPs role in the Portuguese skills system • Stabilise the financial basis of the Portuguese VET system • Engage the General Board in a meaningful way • Support the sectoral councils so that they can meet their duties
United States: Massachusetts' Early Warning Indicator System (EWIS)	• Promoting co-ordination across the whole of government • Building integrated information systems	• Establish a monitoring system to constantly evaluate EWIS • Empower schools and districts to work with information management systems • Improve the usability of EWIS

The recommendations identified in this report as being relevant to a broad range of contexts (and which are described in greater detail in the final chapter of the report) are summarised in Table 1.3.

Table 1.3. Overview of general policy recommendations

Governance challenge	Recommendations
Promoting co-ordination, co-operation and collaboration across the whole of government	Establish co-ordinating committees with a meaningful mandate and clear internal governance structures. • Define a clear mandate • Define mandate with real substance • Establish strong internal governance structures
Engaging with stakeholders throughout the policy cycle	Promote the involvement and commitment of non-governmental stakeholders, while managing the risk of undue influence from special interests. • Promote meaningful stakeholder involvement • Limit the overall number of stakeholders involved • Prevent gridlock and manage the risk of undue influence by special interests • Allow stakeholder engagement to develop over time
Building integrated information systems	Support the establishment of information management systems, but ensure that they provide usable and relevant information to stakeholders and policy makers. • Involve stakeholders in the design of integrated information systems • Use information management systems to inform rather than automate governance decisions • Make use of different kinds of data
Aligning and co-ordinating financing arrangements	Invest and commit the diversified resources needed to strengthen skills policies. • Provide adequate resources by setting long-term budgetary goals • Tap into multiple sources of funding while keeping equity concerns in mind

References

Amable, B. (2003), *The Diversity of Moden Capitalism*, Oxford University Press, Oxford, New York. [23]

Anderson, K. and A. Hassel (2013), "Pathways of change in CMEs: Training regimes in Germany and the Netherlands", in Wren, A. (ed.), *The Political Economy of the Service Transition*, Oxford University Press, Oxford, New York. [24]

Arreman, I. and A. Holm (2011), "Privatisation of public education? The emergence of independent upper secondary schools in Sweden", *Journal of Education Policy*, Vol. 26/2, pp. 225-243. [34]

Becker, G. (1993), *Human Capital: A Theoretical and Empirical Analysis with Special Reference to Education*, University of Chicago Press, Chicago, London. [15]

Bohle, D. and B. Greskovits (2012), *Capitalist Diversity on Europe's Periphery*, Cornell University Press, Ithaca, London. [29]

Busemeyer, M. (2015), *Skills and Inequality: The Political Economy of Education and Training Reforms in Western Welfare States*, Cambridge University Press, Cambridge, New York. [17]

Busemeyer, M. (2009), *Wandel trotz Reformstau: Die Politik der beruflichen Bildung seit 1970 (Change despite a backlog of reforms: The policy of vocational training since 1970)*, Campus Verlag, Frankfurt/New York, http://www.mpi-fg-koeln.mpg.de/pu/mpifg_book/mpifg_bd_65.pdf (accessed on 14 January 2019). [25]

Busemeyer, M. et al. (2018), "Investing in education in Europe: Evidence from a new survey of public opinion", *Journal of European Social Policy*, Vol. 28/1, pp. 34-54, http://dx.doi.org/10.1177/0958928717700562. [8]

Busemeyer, M. and C. Trampusch (2012), *The Political Economy of Collective Skill Formation*, Oxford University Press, Oxford, https://global.oup.com/academic/product/the-political-economy-of-collective-skill-formation-9780199599431?cc=fr&lang=en&# (accessed on 14 January 2019). [4]

Christensen, T. and P. Laegreid (2007), "The Whole-of-Government Approach to Public Sector Reform", *Public Administration Review*, Vol. 67/6, pp. 1059-1066. [5]

Esping-Andersen, G. (1990), *The Three Worlds of Welfare Capitalism*, Polity Press, Cambridge. [2]

Ferrera, M. (1996), "The 'Southern Model' of Welfare in Social Europe", *Journal of European Social Policy*, Vol. 6/1, pp. 17-37. [28]

Gerring, J. (2006), *Case Study Research: Principles and Practices*, Cambridge University Press, Cambridge, New York. [20]

Gingrich, J. (2011), *Making Markets in the Welfare State: The Politics of Varying Market Reforms*, Cambridge University Press, Cambridge, New York. [32]

Hall, P. and D. Soskice (2001), "An Introduction to Varieties of Capitalism", in Hall, P. and D. Soskice (eds.), *Varieties of Capitalism: The Institutional Foundations of Comparative Advantage*, Oxford University Press, Oxford, New York. [3]

Hay, C., M. Lister and D. Marsh (2006), *The State: Theories and Issues*, Red Globe Press, London. [37]

Huber, E. and J. Stephens (2014), "Income inequality and redistribution in post-industrial democracies: Demographic, economic and political determinants", *Socio-Economic Review*, Vol. 12/2, pp. 245-267. [18]

Hudson, C. and A. Lidström (2002), "National School Policy Changes in Britain and Sweden", in Hudson, C. and A. Lidström (eds.), *Local Education Policies: Comparing Sweden and Britain*, Palgrave, Houndmills, Basingstoke, Hampshire, New York. [36]

Kattel, R. and I. Mergel (2018), "Estonia's Digital Transformation: Mission Mystique and the Hiding Hand", *UCL Institute for Innovation and Public Purpose Working Paper*, Vol. 2018-09. [31]

Lehmbruch, G. (1979), "Consociational Democracy, Class Conflict, and the New Corporatism", in Schmitter, P. and G. Lehmbruch (eds.), *Trends Toward Corporatist Intermediation*, Sage, Beverly Hills, London. [9]

Lijphart, A. (1999), *Patterns of Democracy*, Yale University Press, New Haven, CT. [22]

Lundahl, L. (2002), "From Centralisation to Decentralisation: Governance of Education in Sweden", *European Educational Research Journal*, Vol. 1/4, pp. 625-636, http://dx.doi.org/10.2304/eerj.2002.1.4.2. [35]

Lundahl, L. et al. (2010), "Setting Things Right? Swedish Upper Secondary School Reform in a 40-Year Perspective", *European Journal of Education*, Vol. 45/1, pp. 46-59. [27]

Martin, C. and D. Swank (2012), *The Political Construction of Business Interests: Coordination, Growth and Equality*, Cambridge University Press, Cambridge, New York. [26]

Mons, N. (2004), "Politiques de décentralisation en éducation: Diversité internationale, légitimations théoriques et justifications empiriques", *Revue française de pédagogie*, Vol. 146, pp. 41-52. [33]

OECD (2019), *OECD Skills Strategy 2019: Skills to Shape a Better Future*, OECD Publishing, Paris, https://doi.org/10.1787/9789264313835-en. [1]

Offe, C. and H. Wiesenthal (1980), "Two Logics of Collective Action: Theoretical Notes on Social Class and Organizational Form", *Political Power and Social Theory*, Vol. 1, pp. 67-115. [13]

Olson, M. (1965), *The Logic of Collective Action: Public Goods and the Theory of Groups*, Harvard University Press, Cambridge, MA. [12]

Scharpf, F. (1997), *Games Real Actors Play: Actor-centered Institutionalism in Policy Research*, Weastview, Boulder, CO. [7]

Schmitter, P. (1979), "Still the Century of Corporatism?", in Schmitter, P. and G. Lehmbruch (eds.), *Trends Toward Corporatist Intermediation*, Sage, Beverly Hills, London. [10]

Seawright, J. and J. Gerring (2008), "Case Selection Techniques in Case Study Research: A Menu of Qualitative and Quantitative Options", *Political Research Quarterly*, Vol. 61/2, pp. 294-308. [21]

Solga, H. (2014), "Education, economic inequality and the promises of the social investment state", *Socio-Economic Review*, Vol. 12/2, pp. 269-297. [19]

Streeck, W. (1996), "Lean Production in the German Automobile Industry: A Test Case for Convergence Theory", in Dore, R. and S. Berger (eds.), *National Diversity and Global Capitalism*, Cornell University Press, Ithaca, London. [16]

Streeck, W. and D. Mertens (2011), "Fiscal Austerity and Public Investment: Is the Possible the Enemy of the Necessary?", *MPIfG Discussion Paper*, Vol. 11/12. [14]

Streeck, W. and P. Schmitter (1985), "Community, market, state – and associations? The prospective contribution of interest governance to social order", in Streeck, W. and P. Schmitter (eds.), *Private Interest Government: Beyond Market and State*, Sage, London, Beverly Hills, New Delhi. [11]

Toots, A. and T. Lauri (2017), "Varieties of Social Investment Policies on Two Sides of the Baltic Sea: Explaining Routes to Endurance", *Social Policy & Administration*, Vol. 51/4, pp. 550-576. [30]

UNESCO and ILO (2018), *Taking a whole of government approach to skills development*, UNESCO, ILO. [6]

Note

[1] Pork barrel politics refers to policy makers supporting a piece of legislation specifically intended to benefit a particular group/constituency in return for that group's subsequent support (Hay, Lister and Marsh, 2006[37]).

2 Case Study: The Estonian Education Information System (EHIS)

The governance of skill systems is very complex. Thus, evidenced-based decision making requires reliable data. However, establishing and maintaining an integrated information system is challenging and requires commitment of different stakeholders. Estonia is one of the few countries that successfully established and maintains a digital, online and encompassing database that brings together data on important parts of the education system such as schools, pupils, teachers, exams and qualifications. This chapter analyses the Estonian Education Information System (Eesti hariduse infosüsteem) and looks at its history, how data enters the systems and how it is used for policy making. This case shows how well-developed information systems contribute to successful skill governance and develops policy recommendations that will help to develop the information system further.

Introduction

Estonia is acknowledged as having successfully developed one of the most advanced digital societies. For example, 46.7% of Estonians use Internet voting and 99% of public services are available online (E-estonia, 2019[1]). It is therefore not surprising that in the governance of Estonia's skill system, digitalisation plays an important role. All schools in Estonia use "e-school solutions" (E-estonia, 2019[2]) such as digital learning material or web-based school management software. The Ministry of Education and Research, as well as private companies, offer a great variety of online tools. For example, the "e-schoolbag" (*e-Koolikott*) is an online portal that provides digital learning materials for teachers and students across educational levels (E-estonia, 2019[2]).

Another key building block at the state level in Estonia's skills system is the Estonian Education Information System (Eesti hariduse infosüsteem, EHIS). Since 2004, this database has collected data on students, schools, study materials, examinations, curricula and teaching staff. As schools are required to enter the data directly into the system, the data are deemed reliable. EHIS is a personal-identity-based database, which means that each person is registered with an individual identification number. All events related to studies, for example grades and successfully completed certificates, are stored in EHIS. This individual-based approach allows the tracking of each student's development over time. The database is managed by the Ministry of Education and Research. The online platform Educational Eye (HaridusSilm in Estonian) makes aggregated data available to the public. Schools can access their school-specific data and, importantly, policy makers take decisions based on EHIS data, as will be explained in greater detail below.

Estonia's education system is not only one of the most digitalised, it is also one of the most successful (this is explored further in the next section), as reflected in its top performance in the Programme for International Student Assessment (PISA). In the 2018 PISA round, which compared the pupils' science, mathematics and reading skills, Estonia ranked first in science and reading, and third in mathematics among all participating countries (OECD, 2019[3]).

Evidence-based policy making in education is essential, but depends on the availability of reliable data. The case of EHIS in Estonia represents the successful establishment of an encompassing information system used by all stakeholders in the skills system to inform decision-making processes. Thus, with reference to the overall framework of this report, this case study focuses on two of the four dimensions:

- Building integrated information systems.
- Engaging stakeholders throughout the policy cycle.

The emphasis of this case study is on the information system, but it also considers how stakeholders are involved in the governance and usage of the database. The first section introduces Estonia's education system before detailing how the EHIS database functions. The next section analyses the strengths and weaknesses of EHIS based on document research and 11 semi-structured interviews with 20 experts conducted in August and September 2019. The chapter concludes with policy recommendations.

Estonia's skills system

Top performance in PISA

Estonia's skills system is very successful in international assessments of educational performance. Estonia has participated in PISA since 2006 and from the start has performed well above average. In 2018, Estonian students achieved the highest scores in science and reading from all participating countries, and only students from Korea and Japan managed to score higher in mathematics (OECD, 2019[3]). Figure 2.1 shows Estonia's strong performance compared to the OECD average.

Figure 2.1. Estonia's PISA scores, 2018

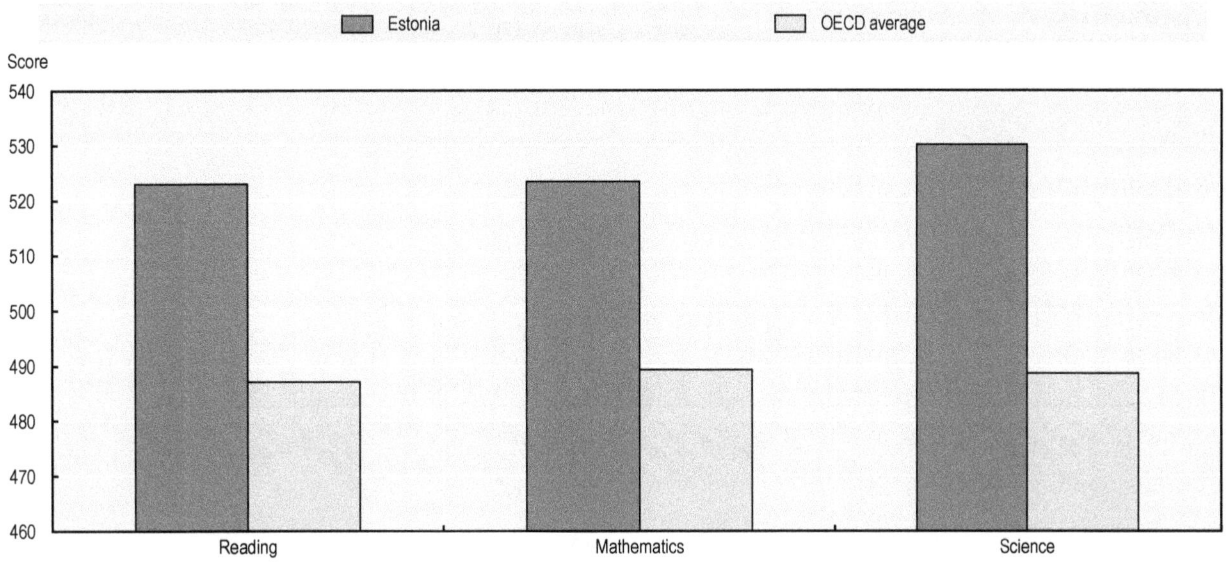

Source: OECD (2019[3]), *PISA 2018 Results (Volume I): What Students Know and Can Do*, https://dx.doi.org/10.1787/5f07c754-en.

StatLink https://doi.org/10.1787/888934112633

Besides high average scores, Estonia has the third highest share of top performers among PISA participating countries, which also increased between 2006 and 2018 (Figure 2.2). At the same time, Estonia has the smallest share of low-achieving students out of all participating countries (Figure 2.2), which implies that Estonia's strong performance in average scores is complemented with a relatively low degree of educational inequality.

The interviewees underlined that Estonia has a very egalitarian education system. The quality of schools does not differ to a great extent, which increases students' chances to receive equally good education regardless of where they live. The PISA results support this impression, showing that the socio-economic status of a student in Estonia has relatively little influence on their opportunity to attain high levels of skills. In Estonia, roughly 5% of variance in reading performance of students is explained by their economic, social and cultural status (ESCS), compared to the OECD average of 12% (OECD, 2019[4]). At the same time, 16% of disadvantaged Estonian students are academically resilient (scoring in the top quarter in reading amongst all Estonian students), which is above the OECD average of 11% (OECD, 2019[4]).

Figure 2.2. Percentage of top performers and low-achievers in science, PISA 2006 and 2018

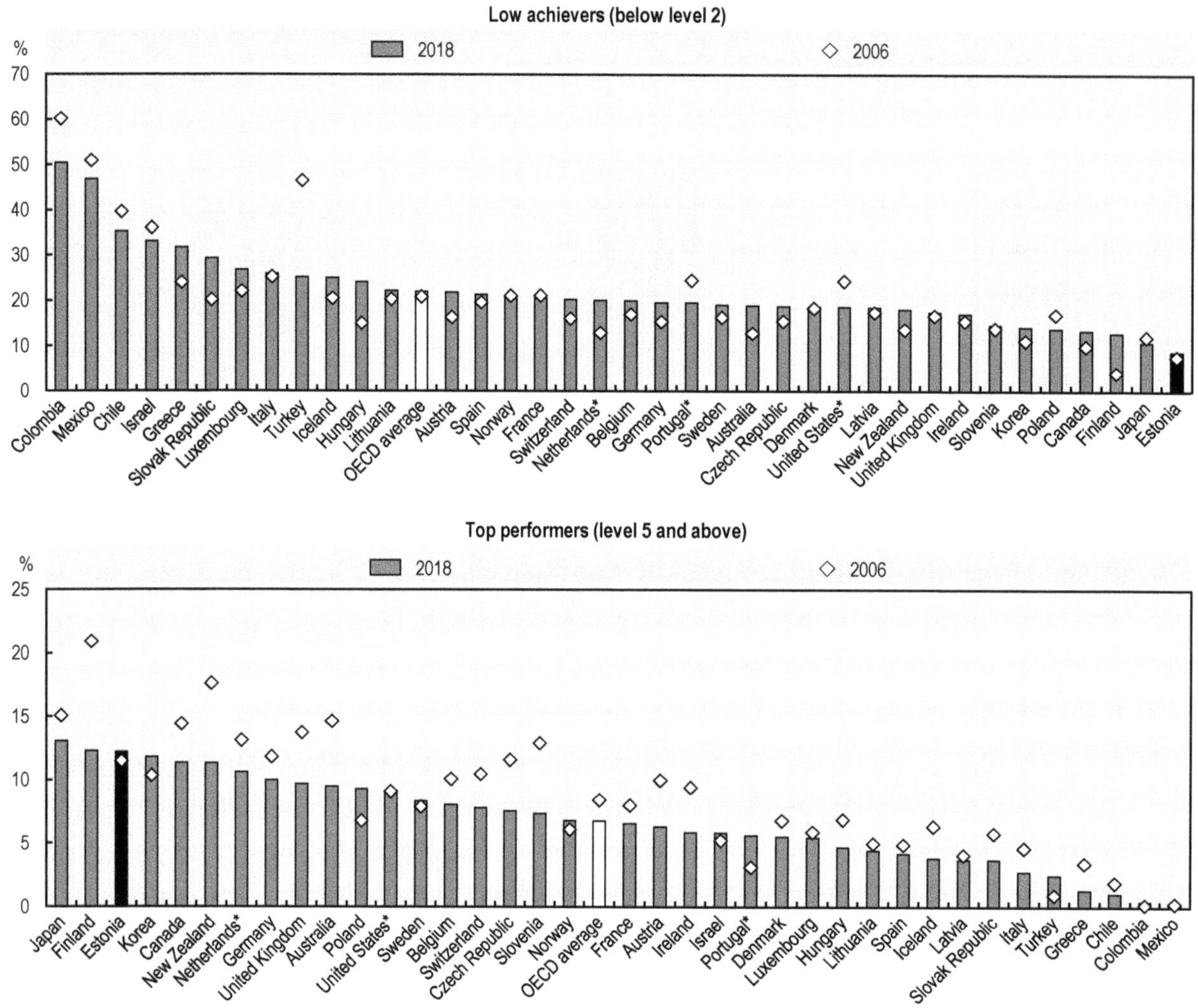

Note: Netherlands, Portugal and the United States: PISA 2018 data did not meet the PISA technical standards but were accepted as largely comparable.
Source: OECD (2019[3]), *PISA 2018 Results (Volume I): What Students Know and Can Do*, https://dx.doi.org/10.1787/5f07c754-en.

StatLink https://doi.org/10.1787/888934112652

E-Estonia and its history

Today, Estonia is one of the most developed e-societies. In order to achieve this, it went through an intense process of change since gaining independence in 1991 after five decades of Soviet rule. The newly independent country faced severe challenges in the 1990s such as steeply rising unemployment, which exceeded 15% in 2000 (OECD, 2020[5]). Digitalisation was virtually non-existent, as the interviewees explained, and the country had very few resources to build on. However, historic ties and a shared identity with the Scandinavian countries, especially Finland, are very strong, and Estonia received significant support from Finland after independence in the form of expertise and economic investments, which helped it nurture and develop its digitalisation strategy.

One of the most influential turning points in the post-Soviet period was the project Tiger Leap (Tiigrihüpe). Tiger leap – a reference to the economic boom of the economies of Hong Kong (China), Korea, the People's Republic of China (hereafter 'China'), Singapore and Chinese Taipei – aimed to establish an up-to-date IT infrastructure in the country, with a special focus on schools, to boost economic growth and improve the education system.

The Tiger Leap programme was launched in 1996 by the Estonian government and was institutionalised with the establishment of the Tiger Leap Foundation in 1997 (HITSA, 2019[6]), which was in place until 2000.

The Tiger Leap programme was financed by the Ministry of Education (renamed the Ministry of Education and Research in 2003) (Ministry of Education and Research, 2019[7]). Its goal was to increase the quality of education in Estonia with the help of information and communication technology (ICT) (Laanpere, 2002[8]). The Tiger Leap programme aimed to:

- Provide each school in Estonia with computers and Internet access.
- Train teachers how to use computers in school and in teaching.
- Develop educational software to enable digital learning.
- Foster students' IT skills.
- Support municipalities in developing an ICT structure.

The programme was largely financed by the state and received about USD 10 million between 1997 and 2000. This money was complemented by about USD 2 million from the European Union (EU) (Laanpere, 2002[8]). More than two-thirds of funding went to ICT infrastructure (Laanpere, 2002[8]). By the end of 2000, all schools had Internet access and were equipped with computers, with about one computer per 25 students, and 65% of teachers had received training in how to use computers (Laanpere, 2002[8]). The Tiger Leap programme was followed by the Tiger Leap Plus programme launched in 2001.

Before the Tiger Leap programme, schools did not use computers, or only to a very limited extent. Interview partners explained that in hindsight, it was an advantage that Estonia started from scratch regarding IT in the 1990s as it allowed the country to enter the process of digitalisation on an already advanced level from a global perspective. The interviewees explained that the country was not trapped in older "legacy" systems of the 1980s. This was an advantage as changing old complex systems can be more difficult than establishing a completely new system. Political support for Tiger Leap was very strong as the President Lennart Meri was greatly in favour of investing in digitalisation. The interviewees noted that he had "a vision" for Estonia to be an advanced, digitalised society.

By 2001, all schools were equipped with computers and connected to the Internet. The Tiger Leap Foundation financially supported local governments by matching their financial contributions (HITSA, 2019[6]). However, interviewees underlined that equipment itself does not bring change: users also need to be trained in how to handle computers and the Internet, as well as be motivated to make use of the new facilities. For this purpose, the Tiger Leap Foundation organised basic computer training courses for teachers that covered 40 hours of training (HITSA, 2019[6]). In 1997, almost 4 000 teachers completed this training, following by many more in the years to come. In the early 2000s, electronic educational materials were developed and shared through the educational portal SchoolLife, established in 2001.

Education was not the only area to undergo an intense significant and quick process of adaptation to digitalisation, other areas of public policy such as taxation, voting and healthcare also experienced rapid change (E-estonia, 2019[1]). In 2002, the digital ID, an ID card that contains a chip that stores important personal information, was introduced in Estonia (E-estonia, 2019[1]). The card functions as the key to e-services. Almost every citizen has their own identification card. Most laptops have a card slot for the ID card that allows the user, together with a password, to identify themselves and access e-services. Furthermore, the Mobile ID – a special mobile SIM card – and the Smart ID – a smartphone application – allow for identification without a card reader (E-estonia, 2019[9]). In the public sector, login is not possible with "just" a user name and password, but also requires either the ID card, the Mobile ID or the Smart ID.

Since the mid-2000s, the Learning Tiger programme has promoted e-learning, for example through the establishment of a web-based learning management system. Subject specific programmes were developed that targeted specific fields in education, and teacher focused training projects such as DigiTiger educated teachers on how to use information technology in learning. TechnoTiger targeted support at teachers of information technology, arts and occupational guidance with the aim of increasing the number of students who continue education in technology. Today, one in ten students in higher education choose to study IT every year (E-estonia, 2019[2]).

The establishment of EHIS took place in the context of this rapid digitalisation of society, in particular the educational system. Interviewees explained that collecting data from schools was not new, although it was previously less granular and detailed, as even in Soviet times schools had to keep a record of relevant educational data, such as the number of students. In the pre-digital times, however, these numbers were written down on paper in tables and books that were passed on to the municipalities, then to the Ministry of Education and Research. Data were also collected by regional authorities and public sector organisations such as the Department for Statistics. This process involved a lot of manual copying, thus it was very time consuming and prone to errors. Data were only collected once a year, which meant that information was not necessarily up to date.

The Tiger Leap programme aimed to provide all schools with computers and Internet access. This task required the Tiger Leap team to have a reliable overview of all schools, including the number of students, teachers, classrooms and existing technical equipment. However, information on schools' technical equipment had thus far not been systematically collected. In addition to the Tiger Leap programme, the Ministry of Education sought professional advice from experienced IT advisors, who suggested strengthening evidence-based decision making; however, this required reliable data on education and the skills system. Interview partners confirmed that the provision of computers and Internet access to schools opened a unique window of opportunity to lay the foundations for an encompassing digital information system. Interviewees reported that the initiative came from the small team who discussed their idea with the Ministry of Education. The minister was supportive and decided to replace paper-based data collection with a digital educational information system. The introduction of EHIS was therefore a top-down decision.

In the present day, the collection of sensitive personal data by the state is hotly debated in many countries. However, in the early 2000s, Estonia was in the middle of an intense digitisation process that brought a great deal of advantages, jobs, new educational opportunities and a bright future perspective for the country. At this time, data security was not of such importance as the Internet was not so well developed, and data leaks and hacks were not seen as potential threats. Against this backdrop, Estonia's e-society was developed and EHIS was one of its many building blocks. A special feature of Estonia's approach to digitalisation is the decentralised nature of the system. Data are stored in many different databases instead of being pooled in one. In order to understand how the e-services in Estonia work and how they are connected to each other, it is essential to look at X-tee, often referred to as X-Road, which is a "technological and organisational environment enabling a secure Internet-based data exchange between information systems" (Authority, 2019[10]). All databases, for example the population register or the tax board, function independently from each other but are (or can be) connected via X-Road (Figure 2.3).

Interviewees explained that an advantage of X-Road is that access to individual databases can be controlled and regulated, with only authorised users able to enter the databases and receive pre-defined content. Some 151 public sector institutions are connected to X-road, and it is used indirectly by 487 enterprises and institutions and about 52 000 organisations (X-tee, 2019[11]).

Figure 2.3. Internet-based data exchange: The X-Road system

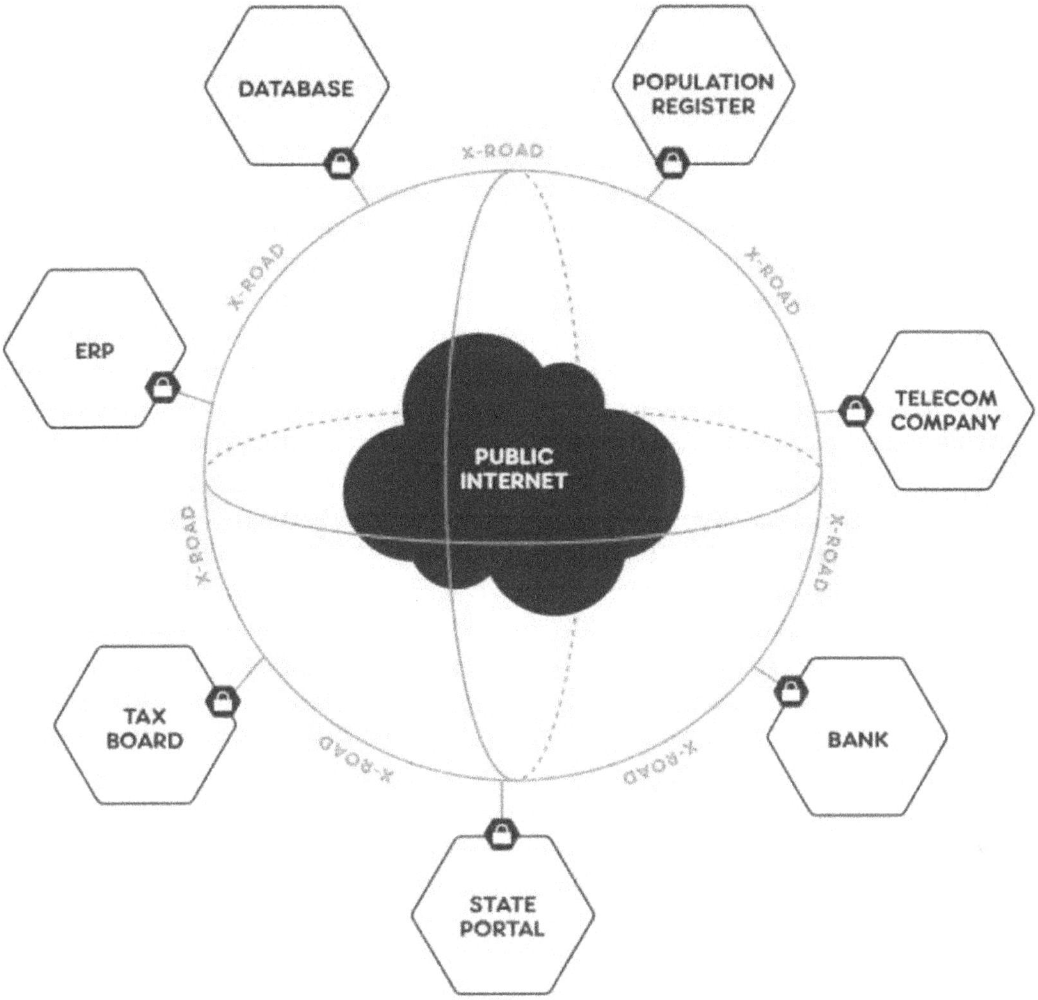

Source: Estonian Information System Authority (2019[10]), *Data Exchange Layer X-tee,* https://www.ria.ee/en/state-information-system/x-tee.html.

Today, a variety of digital online tools are used in Estonia to support education delivery and progression. These tools and platforms can be connected to EHIS via X-Road in order to complement the data in EHIS. Some tools are developed by private providers and some are provided by the Ministry of Education and Research. The following are some of the most important databases and platforms:

- **eKool (eSchool)**: eKool was established in 2002 by the Look@World Foundation and has been run by a private for-profit company since 2005. eKool is an online school management and communication system for pupils, teachers, parents and government bodies (ESchool, 2019[12]). It can be used as a communication platform, to administer learning materials, or teachers can use it to document homework, grades or class absences (ESchool, 2019[12]). Basic features are free of charge for students and parents, but schools and government bodies pay a fee to use the system.
- **Studium**: Similar to eKool, studium is a management and communication tool for teachers, parents and pupils. It is designed for schools, kindergartens and "hobby schools". It is free of charge and free of advertisement for students and parents, but schools pay to use the tool. It can be connected to EHIS and is used by more than 200 institutions. It is run by a for-profit company.

- **e-koolikot (e-schoolbag)**: The e-schoolbag is an online portal run by the Ministry of Education and Research that collects learning materials (E-estonia, 2019[2]). The portal covers materials such as texts, games and examinations for basic, general and vocational education, with users able to search material by keywords, based on curricula. Teachers can create individual collections of learning material and share them with others. Users can also comment on the materials (E-estonia, 2019[2]). The database allows for the creation of statistics on the use of different materials.
- **Study Information System (*Õppeinfosüsteem*, ÕIS)**: The ÕIS is a joint project of different stakeholders (OIS, 2019[13]). Students have to sign up with this system once they are enrolled in their education institution. It contains information about study programmes and timetables, and allows for exam registrations. It is used by vocational schools and applied higher education institutions. The first universities plan to join soon.
- **Estonian Research Portal (*Eesti Teadusinfosüsteem*, ETIS)**: The Ministry of Education and Research operates this portal, with the Estonian Research Council as the authorised processor (Etis, 2019[14]). It contains information on all researchers in Estonia, including research projects, qualifications and publications. All higher education institutions are registered and the portal can be searched by keywords.
- **Admission Information System (*SisseAstumise InfoSüsteem*, SAIS)**: This system is administered by the Information Technology Foundation for Education (HITSA). Applications to educational institutions can be made through SAIS. The portal allows for the upload of required information and can collect data from other databases, if authorised by the user.
- **Examination Information System, (*Eksamite infosüsteem*, EIS)**: The electronic environment EIS is a tool to carry out and evaluate examinations and tests (Innove, 2019[15]). It is designed to be used by students, teachers, parents and examination centre specialists. It is run by Foundation Innove, which was created in 2003 by the Ministry of Education and Research (Innove, 2019[15]).
- **Register of Occupational Qualifications (*Kutseregister*)**: This online register is run by the Estonian Qualifications Authority (Kutsekoda) and owned by the Ministry of Education and Research. Established in 2001 it brings together information on occupational qualification standards, professional councils and awarding bodies (Kutseregister, 2019[16]). The register provides information on professional certificates via X-Road to EHIS.

Governance structure of the skills system

Two governmental levels are important for the governance of education in Estonia: the central (state) level and the municipal level (Santiago et al., 2016[17]). At the state level, the Ministry of Education and Research plays a key role. The state organises vocational training, regulates national curricula and largely finances educational institutions. Furthermore, the central state is responsible for monitoring the system overall and for developing a strategic framework for Estonia's education system (Santiago et al., 2016[17]). For example, the state defines the required professional and pedagogical skill levels of educational staff and sets the minimum wage for teachers (Santiago et al., 2016[17]). The Ministry of Education and Research is divided into 20 departments (as of October 2019). Regarding EHIS, which is the focus of this case study, the Analysis Department and the E-Service Department are the most relevant.

Municipalities are in charge of monitoring and implementing national guidelines at the local level. Each municipality is governed by its own council, which is elected every four years in local elections. There are 79 municipalities in Estonia responsible for pre-primary and general education. This involves, for example, the financing of schools and paying teacher salaries. Financing is thus very decentralised and, in some cases, school directors define the salary level (Santiago et al., 2016[17]). Municipalities also monitor the provision of education by maintaining a network of schools that meet local demands for schooling. There are 15 counties in between municipalities and the national level, but they do not play an important role in the governance of education.

Alongside these two governmental levels, the Estonian Qualifications Authority (Kutsekoda), the Information Technology Foundation for Education (HITSA), Foundation Innove and the Archimedes Foundation perform important tasks in the Estonian skills system.

The Estonian Qualification Authority sits at the intersection between the education system and the labour market. It was founded in 2001 by the Estonian Chamber of Commerce and Industry, the Estonian Confederation of Employers and Industry, the Estonian Employees' Unions' Confederation, the Confederation of Estonian Trade Unions, the Ministry of Social Affairs, and the Ministry of Economic Affairs (Kutsekoda, 2019[18]). It is subordinated to the Ministry of Education and Research, and a member of the ministry is part of the supervisory board. Organisational tasks include analysis of labour and skills demands, and analysis and forecast of skills supply

The Estonian Qualification Authority also implements the OSKA project, launched in 2014 by the Ministry of Education and Research, which aims to match skills provision to labour market needs (OSKA, 2019[19]). OSKA combines qualitative and quantitative research methods to analyse the labour market and the skills system. Its aim is to answer questions about the nature and relative quantity of different skills needed in the future labour market (OSKA, 2019[19]), but also to develop ideas on how to provide necessary skills and how the current skills system needs to be adjusted to meet future skills demands. OSKA applies a sector-centred approach in its work, with sector-level surveys helping to understand and predict future skills needs. Interviewees explained that data are complemented by information from EHIS.

The second important actor in the Estonian skills system is the Information Technology Foundation for Education (HITSA). HITSA was founded in 2000 by the Republic of Estonia, the University of Tartu, Tallinn University of Technology, Eesti Telekom and the Estonian Association of Information Technology and Telecommunications (HITSA, 2019[6]). The establishment of this foundation was initially motivated by the idea of stakeholders opening an IT College. However, the Tiger Leap Foundation then developed even more ambitious goals to modernise and boost IT in Estonia. HITSA aims to equip all students at all educational levels with digital skills. It also supports the use of digital learning tools to enhance the quality of teaching and learning (HITSA, 2019[20]). Interview partners described the foundation as the long, implementing "arm" of the Ministry of Education and Research, as it is financed by the ministry and develops and implements new technological solutions in education for the ministry, while taking into account the needs of the other (founding) stakeholders, such as universities and companies. HITSA supports innovation in digital learning and enables the exchange of information and best-practice examples among stakeholders such as schools, municipalities and companies. Furthermore, it is the official helpdesk for different education online tools developed by the Ministry of Education and Research, including EHIS. Thus, when schools have a question concerning EHIS, they contact HITSA. EHIS data, but also data from other educational online tools that collect data, are very important for HITSA's work, as confirmed by interviewees. For example, teams of developers and researchers on education in HITSA work on new web applications to support personalised learning. For this purpose, personal information on students from EHIS is very important.

Two further foundations under the Ministry of Education and Research are Innove Foundation and the Archimedes Foundation. In 2003, the Ministry of Education and Research created the Foundation Innove, which is responsible for external evaluation, curricular development in general education, and vocational education and training. In 1997, the Estonian government established the Archimedes Foundation, an independent body responsible for the implementation of national and international, especially European, programmes such as Erasmus+ (Archimedes Foundation, 2018[21]).

The Estonian Education Information System (EHIS)

The first EHIS pilot ran in 2004, and by 1 January 2005 it was fully established and available and compulsory for all schools to use. It is a state-run, web-based database that contains live data on education. It covers all educational levels, including kindergarten, primary schools, secondary schools, vocational training, universities, adult education and so called hobby schools that provide classes in, for example, music and art for young people. EHIS covers about 600 data fields. The information is individual-based, which means that each student and teacher is registered with an individual identification number. EHIS collects information on students' grade as well as their performance, state exam results or need for special support. All teachers are registered in EHIS with an identification number, and the system collects information about their qualifications, teaching hours and which grades they teach.

EHIS is connected to X-Road, with two important functions. First, it allows EHIS to complement its data with information collected in other databases. For example, EHIS collects data on the students' place of residence not from the students themselves but from the population register. Second, the connection to X-road allows other databases to complement their data with EHIS data. For example, the Health Insurance Fund uses EHIS data to determine who is eligible for student health insurance.

Some of the many online tools and platforms used by schools, pupils, teachers and parents have been introduced in the previous section. These tools and platforms can also be connected to X-road, which means that their data can be accessed by EHIS, and vice versa. As will be described in more detail below, schools can connect their online school management system to EHIS. This means that schools input information on their students and teachers to their school management system, which automatically reports this information to EHIS. X-road is the connection between all the different databases, but this connection is not automatically established. Access to EHIS data is supervised by the Ministry of Education and Research and requires a legal agreement between the two institutions responsible for the respective databases. The following section further describes how data enter the information system and how the data are used.

How data enter EHIS

EHIS combines data that comes directly from all schools in Estonia, which includes all institutions that provide education following a curriculum. In total, about 2 000 institutions enter data into EHIS. By law, all schools are required to enter the data and keep it up to date. This is an important difference to the Massachusetts' Early Warning Indicator System (EWIS) explored in Chapter 7, the US case study, in which school participate voluntarily. In Estonia, schools are required to update information immediately, for example when a student leaves the school. Schools only receive their funding if the data are complete. School head teachers are required to nominate at least two employees who are responsible for EHIS data. Interviewees explained that this responsibility usually falls to the school secretary.

When data are entered by individual schools, EHIS performs logical consistency checks, as explained by interviewees. For example, a student can only be registered with one school. When a school wants to enter a new student into their system but the "old" school did not de-register the student, the new school will receive an error report and will not be able to register the student. This mechanism helps to ensure that every person in compulsory education is always only linked to one school.

Another example of an internal control mechanism is the checking of demands for special needs. The database stores information on individual students' need for special support and is able to compare the needs of a student with information on them from previous years. If the need suddenly drops from high to zero the electronic system will send an automatic message to the school to check if this information is correct, as it is considered unlikely that a high demand for support will disappear. This feature will be implemented from 2020 onwards. These logical consistency checks, which allow for checking across different schools as well as across time on an individual student level, make the data very reliable and accurate.

There are three ways a school can enter data into EHIS. First, schools in Estonia use several online and digital tools and applications in their daily work, and all schools use digital management software. The two most popular programmes are eKool and studium, which can be connected to EHIS and data can automatically be transferred from the school management system to EHIS without any additional action required. Thus, apart from requiring schools to enter data into EHIS in the first place, the infrastructure is designed to make the process as easy and convenient as possible. Second, schools can generate Excel sheets based on the data in their school management system and upload XML files to EHIS. Third, the data can be manually entered into the EHIS user interface. According to interview partners, the three options are equally popular among schools, with about one-third of schools choosing automatic data transfer, about one-third uploading Excel sheets, and about one-third entering data manually through the EHIS user interface.

The Ministry of Education and Research, however, prefers schools to connect their management systems to EHIS so that all information is automatically transferred. Within the ministry, the Department for E-Services is developing the next version of EHIS in which data exchange works automatically and data transfer does not require nor allow interference by schools. There will be very limited user interface in EHIS 2.0. Some schools argue that non-automatic entry allows the data to be reviewed and verified. However, the Ministry of Education and Research has concerns that such a process might also enable schools to manipulate the data to their advantage. However, this could only happen on a very small scale as the logical consistency checks guarantee the high quality and accuracy of the data. Nevertheless, schools in theory do have an incentive to reduce the number of "missed classes", for example, in order to improve their image. They may also, in theory, report a higher number of students with special needs in order to receive more funding.

If school staff encounter problems with EHIS, there is a help desk run by HITSA. If HITSA is unable to deal with the question, it is forwarded to the E-Service Department of the Ministry of Education and Research. Interviewees argued that the questions received through the help desk help them to reflect upon which aspects, especially regarding user friendliness, should be improved.

User groups and their access to the data

The most important users of EHIS can be categorised into six main groups, as shown in Figure 2.4. Each group has a different way of using EHIS data.

Each school has its own individual online access to EHIS through the user interface, which it can use to enter data. The interface also provides an overview over the information on individual students and teachers. However, schools cannot see information on individual students from other schools. Through Educational Eye, the online platform that makes EHIS data available to the public, schools can compare their performance to all other schools in Estonia, for example the average grade in state exams. However, in interviews it became clear that schools use their own school management systems to monitor their performance and to keep track of their students, instead of using EHIS. One of the key purposes of EHIS is to develop (together with data from other sources) statistics and indicators that allow schools to compare themselves with other schools. This comparison is supposed to incentivise schools to improve their performance. However, interviews revealed that schools hardly ever use Educational Eye data as they are busy with their daily work and undertaking comparison or analysis with other schools would take additional time. Furthermore, interviewees explained that the differences between schools are usually small because Estonia has a relatively egalitarian school system, and the schools that face problems already know that these problems exist without checking the results of other schools. Nevertheless, statistics based on EHIS data in theory offer the opportunity to perform comparative analyses at the school level. This is a very similar challenge to the problems described in Chapter 7, the US case study, on EWIS: the data are available but the schools do not make use of them.

The Educational Eye is a public online platform that contains data on all educational aspects covered by EHIS. For example, the public has access to information on the number of students by educational level, as well as the number of teachers, researchers and scientists. This information can be sorted by local government and county. Furthermore, Educational Eye contains detailed and publicly available information on each school in Estonia. Each school is represented by a "school card" (*Koolikaart*) that contains information on, for example, the type of school, the number of students, the language of instruction and the level of pupil satisfaction (Figure 2.5). The school card shows the average grade reached by pupils in the state exam in comparison to the average grade reached by all pupils who participated in the state exam. Interviewees explained that parents in particular are interested in the school's performance in state exams. This is one of the main challenges of EHIS, as will be discussed in the analysis section of this case study.

Figure 2.4. EHIS user groups and their access to the data

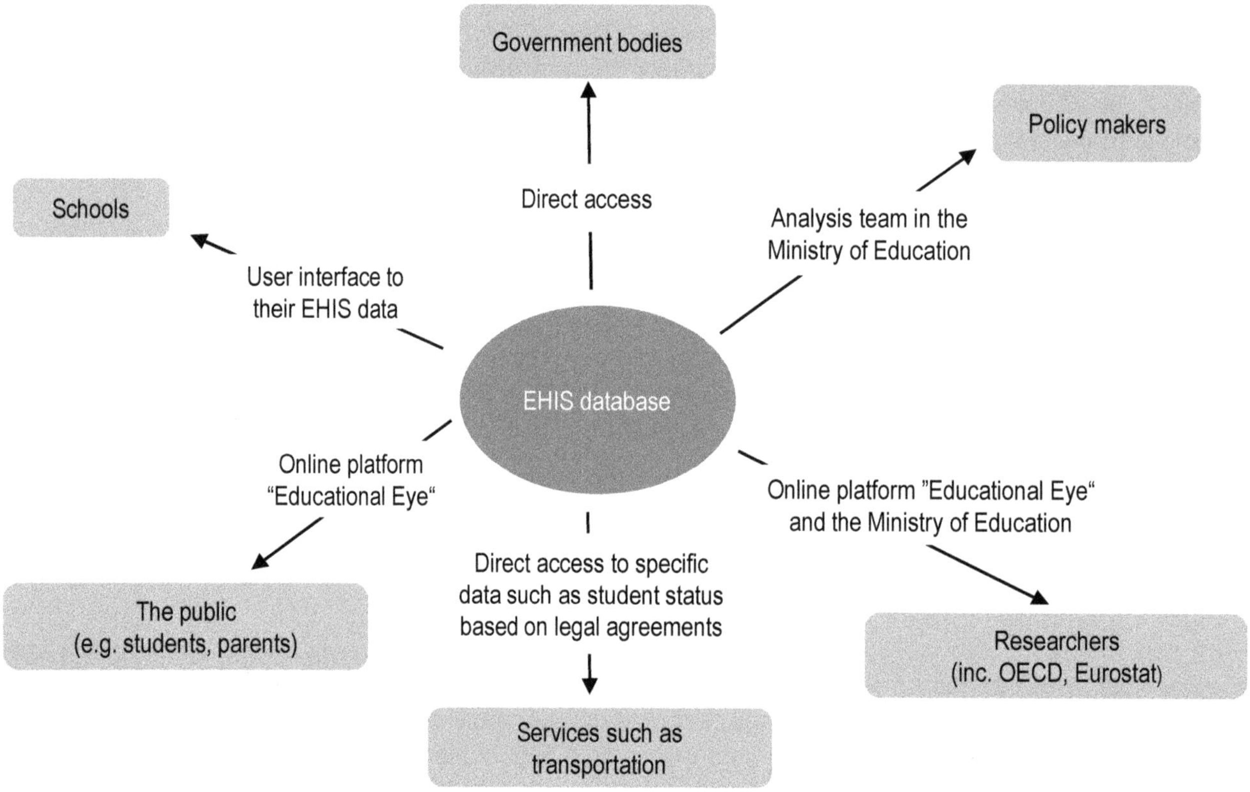

Figure 2.5. Example of a school card and results (fictional) of the state exam in comparison to the average grades

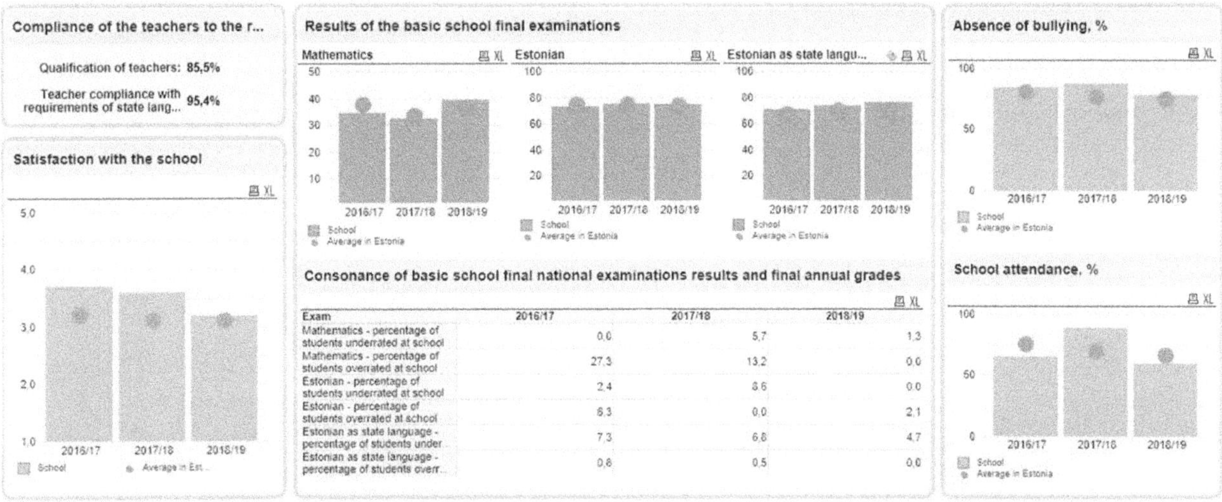

Source: Ministry of Education and Research (2020[22]), *Basic School School Card.*

Specific service providers also make use of EHIS, with access regulated by a legal agreement. In order to enter into a contract with the Ministry of Education and Research, the service provider has to submit an application that specifies the legal basis and how the data will be used by the provider. About 50 organisations have access to EHIS data. For example, as students in Estonia get a discount on public transport, the ticket inspector needs to check the student status of the passenger. For this purpose, transportation providers have an agreement with the Ministry of Education and Research that ticket inspectors have access to live data on student status, which is stored in EHIS. When travelling, the students' ID card is used to check the up-to-date student status in EHIS via X-Road. This process accounts for the highest number of queries to EHIS.

Many other service providers also have access to EHIS data, with access again strictly regulated by legal agreements between the Ministry of Education and Research and the service provider. Only the data specified in the contract can be shared and each query is tracked and documented. The contract also defines how often data can be accessed. Other examples of frequent queries to EHIS data include banks checking the status of students when receiving an application for a student loan or needs-based study allowances financed by the state. To apply for a study allowance, the student has to open an application and allow the system to receive personal information from other databases (Figure 2.6). When EHIS receives the required information, it makes an automated decision based on pre-defined requirements. In case of a positive response, EHIS sends a payout order to the State Support Service Centre (RTK) and the money is automatically transferred to the student's bank account. Interviewees explained that not all students eligible to receive support actually apply for a study allowance, even though the application process is very easy. In theory, the process could be completely automated, meaning that EHIS could technically identify all students eligible to receive a study allowance. However, this would require a change of the legal bases in order to allow the state to perform a matching of data, and would probably also increase the costs for the state.

Figure 2.6. Needs-based study allowance application process

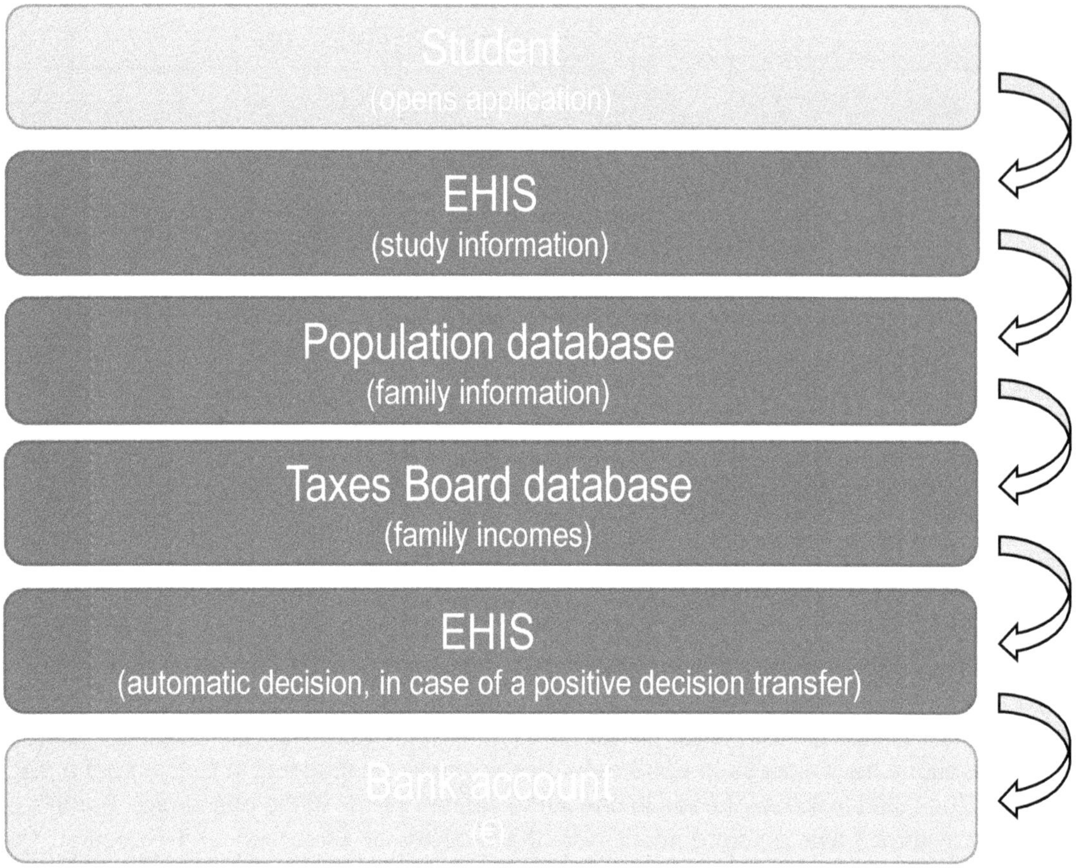

Source: Ministry of Education and Research, (2018[23]), Estonian Education Information System.

In addition to private service providers, EHIS is connected to more than 20 other state-run information systems, including the population register and the taxation register. EHIS needs data from the population register to complete information on student's residence, and the population register needs information on citizens' educational attainment to complement information on the general population. In this way, there is close collaboration and data exchange between the different state-run information systems. However, the legal basis is necessary to allow access to the data of other state-run information systems. Interviewees explained that the responsible employees in the ministries often know each other, and that co-ordination is often informal before drafting a contract that must be signed by the head of the respective ministry. Interviewees noted that in order to reach a legal agreement, the purpose of the data use and the legal basis must be made clear.

Another category of users of EHIS are researchers from Estonian universities and international universities, from international organisations such as the OECD, and from various EU bodies and agencies. Researchers can use the public online platform Educational Eye to access data, but the Ministry of Education and Research can also grant access to more detailed data for research purposes. Similar to service providers, researchers must submit an application that specifies the purpose and extent of the data requested. Additionally, the research plan has to be approved by the ethics committee. If access is granted by the Ministry of Education and Research, a contract is signed and the data can be accessed. The ministry can also specify how the data can be accessed. In cases of very sensitive data, for example information on students with special needs, data might only be accessed in the ministry building, or be anonymised by the ministry before being sent to the researchers.

A central role of EHIS is to facilitate evidence-based policy making. Interviewees explained that EHIS data are the basis for all educational policy decisions, with financing, quality control and monitoring processes all relying on EHIS data. For example, the state uses EHIS data to calculate allocations to the municipalities and state education institutions. Municipalities use EHIS data to calculate the budget needed for their schools and to monitor and plan the development of their school network. OSKA uses data on the number of students and teachers to identify teacher shortages.

One of the few user groups with direct access to EHIS data are government bodies such as the Ministry of Education and Research and the Statistical Office (Statistics Estonia). The main users of EHIS work in the Analysis Department and the E-Service Department of the Ministry of Education and Research. They answer data queries, monitor data quality and conduct the EHIS development process. Before reaching policy makers, data from EHIS go through the Analysis Department, which writes reports and analyses the data regarding questions that are of interest to policy makers. Furthermore, the Analysis Department prepares an annual report on the education system, along with other reports available online, which rely to a large extent on data from EHIS. The Analysis Department also makes sure that the database is in accord with the legal basis. According to interviewees, most changes in data collection are caused by changes in the legal basis on educational policy. For example, if the legal basis for special needs education changes, then the data in EHIS must be adjusted to capture those students who are entitled, according to the new law, to receive additional support at school.

The E-Service Department guarantees the technical functioning of EHIS. It can also make data queries, especially when these queries exceed the standard analyses. However, the development of the EHIS code is outsourced to private IT development firms. The E-Service Department functions as the connection and communication channel between developers and users, and works closely together with the Analysis Department. Changes in data collection that require changes in the code are collected in the E-Service Department and then communicated to the external developers. As described above, users can contact the EHIS helpdesk, which is run by HITSA. Complicated problems that cannot be solved by HITSA are delegated to the E-Service Department. The development of EHIS 2.0 also takes place in the E-Service Department.

Estonian trust and the culture of data usage

In many countries, data privacy concerns are high and there is limited trust in governmental services. However, in Estonia, there are higher levels of trust in the e-society than in other countries, which can be explained by five main aspects: historic context, convenience, reliability, security and transparency.

First, to understand why citizens in Estonia give data to the state so easily, interviewees underlined that the e-society must be seen in a historical context. When the Tiger Leap initiative was launched, with a focus on digitalisation and bringing computers to schools and ministries, data protection and data piracy were not an issue because the Internet and the online connections possible today were not yet on the horizon. Therefore, it was not problematic in the 1990s to establish databases with private data. Once the databases were established and people became used to giving their data – which is often not actively given but collected from the state, with citizens not necessarily aware of which kind of data are collected – the e-society continued down this path. Against this backdrop, interviewees were unsure if the establishment from scratch of such an encompassing e-society would be possible in present-day Estonia due to a higher awareness of data privacy and data leaks than in the 1990s.

Second, e-services are very convenient for people as they replace a lot of paperwork. For example, the application process for a university study programme can be completed easily online. The applicant allows the application platform to connect to EHIS and receive information on their certificates and grades. While in other countries this requires a lot of paperwork, in Estonia, the process is completed in a very short time and can be done from home. The online tax declaration or application for study loans were named as examples of digitalisation and e-services making the lives of Estonians easier. In the context of convenience, the "once only principle" plays an important role. The state can (by law) only ask once for citizens' data. For example, the study application portal should not ask the applicant for information on their name, address or prior schooling because all of this information is already registered in other systems, such as the population database or EHIS. Thus, the applicant only has to identify themselves using an identification card, and the application platform collects the information needed from other databases. The "once only principle" reduces the effort required by users, which goes hand in hand with the fact that citizens are used to giving data to the state and receiving services in return.

The third important building block for citizens' trust in e-services is the reliability and functionality of the services. Interview partners confirmed that services work well and that there are very few errors. For example, there is a website that documents the number of days of "smooth X-Road experience" (X-tee, 2019[11]). As of 1 September 2019, this number stood at 685 days.

Fourth, the state guarantees a high level of security, key to which are the decentralised structure of the databases and X-Road. Decentralisation refers to the fact that citizen data are stored in several different databases. For example, information on taxation is stored in a different database to data on health issues. Access is granted only on the basis of a legal agreement between the owner of the database, for example the Ministry of Education and Research in the case of EHIS, and the user of the data. So far, there have been no major data leaks or hacks. However, security remains an important issue, with security measures needing to be constantly updated as the tools to hack a database continue to develop.

Finally, the high level of transparency increases the trust in the e-services. Citizens can see online in their personal account who accessed which part of their data and when. They have the right to ask state authorities on what basis access was granted to their data. Furthermore, every query to any database is documented by the respective database and marked with a time stamp. This allows the database owners to trace every user of the data.

Analysis

EHIS is a complex database, but also an integral part of e-society in Estonia. However, interviews revealed that as well as the considerable opportunities offered by EHIS, there are also challenges. The strengths and challenges of the system are detailed below.

Strengths

First, one of the biggest strengths of EHIS is the accuracy of the data. EHIS is based on live data from the original source, education providers, and changes such as a new teacher starting work in a school are registered in EHIS the same day they start. Thus, EHIS data are always up to date. Additionally, the logical consistency mechanisms ensure that data are very accurate. For example, students cannot be counted twice because EHIS identifies each individual student with the help of the student's identification number and sends an error message if a school tries to register a student still registered with another school. EHIS is connected to other state-run databases, such as the population database, which allows it to present a wide range of data to its users without needing to ask schools to enter data already available in another database.

Second, the data and structure of EHIS allow for very detailed and diverse analyses, which supports the development of a variety of innovative features in education that is hardly possible in other countries to the same extent, such as the tracking over time of individual students. Furthermore, the structure of the database allows for educational data to be connected to, for example, the tax register, which contains information on income. This allows for an analysis of the effects of educational career on income. These data are naturally very sensitive, but interviewees argued that these kinds of analyses are closely supervised by experts in the Ministry of Education and Research and the Statistical Office (Statistics

Estonia) to safeguard the security of personal data. The personalised data in EHIS also allow the individual learning process to be analysed. For example, HITSA is working on applications that allow for a comparison between the individual usage of learning materials and individual learning outcomes. In Estonia, teachers and students can chose from a variety of online sources and e-learning applications; however, the volume might be overwhelming, and teachers might not always have enough time to find the best materials for their lessons. Information on materials for effective learning and teaching strategies can be used to inform the development of teaching material collections with the help of cross-usage of data collected in EHIS and other sources. This would allow teachers to find study materials faster and receive automated recommendations on other materials related to the same topic or student skill level. EHIS is the foundation for data personalisation and contextualisation that allows for these types of analyses and deep learning.

Third, EHIS enables evidence-based decision making – not only for policy makers but also for citizens. The public can access anonymised and aggregated EHIS data through the online platform Educational Eye. Based on this information they can take informed decisions concerning their own or their children's educational career. For example, information is available on employment rates and average income level for graduates of certain study programmes or vocational training courses. Information on which schools or universities provide which type of training are also collected and made available online. Educational Eye allows the public to get involved in the monitoring of the education system in general. EHIS is also an important tool for policy makers and enables them to take evidence-based decisions. Policy makers receive analyses and reports from experts in the Analysis Department of the Ministry of Education and Research. Interviews revealed that the Analysis Department is well connected to other internal departments and to other ministries. The administrative body in Estonia is small compared to very large countries, and information channels are often informal and short. This enhances the accessibility to information for policy makers.

Fourth, competences in the governance of EHIS are clearly defined, which allows for efficient decision making. EHIS is state-run and state-financed. The Ministry of Education and Research owns the database and is the only legal partner that users can enter into a contract with to access data. This makes it easier for stakeholders to file an application to receive access to the data. The main tasks concerning EHIS, such as technical and conceptual development, are performed in the Analysis Department and the E-Service Department. Both departments work closely together and are well connected to policy makers. Thus, competences are combined, which allows for an efficient usage and development of EHIS. Even though stakeholders such as private companies or schools are not directly involved in the governance of EHIS, feedback channels allow them to state their opinion and concerns concerning the system. For example, interview partners noted that the EHIS helpdesks – there is one run by HITSA and one by the E-Service Department for more complicated issues – are an important tool to collect feedback on EHIS, which is taken into account in its further development. Furthermore, schools can participate in pilot projects to test new features of EHIS. Interviews with schools confirmed that they feel well informed and competent to use EHIS and give feedback to the Ministry of Education and Research. Nevertheless, stakeholder involvement in the governance of EHIS is very limited. But the case of EHIS shows that, even though stakeholder engagement is desirable and could be improved, it is not always necessary to build and govern an integrated information system.

Challenges

The first of the main challenges of EHIS is the unused potential for evidence-based decision making by schools. Schools enter data because they are obliged to, but they show little interest in EHIS. This is a very similar challenge to that identified in the case of EWIS explored in Chapter 7, the US case study. One of the main objectives of EHIS is to facilitate the comparison of school performance and, as a result, incentivise school improvement. However, EHIS does not fully meet this aim. While institutions in higher education and vocational education do seem to compare performance, schools providing general education rely on their own experience and internal school management systems instead of analyses based on EHIS data. Thus, a great potential to use general education system data for evidence-based decision making at the school level is not fulfilled.

Second, stakeholder involvement could be extended and institutionalised, especially regarding the development of data-based e-services, deep learning tools and other applications. The increased involvement of schools, teachers, universities, pupils and other stakeholders in the development process would improve the quality and user friendliness of new features. Users know best about their needs. Instead of developing a "ready to use" product with little stakeholder involvement, integrating them into the development phase would allow for the tailoring of new features to their needs and demands. Feedback tools or personalised skill assessment tools would best be designed together with other stakeholders, who should be able to regularly voice their feedback.

Third, the detailed information in EHIS allows for extensive and sophisticated analyses. EHIS data are mainly used for standard reports and specific requests from policy makers, and the full analytic potential from the ability to connect EHIS data to other databases is not yet being used. The Ministry of Education and Research has started to tackle this issue and is working on more sophisticated analyses, including the tracking of teachers' careers and analysing pathways of drop-out candidates. Implementing bodies such as HITSA and the Innove Foundation have also started to consider new ways of analysing the rich EHIS data, but the process is slow. For example, data on student learning behaviour, which includes the selection of specific subjects, can be linked to career development. These are sensitive data which must be treated very carefully.

Fourth, how EHIS data is displayed to the public might lead to a limited and one-sided interpretation of the data. Educational Eye provides information on each school in Estonia in the form of a school card that summarises key indicators such as number of students or the average grade in the state exams. However, these key indicators do not represent the full range of qualities that education and schools have to offer. Interviewees explained that parents in particular pay too much attention to the grades in the state exams. The extent to which a school promotes personal development or fosters a child's interest in learning is not displayed on the school card.

Fifth, the process of how data enter EHIS is partly sensitive to errors. As described above, schools can choose between three options on how to enter data to EHIS: uploading Excel sheets, manual entering through the user interface, or automated data exchange between the schools' management software and EHIS. The first two options, however, allow schools to "check" and "correct" the data before submitting to EHIS. This means that there is the possibility to influence the data, intentionally or unintentionally, as errors might occur in the process of entering the data into the system. Furthermore, although it is a legal requirement, there are schools that do not always update the data immediately. This means that the live data in EHIS are not as live as they could and should be. However, such "manipulation" of the data is limited by the logical consistency check functions of EHIS, such as the automatic warning message if a school tries to register a student who is registered with another school, or who is not registered in the population register.

Summary

This case study on EHIS covers two policy dimensions – building integrated information systems and engaging stakeholders throughout the policy cycle. The emphasis of the analysis is on the first of these two dimensions as EHIS is a successful example of an integrated information system. As the analysis has shown, EHIS collects reliable live and personalised data that allow for detailed and even longitudinal analyses of the education system. EHIS enables policy makers to take informed and evidence-based decisions, and the analysis revealed that EHIS data are a very important source of information for policy makers. However, the analytic potential that EHIS offers is not yet fully used. One of the aims of EHIS was to incentivise schools to compare their performance with other schools, and thus stimulate efforts for further development and improvement; however, this aim is not met by EHIS due to a lack of interest by schools in EHIS data.

Although this case study also touches on the policy dimension of engaging stakeholders throughout the policy cycle, in contrast to the other cases in this report EHIS is an example of very limited stakeholder engagement. Stakeholders such as schools or private companies can access EHIS data, and the governance of EHIS offers feedback channels such as help desks, workshops and pilot projects. However, stakeholders are not systematically involved directly in decision making, for example in how to use EHIS data and the further development of EHIS. Although the centralisation of governance competences in the Ministry of Education and Research simplifies development processes, such as the application for access to data because there is only one party responsible, opening up governance to other stakeholders might increase the use of EHIS.

Policy recommendations

Use questions as drivers of data collection

One of the most important lessons learned from this case study is that successful information systems require more than just data collection: data should also answer important questions. Thus, questions to the education systems should be the driver of data collection, not the data collection itself. The case of EWIS explored in Chapter 7, the US case study, is a good example of how a concrete question, for example which student is likely to drop out of school and thus might need support, can drive data collection. EHIS was implemented and is governed by a top-down approach by the Ministry of Education and Research, as discussed in the main section on EHIS. In the foundation phase of EHIS, concrete questions such as how many schools have access to the Internet motivated data collection. Today, EHIS answers a lot of questions discussed in reports by the Ministry of Education and Research. It seems clear to the ministry what questions EHIS answers; however, schools and other stakeholders do not seem to know about the questions driving data collection. This should be made more transparent as it would increase the visibility of EHIS.

Support innovative data analyses

EHIS generates and collects a great deal data that allow for very detailed and innovative analyses. However, as discussed in the analysis section, the analytic potential is not fully used. HITSA explores new ways of connecting databases to generate new insights in learning processes and career development. This, however, should only be the beginning of innovative research. Estonia has the potential to generate very useful new insights into learning behaviour, learning materials and the effects of educational attainment on careers. These efforts could be intensified by investing in research teams that develop new questions for educational systems.

Put the data into perspective

The value of data comes with how they are interpreted and used, not merely with the collection. However, data interpretation can be difficult, and there is often more than one way. One example of problematic data interpretation concerns the school cards described previously, which summarise key indicators for a school such as the average grade of the pupils in state exams. It is essential to put these data into perspective, and users might need help with the interpretation of data and to understand that good education is more than just the final grade in the state exam. This can be achieved by, for example, educating users about the context of certain indicators, such as additional explanations in written form to help users to put numbers into perspective. Furthermore, the analysts who compile the data for the public should be aware of this challenge and consider how to provide further information, as well as which indicators are published.

The Ministry of Education and Research is aware of this problem and has started to complement information on the school with aspects such as pupil satisfaction. Ministry reports should explain the complexity of educational systems and not focus too much on certain numbers.

Streamline and automate the data collection process

As discussed in the analysis section, errors are most likely to occur in EHIS when schools enter their data. From the perspective of the schools, entering the data is an extra burden as most schools do not use the automated connection between their management system and EHIS. For some schools, this option is not available, and some schools prefer to have a final look at the data before submitting to EHIS. Thus, there are different ways to enter the data, and many manual steps that might lead to mistakes in the data. The Ministry of Education and Research has identified this problem and is working on EHIS 2.0. The new version of EHIS is supposed to collect the data automatically from the school's management systems and to remove human interaction in the data collection. A streamlined and automated data collection process would reduce the chances of errors entering the data, but it would also require getting the schools on board and establishing a process that they understand and support. For this purpose, schools need to be open to use new e-school management systems and be convinced that it is not necessary to check the data in person before submitting to EHIS. Moreover, streamlined and automated data collection would require streamlining the e-solutions, which is the task of the Ministry of Education and Research and private providers.

Promote the use of EHIS data among schools

Schools are the source of the data and the providers of education, and therefore are key players. Getting them on board in the data collection process is essential, and getting them to use EHIS data is important as it was one of the main goals of EHIS. The Ministry of Education and Research is working on how schools can be motivated to use EHIS data. One important aspect is to avoid increasing the burden of schools by using existing mechanisms and channels of communication. Schools rely on their own internal online management systems for evidence-based decision making. EHIS offers two advantages compared to the school management systems: it can connect to other databases and it contains data on other schools. Thus, EHIS allows schools to put themselves in a much broader context. Schools need to be educated about these advantages and need easy access to EHIS data that is of use to them.

Increase user friendliness

One way to make EHIS data more attractive is to increase the user friendliness of the access points. For example, the online platform Educational Eye contains a great deal of data but is not always easy to use. Citizens most likely do not use these tools on a daily basis, so the portal must be as intuitive as possible. User friendliness is important to make data accessible, and thereby lay the foundation for data collection in general. Increasing user friendliness requires research on the needs and behaviour of the users. In the case of EHIS this could be a challenge as a great variety of users access EHIS data. Thus, the portal has to be able to speak to many different perspectives. User friendliness is also one of the aspects of governance to be improved in the case of EWIS which is described in Chapter 7, the US case study.

References

Archimedes Foundation (2018), *Archimedes Foundation - Homepage*, http://archimedes.ee/en/archimedes-foundation (accessed on 3 January 2020). [21]

Authority, E. (2019), *Data Exchange Layer X-tee*, https://www.ria.ee/en/state-information-system/x-tee.html. [10]

E-estonia (2019), *Education*, https://e-estonia.com/solutions/education/. [2]

E-estonia (2019), *E-identity*, https://e-estonia.com/solutions/e-identity/smart-id. [9]

E-estonia (2019), *We have built a digital society and so can you*, https://e-estonia.com/. [1]

ESchool (2019), *About eKool*, https://ekool.eu/index_en.html. [12]

Etis (2019), *Terms and conditions of use*, https://www.etis.ee/Portal/Article/Index/f214f72b-3333-4426-8f31-2db3f1cb0b52?lang=ENG. [14]

HITSA (2019), *About us*, https://www.hitsa.ee/about-us. [20]

HITSA (2019), *Historical overview 1997-2017*, https://www.hitsa.ee/about-us/historical-overview. [6]

Innove (2019), *About Innove*, https://www.innove.ee/en/about-innove/. [15]

Kutsekoda (2019), *About Estonian Qualifications Authority*, https://www.kutsekoda.ee/en/about-kutsekoda/. [18]

Kutseregister (2019), *Avaleht (Home Page)*, https://www.kutseregister.ee/. [16]

Laanpere, M. (2002), "Tiger Leap Plus – an ICT Strategy for Estonian Schools, 2001 – 2005", *Baltic IT&T Review*, Vol. 01/24. [8]

Ministry of Education and Research (2020), *Basic School School Card.* [22]

Ministry of Education and Research (2018), *Estonian Education Information System.* [23]

Ministry of Education and Research (2019), *Contacts*, https://www.hm.ee/en/contact. [7]

OECD (2020), *Unemployment rate* (indicator), https://dx.doi.org/10.1787/997c8750-en (accessed on 28 January 2020). [5]

OECD (2019), *PISA 2018 Results (Volume I): What Students Know and Can Do*, PISA, OECD Publishing, Paris, https://dx.doi.org/10.1787/5f07c754-en. [3]

OECD (2019), *PISA 2018 Results (Volume II): Where All Students Can Succeed*, PISA, OECD Publishing, Paris, https://dx.doi.org/10.1787/b5fd1b8f-en. [4]

OIS (2019), *Õppeinfosüsteem (Study Information System)*, https://www.ois.ee/. [13]

OSKA (2019), *What is OSKA*, https://oska.kutsekoda.ee/en/. [19]

Santiago, P. et al. (2016), *OECD Reviews of School Resources: Estonia 2016*, OECD Reviews of School Resources, OECD Publishing, Paris, https://dx.doi.org/10.1787/9789264251731-en. [17]

X-tee (2019), *X-tee factsheet*, https://www.x-tee.ee/factsheets/EE/#eng. [11]

3 Case study: The Alliance for Initial and Further Training in Germany

This chapter discusses recent efforts to strengthen the governance of skills policy for the case of Germany. Building on the analytical framework developed in the introductory chapter, the German case study explores the case of the Alliance for Initial and Further Training, which was established in its present form in 2014. The Alliance brings together a broad range of stakeholders, i.e. state actors from different levels of government, representatives from unions and employers' association as well as other civil society groups. Even though Germany has a long tradition of collective decision-making in skills policy, the Alliance brings added value by effectively pursuing a "whole-of-government" approach in promoting collaboration between stakeholders. This chapter introduces the Alliance in detail as well as how it fits into the broader landscape of skills governance in Germany. It further discusses the Alliance's contribution to innovation in skills policy and ongoing challenges.

Introduction

The German skills regime, in particular the dual system of apprenticeship training, is widely perceived as a successful model that supports the effective development of skills. The success and popularity of the German "skills machine" (Culpepper, 1999[1]) rests on its ability to mobilise and involve employers in the financing and provision of vocational education and training (VET) to a much larger extent than in other countries. The strong involvement of employers in skills development and use is supported by a high degree of public commitment to VET. Apprenticeship training in firms is complemented with theoretical education in vocational schools, and training firms are supported by various means and measures so that they can provide training for disadvantaged young people. The governance structure of the skills system involves a multitude of stakeholders from local, regional and federal levels of government, as well as employer and craft associations and unions, which compels them to work together to address current challenges in the skills system and to continuously update and adapt the system to the changing socio-economic environment. Germany is considered to be a prime example of a "collective" skills regime (Busemeyer and Trampusch, 2012[2]) as it requires the continuous interaction between, and commitment from, these different stakeholders.

This case study provides a broad introduction to the governance of the German skills system and presents a relatively recent innovation within this structure: the Alliance for Initial and Further Training (Allianz für Aus- und Weiterbildung, hereafter "the Alliance"), which was established in its current form in 2014. This alliance builds on various preceding Pacts for Vocational Education and Training, the first of which was passed in 2004. Even though the governance of the German skills system already offers a multitude of entry points for stakeholders to get involved, there are several advantages of the new pact instrument that are particularly relevant for improving co-ordination across levels of government and different sectors of the skills system. Furthermore, the Alliance includes the top levels of the political hierarchy, whereas the regular governance bodies of the training system are somewhat removed from the top strata of politics. The Alliance has been an effective instrument in raising the priority of skills policy on the government's agenda and in devising new policy instruments and solutions to co-ordination problems that could not have been addressed in the regular governance structures.

Within the overall framework of this report, this case study focuses in particular on the dimensions of:

- Promoting co-ordination, co-operation and collaboration across the whole of government.
- Engaging stakeholders throughout the policy cycle.
- Aligning and co-ordinating financing arrangements.

Aligning financial incentives will receive somewhat less attention than the first two dimensions as the instrument of the Alliance is mostly about stakeholder involvement and co-ordination. The next section of this case study provides a short introduction to the governance of the German training system, before exploring the Alliance in greater detail. The analysis that follows is based on insights from interviews with stakeholder representatives and experts conducted in June/July 2019 in Berlin and via telephone. The final section of the case study gives a number of policy recommendations for the future development of governance in the German skills system.

Germany's education and training system

The German VET system – in particular dual apprenticeship training – is often regarded as a role model in education reform as it produces low levels of youth unemployment, a highly trained workforce at the intermediate skills level and – as a consequence – high levels of competitiveness among firms in certain product markets, such as high-quality manufacturing. More recently, scholars have argued that it also contributes to lower levels of socio-economic inequality as it provides access to well-paid and relatively secure employment for practically talented youth (Busemeyer, 2015[3]; Estévez-Abe, Iversen and Soskice, 2001[4]).

The German VET system also encompasses various forms of full-time vocational education in schools, but its core strength (and characteristic) is the dual apprenticeship training system. Despite the continued attraction of academic higher education, vocational training remains a popular choice for young people, even those with a general university entrance qualification. The number of new entries into the apprenticeship system has varied over the years, partly because the number of available training slots depends on business cycles and prevailing economic conditions as employers freely decide whether to hire apprentices and in which occupations they should be trained.

Figure 3.1 shows the number of new entries per year into the apprenticeship system compared to the number of new entries into academic higher (tertiary) education. There are two key observations to be made from this information. The first is that even after decades of educational expansion and "academic drift" towards tertiary education, the number of new entries into the apprenticeship system was still significantly higher than entries into higher education until 2011, and has remained at a comparable level since then. This confirms that vocational training is still an attractive choice for a large share of youth, as well as the relatively low share of young adults who choose to pursue academic tertiary education, which is exceptional in international comparison (Powell and Solga, 2011[5]). It should also be noted that there is a sizeable share of apprenticeship graduates that move on to pursue higher education studies afterwards. The second important observation is that in the year 2013, the number of new entries into academic higher education was – for the first time in history – higher than the number of new entries into the apprenticeship system. Furthermore, the number of entries into higher education increased relatively rapidly within a short period of time, reflecting the strong demand from employers for university graduates, as well as rising educational aspirations of parents and students. Given the continued attraction of higher education, this development is not likely to reverse soon, which indicates a new kind and level of competition between academic higher education and post-secondary vocational education. In response to these developments, hybrid forms of post-secondary education that combine dual apprenticeship training with higher education studies in the dual study programmes have been expanding rapidly (Graf, 2018[6]).

Figure 3.1. Number of new apprentices vs. number of new students per year, 2005 to 2016

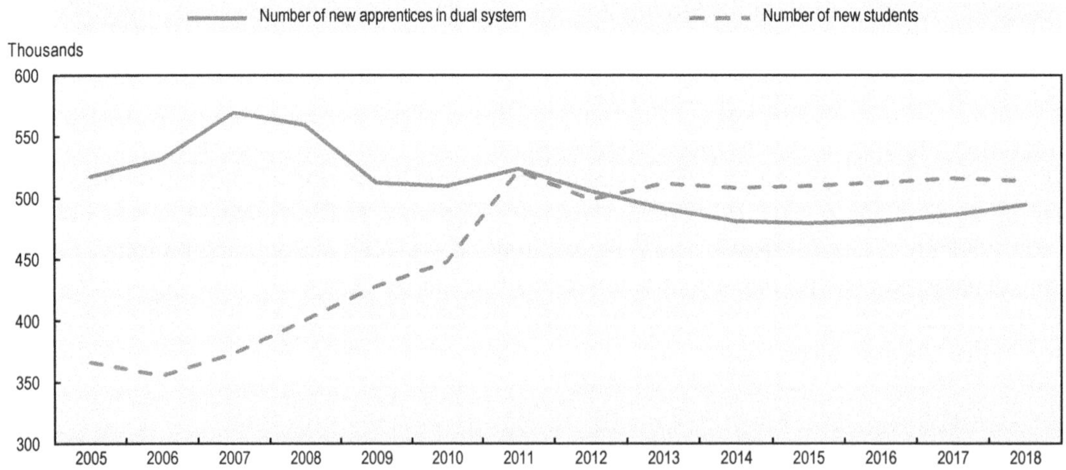

Source: BMBF (2017[7]), Datenreport zum Berufsbildungsbericht 2017: Informationen und Analysen zur Entwicklung der beruflichen Bildung (Data report on the Vocational Education and Training Report 2017: Information and analyses on the development of VET), https://www.fachportal-paedagogik.de/literatur/vollanzeige.html?FId=1137539#vollanzeige.

StatLink https://doi.org/10.1787/888934112671

Despite these recent changes, the dual model of apprenticeship training remains at the core of the German skills system. In this model, practical training in the workplace is combined with theoretical training in vocational schools and colleges. Most importantly, this kind of dual training is organised in an integrated manner, so that apprentices usually spend one or two days per week in school and the remainder of the week in the firm. This way, apprentices can immediately apply their theoretical knowledge in a practical setting, as well as reflect on their practical experiences jointly in a classroom setting. This kind of integrated learning has many advantages compared to sequential learning, which is more common in other countries such as Norway (see case study in Chapter 5 of this report), where students first spend an extended period of time in school before starting work in a firm, without necessarily receiving additional training while on the job.

One advantage of integrated learning is that apprentices gain "polyvalent skills" (Streeck, 1996[8]). These are skills that are specific to a particular firm context as well as sufficiently broad and versatile, often going beyond the immediate skills needs of the training firm. For example, apprentices in car manufacturing would not only be trained in how to use a particular machine or master a particular production process in one specific firm, but rather about the general principles of how to build a car engine, which can then be applied in a particular firm context. In a sense, the dual apprenticeship model involves training "above need", which may be criticised by employers in the short term as it is costly. In the long term, however, it contributes to developing a highly trained workforce that is more able to adapt to changing circumstances than a workforce which only receives short-term on-the-job training. Not surprisingly, unions have been more forthcoming in demanding training regulations that promote polyvalent rather than firm-specific skills in order to ensure that apprenticeship graduates are employable in range of different firms, rather than being tied to one particular employer (Streeck, 1996[8]).

Dual training also provides apprentices with a sense of responsibility for managing their own affairs, and contributes to the development of a number of tacit social and emotional skills (OECD, 2015[9]), such as coming to work on time, meeting deadlines, engaging with customers and taking responsibility for production processes. In the long term, this kind of engagement and involvement leads to a more motivated and committed workforce.

The curricula for the firm-based and school-based part of dual training are decided in a complex process of negotiation that involves business and professional associations, trade unions, the Federal Institute for Vocational Education and Training (Bundesinstitut für Berufsbildung, BIBB), the state (*Länder*) governments, and different federal ministries, depending on the particular occupation. Figure 3.2 is a simplified depiction of this process. The content of the workplace component is regulated in training ordinances (*Ausbildungsordnungen*), which are formal decrees issued by the federal government. Training ordinances regulate the firm-based part of apprenticeship training as they contain relatively detailed regulations on the content of training. The school-based component is regulated in framework curricula (*Rahmenlehrpläne*), which are issued by the individual states (*Bundesländer*). This is because Germany is a federalist country, and the states have the main legal responsibility for education policy. During the negotiation process, individual state governments co-ordinate with each other, as well as with the federal government and social partners (employers and unions), to ensure that the school-based and work-based components complement each other.

Within the federal government, several ministries are involved in skills policy. The Federal Ministry for Economic Affairs and Energy (Bundesministerium für Wirtschaft und Energie, BMWi) is formally responsible for issuing most of the training ordinances, in co-ordination with the Federal Ministry for Education and Research (Bundesministerium für Bildung und Forschung, BMBF). Broadly speaking, the BMWi is responsible for ensuring that training ordinances match the actual needs of labour market actors, whereas the BMBF is more concerned with how training ordinances fit with the needs of educational actors. The Federal Ministry for Labour and Social Affairs (Bundesministerium für Arbeit und Soziales, BMAS) has competencies in the area of adult learning, and is also involved as a central actor in the various initiatives further discussed below.

Compared to other sectors of the education system, VET is much more co-ordinated and centralised across the different *Länder*. As the training ordinances regulating the firm-based part of training is the same throughout the whole of Germany, the curricula for vocational schools also need to be harmonised. This is achieved by the *Länder*'s acceptance that in the case of VET, the social partners act as "first movers" in defining the needs and broad content of new or updated training ordinances.

Horizontal co-ordination across *Länder* is further facilitated by the Standing Conference of the Ministers of Education and Cultural Affairs of the Länder (Kultusministerkonferenz, KMK). The KMK was established in 1948 as a body of voluntary co-ordination between *Länder* in the policy area of education, in which the *Länder* enjoy a great deal of autonomy in policy making. Its purpose is to issue recommendations to the *Länder* in order to achieve a certain degree of harmonisation of educational standards, procedures and institutions, while also maintaining the autonomy of *Länder* to devise their own education policy. The recommendations do not have a legally binding character, even though in practice they are followed. The KMK's work is based on the consensus principle, which means that all *Länder* have to agree before a recommendation is passed. The strong emphasis on consensus-based decision making is identified by critics as a reason for decision making in the KMK often being perceived as slow and cumbersome.

Figure 3.2. The process of devising apprenticeship training curricula in Germany

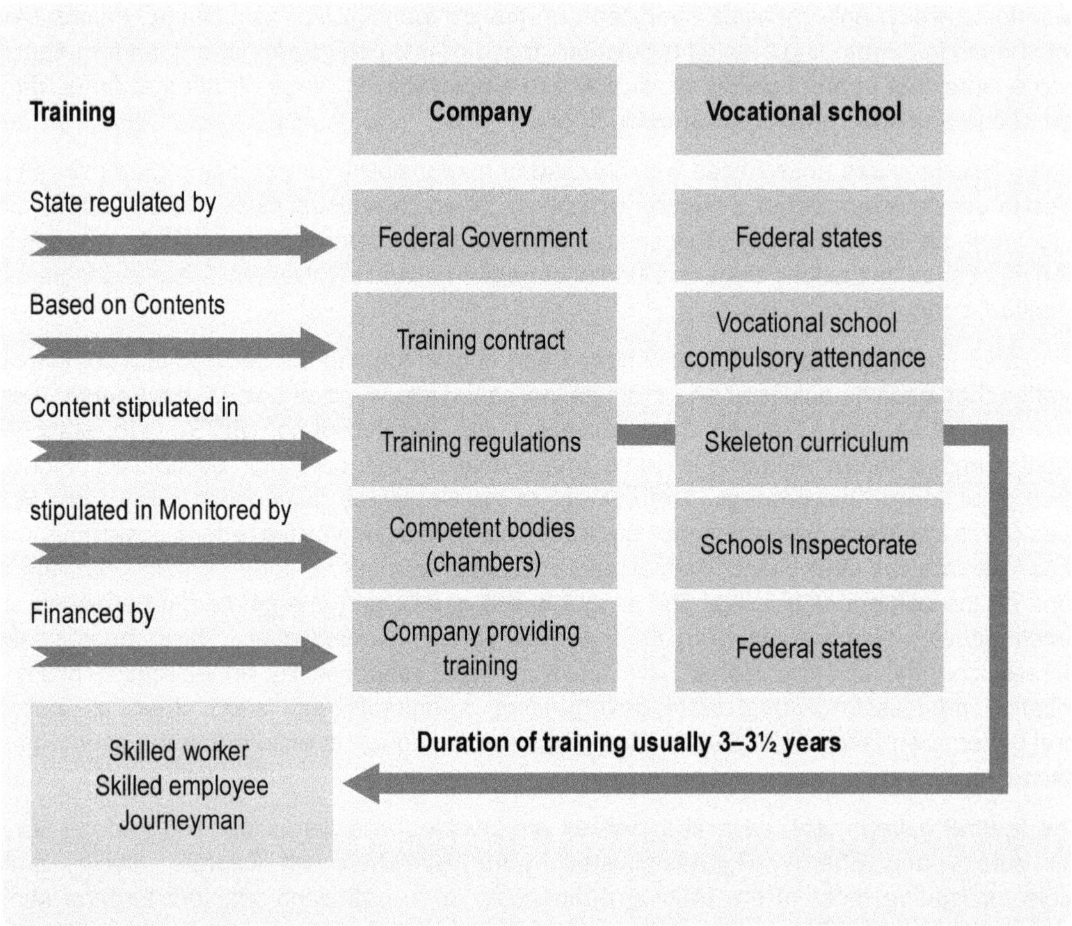

Source: Bundesinstitut für Berufsbildung, BIBB (2014[10]), *Training Regulations and How They Come About*, https://www.bibb.de/veroeffentlichungen/de/publication/show/7324.

In the domain of dual training, the secretariat of the KMK plays an important role in facilitating the harmonisation and co-ordination process of framework curricula for the school-based part of dual training.

Even though separate committees are set up to update and regulate the firm-based and school-based part of a dual training occupation, there is a clearly defined process (agreed on in the form of a "joint protocol" in 1972) that ensures multiple interactions between these two committees. Among other things, this process foresees that the heads of the two different committees participate in an observing capacity in the meetings of the other committee.

Researchers are also involved in the process of updating training regulations. In this regard, the BIBB plays a central role – both as a moderator of the overall process and as a source of research input. Innovation of training standards occurs mostly in the process of revising the work-based component. In this process, employers' associations and unions (the social partners) and the BIBB co-operate to identify current and future skills needs (Figure 3.3). Social partners have expertise and practical experience with the current set of training regulations. If these are outdated and/or new training needs arise, they can approach the BIBB to set in motion a revision process. The BIBB has a dual function: it acts as a moderator and process manager for negotiations between unions and employers, and provides research and technical expertise during this process. For instance, it conducts surveys among firms to verify whether new skills needs and demands have arisen.

Employers and unions – as well as the different levels of government – bring different perspectives and pursue different interests in this process. Employers and their particular associations are often interested in devising more specific training profiles to ensure that training regulations meet their immediate needs. Unions, in contrast, tend to be more interested in devising broader skills profiles so that apprenticeship graduates from the same occupation have the necessary skills to work in different types of firms. Over the years, both employers and unions have accumulated institutional knowledge and learning experiences so that new or reformed training occupations represent a good compromise between employer needs for specific skills and union demands for labour mobility. State actors largely refrain from direct intervention in this process, even in cases of disagreement, but may put political pressure on social partners to reach consensus (Busemeyer, 2009[11]). *Länder* governments are responsible for implementing the school-based part of dual training. They have an interest in devising occupational profile that are not too specific, as organising classes in vocational schools for very specific occupations is challenging as the number of apprentices/students is very small. Occupation-specific classes in vocational schools often need to include apprentices from a wide geographical area in order to fill up classes with a sufficient number of students, which creates additional organisational problems regarding transport and accommodation.

Figure 3.3. Co-operation between research, government and social partners in training reform

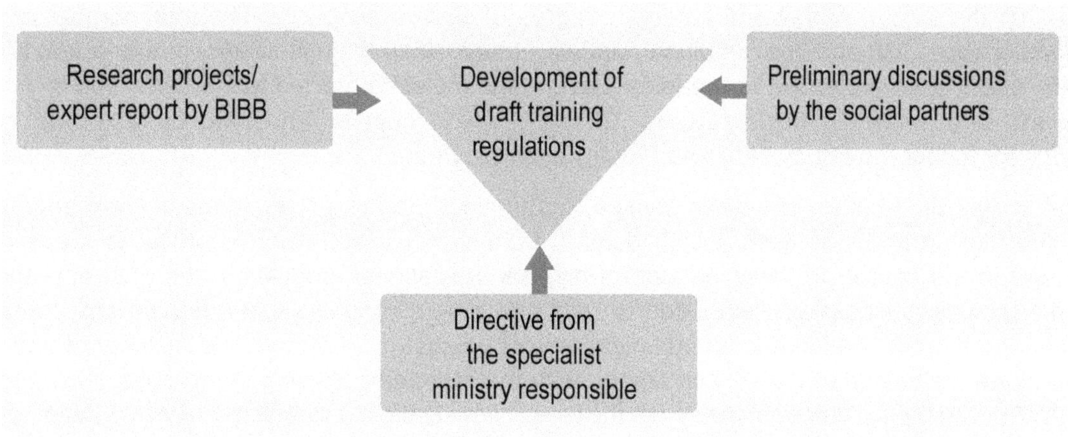

Source: Bundesinstitut für Berufsbildung, BIBB (2014[10]), *Training Regulations and How They Come About*, https://www.bibb.de/veroeffentlichungen/de/publication/show/7324.

Within the BIBB, the Board (Hauptausschuss) is the central governance body that oversees its activities, with an emphasis on its work in the field of updating and creating new training occupations (the so-called *Neuordnungspolitik*). The Board is a classic example of a corporatist decision-making body. The 32 seats (or rather "voices" or voting rights as the number of actual members/persons might be different) are distributed equally across four "banks", with eight seats/voices each for employers, unions, the *Länder* and the federal government. The Board is also responsible for the BIBB's research programme. Besides providing research on training occupations, as explained above, the BIBB also provides analyses on broader issues in the governance of VET, such as the costs and benefits of training or how conditions of access to training vary across regions and time periods. The BIBB is also responsible for publishing the annual report on VET (*Berufsbildungsbericht*), which contains both a data-based report on current developments in VET and a political section on future priorities for policy making.

For the system as a whole, there are advantages and disadvantages to the corporatist process of training reform. A significant disadvantage – particularly in the past when actors were less experienced – is that it can take a long time to revise training regulations as the process is complex and involves many stakeholders with divergent interests. For instance, the process of updating occupational profiles in the metal and electrical sector that took place in the 1980s took almost 15 years to complete (Busemeyer, 2009[11]). However, social partners and the BIBB now have more experience in this process, and may even have become more willing to compromise and work together as they perceive a joint interest in quickly adapting training regulations to changing market needs. The process of updating or creating a training occupation now takes about one to two years, although there are usually informal preparatory negotiations among the social partners before they officially approach the ministry to set in motion the formal process. In the background interviews for this case study it became clear that the involved actors have developed a significant degree of trust in the process and each other, which facilitates the search for objectively good solutions, while also recognising the different interests of the stakeholders involved. It also ensures a high degree of policy stability in the system as the basic structures and processes have been in place since the early 1970s.

A significant advantage of the corporatist approach is that the system remains sufficiently flexible to adapt to changing training needs as policy makers in government pay attention to the skills needs of labour market actors. Training reforms are based on solid research to provide an objective foundation to the subjectively voiced needs. As training reforms are usually based on compromise between unions and employers, potential conflicts in the implementation phase are effectively prevented. Furthermore, the central role of the BIBB as process manager and co-ordinator ensures that the number of training occupations does not get too high, which is important to maintain the usage value of apprenticeship certificates on the labour market and a certain degree of system simplicity. The total number of training occupations is about 330 and has remained relatively stable since the mid-1990s. In the United Kingdom, in contrast, a lack of co-ordination between employers and the state has led to a proliferation of vocational qualifications and awarding bodies (Keep, 2015[12]) which impairs transparency and has negative implications for labour market mobility and (youth) unemployment.

Figure 3.4 shows the number of new or revised (modernised) training regulations in Germany per year. It shows that the early 2000s were a high point in training regulation reform, similar to the mid-1990s (not included in the figure). In these periods of intense educational innovation, the dual apprenticeship training model was (successfully) extended to new and emerging sectors of the economy, in particular the service and the information and communication technology (ICT) sector. The majority of apprentices (63%) are currently trained in the service sector, with the rest being training in the productive (industrial) sector (BMBF, 2017[7]). Although many of these service sector occupations are low-level services, there are also a number of high-skill service sector occupations in the banking, insurance, consulting and ICT sectors, which lead to employment positions occupied by tertiary graduates in other countries. As a consequence, many young students with a university entrance qualification opt for VET instead of academic higher education (college or university). In 2009, 27.7% of apprentices have obtained a university entrance qualification – up from 20.3% (BMBF, 2017[7]). These figures show that VET has remained an attractive option even for students with an academic background, which is related to the system's ability to innovate and adapt to changing circumstances and training needs.

Figure 3.4. Revised and new training regulations in Germany per year, 2001 to 2013

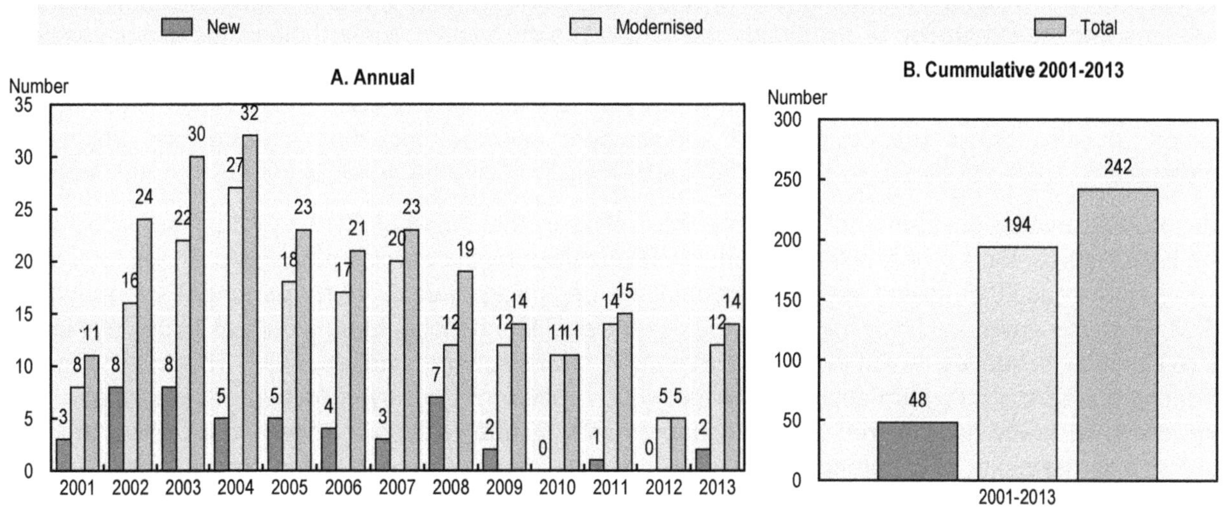

Source: Bundesinstitut für Berufsbildung, BIBB (2014[10]), *Training regulations and how they come about*, https://www.bibb.de/veroeffentlichungen/de/publication/show/7324.

StatLink https://doi.org/10.1787/888934112690

The corporatist model of dual apprenticeship training is accompanied by a cost-sharing arrangement between training firms and the state. The state – in particular the *Länder* – is responsible for financing vocational schools and colleges, including preparatory classes at these institutions. The federal government is mostly responsible for the costs of firm-based preparatory qualification measures related to labour market activation strategies. The training firms themselves, however, take on the largest share of financing. A recent survey of relative costs and benefits of training in firms concluded that, on average, firms spent EUR 17 933 on each apprentice per year, which is almost three times the amount that Germany spends on each student, on average, in the university sector (EUR 6 200 in 2012) (Statistisches Bundesamt, 2015[13]). However, when assessing these figures it is important to note that the gross costs of apprenticeship training are significantly reduced for firms through the productive contributions of apprentices. Apprentices, particularly in the last stages of their training, take on responsibilities of semi-skilled and skilled workers. Since apprentices are paid at lower rates, this amounts to significant cost savings for training firms. It is estimated that the real net costs (on average) are actually EUR 5 398, thus comparable to per-student expenditure. There is, however, a large degree of variation: productive contributions are highest for firms and training occupations in the crafts sector and lowest in large firms in the industrial sector. For firms in the industrial sector, investing in apprenticeships is a strategy to recruit future skilled workers, whereas for those in the craft sector it also amounts to a cost-saving strategy.

Over time, the legal foundations of the German VET system have been remarkably stable. Some critics have repeatedly warned that the resistance of the German VET system to change would eventually lead to its demise (Baethge, Solga and Wieck, 2007[14]; Kern and Sabel, 1994[15]; Greinert, 1998[16]), whereas others have identified its continued flexibility and adaptability to a changing socio-economic environment (Thelen, 2007[17]). The legal foundations of the modern dual apprenticeship system go back to the enactment of the Federal Law for Vocational Education and Training (Berufsbildungsgesetzes, BBiG) in 1969, and the above mentioned "joint protocol" in 1972. The first large reform of the BBiG took place in 2004/05, when the system was adjusted to allow for more flexibility (e.g. in terms of examination procedures) within the system. This reform also opened up the system to international and European influences, such as by allowing apprentices to undertake some of their training abroad. In 2016, the BMBF published the results of an evaluation of the 2005 BBiG reform (BMBF, 2016[18]). This evaluation did not identify major need for reform as the relevant stakeholders continued to be highly supportive of the system, even though union representatives tended to be somewhat more critical and pointed to remaining structural problems with the integration of disadvantaged youths into the system. Nevertheless, the evaluation report recommended only "technical and optimising reforms" in the detailed regulations of the BBiG law rather than large-scale change (BMBF, 2016[18]). Interview partners for this case study reconfirmed that the system receives broad support from all stakeholders involved, including state actors, unions and employers.

The grand coalition government that came into office in the spring of 2018 took up this issue again. The BMBF presented a proposal for a reform law (Berufsbildungsmodernisierungsgesetz, BBiMoG) shortly before Christmas 2018, giving stakeholders until the beginning of January to respond. Even though the BBiMoG mostly envisioned only minor changes to the legal foundations, there were two issues that implied more significant changes, which triggered contentious responses from stakeholders. The first change was to define a statutory minimum apprentice wage, which is currently set by collective wage agreements, or individually in areas not covered by these agreements, although even in these cases there are often collective agreements as reference point. The new minimum wage regulation for apprentices sets a minimum wage level for regions, sectors and firms that do not subscribe to collective wage agreements, meaning that where collective agreements are available they would still effectively set apprentice wages, reflecting the long tradition of social partnership in Germany. The second measure proposed in the BBiMoG was to rename vocational certificates in further/higher vocational education. Instead of (or in addition to) using traditional names such as *Industriemeister* or *Polier*, certificates would be awarded with associations to higher education degrees such as Bachelor Professional or Master Professional (vocational bachelor or master degree). Again, employers (although not necessarily from the crafts sector) are most critical about this proposal. Negotiations about the BBiMoG continued through 2019, thereby affecting the process to achieve a new agreement on the prolongation of the Alliance for Initial and Further Training (see below).

This brief review of the basic governance structure of VET in Germany shows that there is a long tradition of corporatist decision making in Germany, which is widely perceived as a strength of the system. Over time, the continuous interaction between stakeholders in different contexts has contributed to the development of a level of mutual trust among the actors involved. At the same time, there is still potential for conflict when interests diverge, as will be explored in the next section. The development of trust and the establishment of well-functioning corporatist governance bodies take time. In public debates about the transferability of the dual training model, such transferability is often negated with reference to the long tradition of apprenticeship training in Germany, going back to medieval times. Even though there is some truth to this claim, the institutional foundations of the current "modern" dual training system were laid in the 1960s and the 1970s, as explained above. Nevertheless, the strong tradition of corporatism clearly facilitates current efforts to revitalise social partnerships through other instruments, such as the Alliance for Initial and Further Training, which is explored in the following section.

The Alliance for Initial and Further Training

Overview and history of the Alliance

The Alliance for Initial and Further Training in its present form and composition was formed in December 2014 with a mandate for the time period from 2015 to 2018. However, in order to fully understand its role in the governance of skills policy in Germany, it is necessary to go back to the origins of its predecessor in 2004 (see Busemeyer (2009[11]; 2015[3]) for further details).

In 2004, economic conditions in the market for apprenticeships were very different to now. As mentioned above, employers are, in principle, free to decide whether to hire apprentices, and in which occupations these apprentices should be trained. As a consequence, business cycles have a strong impact on the number of available training slots, with business being more reluctant to hire apprentices in difficult economic circumstances. During the economic crisis following the end of the dot-com bubble in the early 2000s, the mismatch between the supply of training opportunities offered by firms and the demand from youth and apprenticeship applicants was particularly severe. A strong increase in formal youth unemployment could partly be compensated by expanding the so-called transition sector – a fragmented "system" of labour market activation and school-based stop-gap measures for youth unable to secure an apprenticeship (Baethge, Solga and Wieck, 2007[14]). However, the government coalition of the Social Democratic Party (SPD) and the Greens was under pressure to come up with measures to counter the lack of training slots without endangering the basic foundations of the dual training system.

One instrument prominently discussed by the government was the introduction of a training levy. The basic concept of a training levy is a requirement for firms to pay into a joint training fund, which can then be used to reimburse firms that engage in training activities. If properly designed and implemented, this system should set strong incentives for firms to engage in training as they will get reimbursed for their costs. Non-training firms are still required to pay into the joint fund in compensation for other firms taking responsibility for the collective good of having a well-trained workforce.

Even though levy-grant schemes have been introduced in other European countries (e.g. Denmark, France and the United Kingdom), as well as in some sectors of the German economy (i.e. in the construction industry), the establishment of a similar levy-grant scheme at the national level has always been very contentious in Germany. Employers and their related associations, as well as the Christian Democratic (CDU) and the Liberal (FDP) Party, have been critical of this idea as they feared that burdening business with further levies, or making their willingness to participate in training dependent on subsidies from the training fund, would endanger their continued commitment to apprenticeship training in the long run. In contrast, proposals to pass a training levy were always more popular with the unions and the SPD, in particular its left wing.

When faced with the continued crisis in the training market in 2003/04, the SPD/Green government moved ahead to develop a proposal to establish a levy-grant scheme. As expected, and as was also the case with previous proposals to establish a levy-grant scheme, the proposal met with fierce opposition from businesses and the Conservative-Liberal opposition. The government coalition and the unions themselves were also divided on the issue, but as the crisis on the training market persisted, there was an urgent need for government action.

The solution found was the enactment of the first National Pact for Vocational Training and the Qualification of Skilled Workers in Germany (*Nationaler Pakt für Ausbildung und Fachkräftenachwuchs in Deutschland*) in 2004. The pact was signed by the Federal Minister for Federal Minister of Economics and Labour, Wolfgang Clement (SPD), the Federal Minister for Education and Research, Edelgard Bulmahn (SPD), as well as the heads of the Association of German Chambers of Commerce and Industry (Deutscher Industrie- und Handelskammertag, DIHK), the Federal Association of German Industry (Bundesverband der Deutschen Industrie, BDI), the Central Association of the German Confederation of Skilled Crafts (Zentralverband des Deutschen Handwerks, ZDH) and the Federal Association of German Employers' Associations (Bundesvereinigung der Deutschen Arbeitgeberverbände, BDA). Most notably, the signatories of the pact did not include union representatives, who decided against participating as they did not believe it to be an effective instrument in response to the lack of training places. Thus, in the following years the pact established a new governance structure besides and in parallel to the formal decision-making bodies described in the previous section, in which the unions continued to participate. This first pact also did not include the *Länder* governments.

The first pact ran for three years (from 2004 to 2007). It's core element was a joint commitment from the pact signatories to provide each "willing and able" youth the opportunity to participate in training, preferably (but not necessarily) in the dual apprenticeship system (Ausbildungspakt, 2004[19]). To achieve this goal, the pact business partners committed to creating 30 000 "new" apprenticeships per year, as well as 25 000 newly designed "entry qualifications" to facilitate the transition from school to training for disadvantaged youths. The federal government would provide financial support for this new type of qualification, as well as further subsidies for training collectives (groups of training firms).

In the years that followed, the performance of the pact in achieving its goals was perceived differently by the different stakeholders in the system. The initial signatories naturally perceived it in a more positive light, i.e. as an instrument that effectively mobilised the "corporatist spirit" of the system to address a supposedly temporary shortage of training places, without fundamentally challenging the basic logic of the firm-based apprenticeship training system as the levy might have done. Unions, in contrast, were more critical regarding the contribution of the pact. In particular they noted that employers' commitment to create 30 000 "new" instead of "additional" training places was misleading. Due to natural fluctuations in the training system, it was possible (and relatively easy) to create new training slots (i.e. slots that had not been offered in the year before), while at the same time the overall number of training slots might still decline (as other slots get eliminated). As shown in Figure 3.1 above, this can happen, particularly in tightening economic conditions. The training market crisis persisted until 2005/06, when an upswing in the business cycle led to a significant improvement in the training market. This positive trend was temporarily halted during the crisis years of 2009/10, but quickly picked up again so that the dominant problem in the training market is no longer a persistent and structural gap between the overall demand and supply of training places, but rather a significant degree of regional imbalances and "mismatching", with some regions (and sectors) suffering from a lack of skilled applicants for apprenticeships, and other regions (and sectors) experiencing a greater demand from youth than supply of available training slots.

Despite continued criticism, the government (now a grand coalition government between the SPD and CDU/CSU) decided to extend the pact in 2007. In the renewed pact, which ran from 2007 to 2010, business actors increased their commitment to provide 60 000 new apprenticeship slots per year and 40 000 places for "entry qualifications", as well as recruit 30 000 new training firms (i.e. firms that had not offered or participated in training before) (Ausbildungspakt, 2007[20]). The federal government committed to provide the necessary funding for the expansion of qualification measures, and the Federal Employment Agency (Bundesagentur für Arbeit, BA) promised to increase efforts and funding to promote the placement of disadvantaged youth, in particular those with an immigrant background. In line with the increased involvement of the BA, the Federal Ministry of Labour and Social Affairs joined the other two federal ministries as formal pact partners. The Federal Association of Free Vocations (Bundesverband Freier Berufe, BfB) also joined as an important stakeholder for small and medium-sized enterprises in the service sector.

The pact was renewed for a third time in 2010, this time under the leadership of a government coalition of Christian Democrats (CDU/CSU) and Liberals (FDP) (Ausbildungspakt, 2010[21]). The number of formal signatories was extended to include a representative of the KMK, i.e. the *Länder* education ministries, as well as the State Secretariat for Migration, Refugees and Integration as the inclusion of youth with an immigrant background became a more important topic for pact signatories. This was partly because demographic changes had accumulated and contributed to a slow but continuous decline in the number of school leavers, which made employers increasingly worried about the future supply of skilled workers. Consequently, the priorities of the revised pact were primarily to improve vocational consulting in schools to lower the rate of school drop outs, particularly among youth with an immigrant background, to mobilise so-called *Altbewerber*, i.e. applicants who had been unsuccessful in securing an apprenticeship place in previous years, as well as to invest greater efforts in recruiting highly talented school leavers for vocational training rather than academic education.

In 2014, the Alliance for Initial and Further Training was established as the successor to the previous pacts. It is important to emphasise that the Alliance is both a document signed by the various partners and a body or discussion forum established to accompany and supervise the implementation of the policies and initiatives agreed upon in the pact document. In many ways, the Alliance signalled a re-start of the pact instrument in skills policy, which is indicated by the change in name and by the expansion of the range and number of pact signatories. Most importantly, unions officially joined the Alliance as pact partners. As some interview partners noted, this can be regarded as a response to increasing worries in previous pacts that unions might be excluded from important agreements between employers and state actors. Unions are formally represented by the German Trade Union Confederation (Deutscher Gewerkschaftsbund, DGB), which co-ordinates directly with major unions such as the IG Metall (Industriegewerkschaft Metall), ver.di (Vereinte Dienstleistungsgewerkschaft), IG BCE (Industriegewerkschaft Bergbau, Chemie, Energie) and IG BAU (Industriegewerkschaft Bauen-Agrar-Umwelt) who are involved as member organisations of the DGB. Moreover, the representation of *Länder* governments is expanded in the Alliance. In addition to the KMK as representative of the *Länder* education ministries, the Alliance includes a representative of the conference of *Länder* ministries for economic affairs and the conference of labour and social affairs ministries. The Federal Employment Agency (Bundesagentur für Arbeit, BA) is also now an official pact partner. All previous pact partners, i.e. representatives from the various employer organisations and government departments, continue to participate.

Innovation in the governance of skills policies

The Alliance encompasses an impressive range of stakeholders, effectively bringing together different government departments (education, business and labour), levels of government and stakeholders. Regarding its internal governance structure, the Alliance combines annual plenary meetings involving the top political levels with more regular meetings of working groups at the lower level. Furthermore, as becomes apparent when comparing the agreements of the Alliance with the previous pacts, the Alliance agreement contains a significantly higher degree of detail regarding specific policy instruments and issues to be further discussed. Over the years, the Alliance at the federal level has been complemented with numerous similar alliances at the regional *Länder* level, which ensure that the activities of the federal Alliance are complemented with regional alliances. Broadly speaking, the activities of the regional alliances are very similar to the federal alliance, for example to improve consulting and placement services for disadvantaged youth, to develop regional strategies to ensure a sufficient supply of skilled workers, and to develop new initiatives to promote adult learning.

The Alliance continues along of the lines of the previous pacts in terms of substance and topics, albeit with a certain rearrangement of priorities, which partly reflect the changing composition of pact partners and the changing conditions in the training market (Allianz für Aus- und Weiterbildung, 2014[22]). For instance, unlike the 2010 pact, but more in line with the pacts before then, the issue of ensuring a sufficient supply of training places receives more attention. More specifically, the business partners in the Alliance have committed to providing 20 000 "additional" (rather than simply "new") apprenticeship training slots per year from 2015, as well as 500 000 internship places for students and pupils. Furthermore, the Alliance partners have re-stated their commitment to provide a training opportunity to every applicant, preferably in firm-based training. The business partners in the Alliance commit to providing three offers for firm-based apprenticeship training to youth who did not manage to secure a training place by 30 September (the official starting date of the training cycle), although with the important modification that youth are expected to be regionally mobile. This points to the significant regional imbalances in the system: there are some regions (and occupations) where employers struggle to find applicants to fill the available training slots, and others where there are more applicants than available slots (BMBF, 2019[23]). Hence, providing training offers to youth if they are willing to move or accept training in a different occupation than they initially preferred is less challenging than the goal of providing each youth with a training slot in their preferred occupation and region, although it still represents a significant commitment on the part of employers. The Alliance has committed to doing more to counter persistent regional imbalances in the provision of training across German *Länder*.

An important innovation in terms of policy instruments that the Alliance agreement introduced was the "assisted apprenticeship" (*assistierte Ausbildung*), which is directed at improving the integration of disadvantaged youth into the training system. Before the Alliance agreement was enacted there were numerous instruments available to support the integration of youth who struggled to find a regular apprenticeship training slot in the open market. The assisted apprenticeship scheme, however, addresses an important gap in supporting measures by providing direct support, in the form of dedicated personnel with specialised social and pedagogical skills, for training firms that hire disadvantaged youth on a regular apprenticeship. The support is available for the entire training period. As youth are employed as regular apprentices within firms (rather than visiting out-of-firm training courses, for instance), their chances of securing employment after training is increased. The instrument of assisted apprenticeship is broadly supported by unions, employers and state actors. In the Alliance agreement, the government (i.e. the Federal Employment Agency) committed to financing 10 000 places for assisted apprenticeships in the first year of the Alliance period, and the pact signatories agreed that the instrument should become a regular element in the statutory toolbox of labour and training market policies soon thereafter.

Another example of concrete action in the context of the Alliance was a special agreement on the integration of refugees into the German education and training system (Allianz für Aus- und Weiterbildung, 2014[24]). When Germany experienced a major influx of refugees in the years 2014-2016, policy makers and stakeholders broadly agreed that education and training policies played a crucial role in integrating young refugees into German society and the labour market. Although many refugees lacked important qualifications and competencies required for the German labour market, an increasing number of German firms – in particular in the crafts sector – struggled to find skilled workers and apprentices. Hence, opening up the apprenticeship system to refugees had the potential to play a crucial role in promoting their integration and in mitigating the shortage of skilled labour, at least in the short run. As one interview partner noted, the Alliance provided important political leverage at this point, which regular bodies such as the BIBB Board would not have been able to provide. The role of the agreement of the Alliance partners on developing "perspectives" for refugees documents the broad willingness of relevant stakeholders in the system to acknowledge and agree on the challenges ahead, and to list and document policy responses that should be given priority, such as promoting language courses and educational consulting, setting up a system of "welcome officers" (*Willkommenslotsen*) to provide individual guidance and counselling to refugees, and recognising formal foreign qualifications and informally obtained prior knowledge.

As will be discussed in greater detail in the next, more analytical, section, the Alliance is broadly supported by the major stakeholders in the system but its future is not certain. The last Alliance agreement officially lasted until the end of 2018. The coalition agreement of the currently governing grand coalition between the CDU/CSU and the SPD contains a commitment to extend and renew the Alliance for another period of several more years. According to interview partners, the signing of a new version of the Alliance agreement was significantly delayed for a number of reasons, particularly the protracted start of the last federal government, which only took up office in the spring of 2018, and the parallel negotiations about the reform of the Federal Law on Vocational Education and Training (BBiMoG) (see above). As the BBiMoG reform involved some contentious issues, the relevant stakeholders, in particular employers, were reluctant to negotiate the renewal of the Alliance agreement before final decisions regarding the BBiMoG had been made. In spite of this state of affairs. Nevertheless, there has always been broad agreement among the stakeholders that the Alliance should be continued, as our interview partners repeatedly confirmed.

On 26 August 2019, a new Alliance agreement was signed that renewed the commitment of the Alliance partners until the year 2021 (Allianz für Aus- und Weiterbildung, 2019[25]), when the next federal elections are scheduled due to take place. The renewed Alliance agreement continues along the lines of the 2014 agreement. First, the Alliance signatories have committed to strengthening firm-based apprenticeship training, for example by intensifying efforts to recruit employers, particularly small and medium-sized enterprises, to offer apprenticeship training, and by expanding guidance counselling in schools and local chambers of commerce. Second, the agreement reinforces the commitment of the Alliance partners to improve and further develop measures that support the transition from school to training. More specifically, the above mentioned assisted apprenticeship instrument piloted in the 2014 Alliance will be further expanded and established as a regular policy instrument, rather than an experimental pilot scheme. Finally, the new Alliance pact puts a focus on promoting higher VET, i.e. types of further education and training that typically follow initial training in VET. In this way, the signatories aim to preserve and promote the attractiveness of VET relative to academic higher education.

Analysis

Opportunities for innovative governance reforms

When considering opportunities for innovative governance reforms it is useful to consider the "added value" of the Alliance, given that the governance of the German skills system had already promoted multiple ways of stakeholder engagement and co-ordination across levels of government. A first observation in this context is that the Alliance and its predecessor pacts have proven surprisingly resilient, as the first pact was passed back in 2004. Furthermore, even though the primary and relatively political purpose of the first pact was to provide some form of compensation for the failure of attempts to establish a levy-grant scheme, the pact instrument has apparently proven its value from the perspective of those directly involved, evolving into a much broader forum for exchange and debate about current and future priorities for skills policy in Germany.

Assessing the added value of the Alliance primarily involves comparing it to the BIBB Board, which is the main decision-making body in the traditional governance structure of the German VET system and includes representatives from employers, unions, the *Länder* and the federal government.

As emphasised by interview partners, a first – and arguably the most important – added value of the Alliance compared to the work of the BIBB Board is that the Alliance directly involves the top of the political hierarchy (i.e. ministers and the government as a whole). In this sense, it is a unique committee at the federal level, and significantly different from existing boards and committees. The signing and renewal agreement of the Alliance agreement and – to a lesser extent – the yearly meetings of the Alliance plenary are major political events that create a significant amount of media attention. Hence, the Alliance helps to put skills policy at the top of the government's agenda during these focal points, and represents a government instrument that shows it takes skills policy seriously. In contrast, the activities of the BIBB Board rarely make the news as they fall under the domain of day-to-day government activities.

Second, there are important differences regarding the dynamic of agenda setting and policy innovation. As explained above, the BIBB Board is the main decision-making body in the process of reforming, revising and passing new training ordinances. As a consequence, its agenda is largely determined by issues related to this process, even though broader issues on the governance of the VET system are also discussed, particularly in relation to the annual publication of the "Report on Vocational Education and Training". Nevertheless, it is important to emphasise that simply for legal reasons, the remit of the BIBB Board is limited to issues concerning the dual apprenticeship system itself, which, although important, is only one part of the overall skills system.

In contrast, the agenda of the Alliance, given that it is mainly a political body with no statutorily defined limitations, is much broader, and social partners have a stronger influence in setting priorities and topics compared to the BIBB Board. For example Alliance discussions cover labour market integration and activation measures, apprenticeship training, and further and continuous training. As interviewees confirmed, the range of topics usually goes beyond what was included in the original Alliance or pact agreement as new issues emerge. By linking initial and further training, the Alliance responds to a traditionally weak spot in the governance of skills policy, namely the connection between initial and further training. This connection is only well-developed for further education routes defined in the statutory foundations of the VET system, namely the BBiG and the associated regulation for the crafts sector (Trade and Crafts Code, Handwerksordnung, HwO). These regulations, however, cover only a certain segment of the growing market for further education, which is increasingly important in times of major technological change. In the long term, the Alliance could help to prepare the ground to establish a more encompassing legal foundation for a comprehensive framework that covers all sectors of initial and further training.

The Alliance provides a forum for discussion and exchange to enable stakeholders to consider the priorities for skills policy in more conceptual terms and, to some extent, independent of the current legal limitations. Compared to previous pacts, the broad involvement of stakeholders is an advantage, even though it may slow down decision-making processes to some extent. Background interviews revealed that even the signatories of the previous pacts support including more partners and stakeholders, such as unions, and a broader involvement of the *Länder* in the renewed Alliance as it has a positive effect on the relevance and effectiveness of the Alliance in the long run. Getting critical voices on board (as mentioned above, unions had been critical of the previous pacts) also helps to achieve a broad consensus and sense of ownership among stakeholders.

The Alliance has become a kind of laboratory for innovative policy instruments, such as the assisted apprenticeship scheme, initiatives to facilitate the integration of refugees into apprenticeship training, new policy instruments to facilitate the transition of disadvantaged youth from school to training (*Einstiegsqualifizierung*, EQ), and the development of joint criteria in placement services for youth in earlier pacts. Since the agencies and ministries in charge of these policies are directly involved as equal partners in the Alliance, these ideas can be tested before being eventually transformed into binding law by the responsible state actors (or not if they do not work). Thus, a supporting condition for corporatist bodies such as the Alliance to work is that state actors are involved on an equal footing and with the same degree of commitment as non-state actors. If and when the Alliance partners commit and agree to joint initiatives, they can easily be transferred from the Alliance level to policy making and implementation. Given the corporatist legacy of the German skills system, achieving this kind of agreement is more likely than in systems without such a tradition. The corporatist tradition also means that the involved partners maintain some degree of autonomy in regulating their own affairs within their domains, which implies that they have the necessary resources at their disposal.

A third issue relates to the internal governance of the Alliance compared to the BIBB Board (and other committees in the system). Although regular meetings and exchanges between stakeholders are helpful in creating mutual trust between those involved, creating trust does not necessarily mean that all stakeholders have to agree to the same thing. Establishing mutual trust in a corporatist decision-making process instead signifies developing a mutual recognition of each other's interests and position, while still remaining committed to joint problem solving and the search for mutually beneficial solutions. The building of trust is also helped by the fact that those involved in the policy network of skills policy often remain in their position for many years, which also leads to a development of trust on a personal rather than institutional level. A potential cost of this might be the development of "group think" mechanisms that prevent the emergence of genuinely new ideas.

Even though stakeholders have met often and repeatedly in the committees of the BIBB, and on other occasions, interview partners indicated that the internal governance of the Alliance provides additional benefits. Most importantly, and somewhat in contrast to the previous pacts, the Alliance organises regular meetings at the working level in one central and several subsidiary working groups dedicated to particular topics, which allows for more continuous and "problem-oriented" forms of exchange. For instance, unions and employers have traditionally disagreed on how exactly to measure the number of youth in need of an apprenticeship training slot. Interviewees indicated that the Alliance was helpful in achieving a joint understanding of these basic facts. The internal governance of the Alliance is also helpful in solving conflicts by shifting venues: if there is conflict at the working level (which rarely happens), contentious issues are delegated to higher levels in the ministerial hierarchy. If issues are contested at a political level, they can be delegated down to the working level to address them from a more problem-oriented and pragmatic angle.

The fourth added value of the Alliance regards its role in facilitating co-ordination across levels of government. As mentioned above, the role of the *Länder* in the process of training reform is usually confined to devising the framework curricula for the school-based part of VET. Given that the BA, which is in charge of the bulk of labour market activation and supporting measures, is a federal agency, the role of the *Länder* is limited in this area. The Alliance has opened up new ways for *Länder* to get involved in skills policy more broadly. Whereas the previous pact only included the KMK as a representative of the *Länder* education ministries, the 2014 Alliance (as well as the 2019 follow-up) also included representatives from the *Länder* ministries of economic affairs and the ministries for labour and social affairs, signalling a much broader understanding of skills policy that goes significantly beyond education and training institutions in the narrow sense. According to interviewees, the co-ordination of positions on the part of the three conferences of *Länder* ministries is challenging, but mostly works well, although other pact partners might perceive it as slow and cumbersome.

The federal Alliance is connected to emerging regional alliances constructed according to the role model of the federal alliance. As mentioned above, these regional alliances essentially translate the goals and strategies of the federal Alliance into a regional context, facilitating the collaboration between regional policy makers and stakeholders. Even though the federal Alliance provides a loose framework to help guide these regional processes, the co-ordination is sufficiently flexible to allow regional actors to set their own priorities.

To sum up, the Alliance for Initial and Further Training is widely supported by the relevant stakeholders in the system, and there is basic agreement that it should be continued. However, there are a number of challenges that should be addressed in further developing governance arrangements in the area of skills policy.

Ongoing challenges of the Alliance

The temporary nature of the Alliance (and the previous pacts) can make it dependent on prevailing political conditions at a certain moment in time, i.e. when the previous Alliance needs to be renewed and revised. As discussed above, even if there is basic agreement among stakeholders, the continuation of the Alliance can become entangled with other potentially more pressing and/or contentious issues on the political agenda. The delay in passing the most recent Alliance agreement did not threaten its continuation as a new agreement was signed within a few months, but as long as the Alliance is not permanent, there is always the potential that renewal attempts might fail, even if it is widely supported by stakeholders.

Some interview partners reported that the temporary nature of the Alliance can also have advantages. For example, it is possible to significantly expand the scope of the Alliance from one iteration to the next, bringing new stakeholders on board and new issues onto the agenda. The temporary nature of the agreement also implies that when a new Alliance is forged its issue are much more likely to rise to the top of the government's agenda compared to if the Alliance is transformed into a regular body of government decision making.

A second challenge is the multiplication of committees and decision-making bodies. Although, as explained above, there is broad agreement among stakeholders that the Alliance provides additional benefits and complements existing governance bodies, there is still a danger that the establishment of additional committees and governance bodies might at some point make decision making too cumbersome and slow, and contribute to overlap between competing bodies.

For instance, in parallel to the negotiations regarding the renewal of the Alliance and the reform of the BBiG, the federal government passed a National Strategy for Further Education (Nationale Weiterbildungsstrategie) on 12 June 2019. All major stakeholders were involved in devising this strategy, which at first sight at least partly overlaps with the mandate of the Alliance. However, in contrast to the Alliance, the National Strategy approaches the issue of further education more from a labour market perspective than an educational perspective, which is related to the fact that the BMAS has taken the lead on the project. Thus, the official division of labour is that the Alliance focuses on types of further education and training that are legally recognised as follow-up training to initial VET, whereas the National Strategy for Further Education focuses on other types of further education and lifelong learning. On a practical level, these different types of further education are clearly related and should therefore be addressed from a more comprehensive perspective. Hence, as interviewees confirmed, although the division of labour between the two bodies – the National Strategy for Further Education and the Alliance – is formally clear, it is practically somewhat entangled.

Although interview partners perceived a certain risk of having too many committees, there was widespread agreement that the Alliance should remain independent and not, for instance, be merged with the BIBB Board, confirming that the actors involved see added value in the Alliance. However, there were also critical voices among interview partners stating that the Alliance may no longer be needed. The initial purpose of the various pacts and the Alliance was to deal with a temporary shortage of training places, which is no longer a major concern. These critical voices also argued that some of the innovations developed in the context of the Alliance are likely to have come about even without the Alliance. Hence, the challenge in this respect is to give the Alliance a clear mandate that would justify its continued existence on a more permanent basis (more on this below).

A third challenge regards the potential of the Alliance to promote innovation in terms of policies and governance instruments. On the one hand, the political nature of the Alliance means that actors can discuss broader conceptual issues independent of statutory limitations. On the other hand, this political nature also means that the actual degree of innovation in terms of policies and instruments promoted by the Alliance is inherently limited, and confined by the discretionary leeway of stakeholders acting within their respective domains.

This means that broadly speaking, the Alliance does not have the task or mandate to develop proposals for large-scale policy reforms, but rather to improve the functioning of the system given the current distribution of competencies and responsibilities. At the same time, reform discussions at the higher political and policy-making level affect the working of the Alliance. For instance, the reform of the BBiMoG mentioned above had concrete consequences for the renewal of the Alliance (namely delaying the enactment of a new Alliance agreement); however, this reform project was not discussed and debated within the Alliance, but through the traditional channels of stakeholder engagement in law making.

Therefore, much of the work of the Alliance amounts to incremental improvements of current practices in labour market and training policies, but usually not proposals for large-scale reforms, not least because this kind of agreement would be politically difficult to achieve. If, however, the actual work of the Alliance is mostly confined to incrementally improving the performance of the system, involved stakeholders might at some point begin to doubt the genuine added value of the pact – in the worst case dropping out altogether – as was also occasionally indicated in interviews.

Furthermore, the degree of innovation that results from Alliance agreements is inherently limited by the fact that it involves stakeholders with strong vested interests in the continued existence of the current system. As decisions are based on the corporatist consensus principle, there is a further risk that solutions will amount to lowest common denominator policies rather than genuine innovations. However, it should be emphasised that the Alliance has on the whole come up with a number of innovative ideas and proposals in recent years, and has effectively mobilised the joint problem-solving potential of the involved actors to some degree.

The final challenge is the information base of decision making in the Alliance. Although the Alliance can and does draw on the expertise provided by established institutions in the field of education, training and labour market policies, such as the BIBB, the research institute of the BA (the Institute for Employment Research, IAB) and various non-governmental research institutes, there is no explicitly formalised input from research to the debates and negotiations of the Alliance at the political level, in contrast to countries such as Norway (see Chapter 5). However, adding an external perspective by, for instance, involving non-partisan experts and researchers in debates could itself become a source of innovation, and partly mitigate the risk of "insider" bias.

Summary

The Alliance for Initial and Further Training responds to the three dimensions of governance identified in the introduction to this chapter in the following ways. First, it promotes co-ordination across levels of government by involving representatives from the *Länder* and the federal government. At the same time, it involves representatives from different departments at these different levels, i.e. education, economic affairs and labour/social affairs. Using these multiple forms of co-ordination and collaboration in an effective manner is demanding on the part of the actors involved, and facilitated by the long tradition of cross-level collaboration within German federalism.

Second, the Alliance engages stakeholders throughout the policy cycle. Due to its long tradition of corporatist decision making, non-governmental stakeholders are regularly involved in policy making through various channels. The Alliance is another channel primarily focused on the implementation and policy formulation stages of the policy cycle. Regarding implementation, Alliance partners devise new and innovative ways and instruments to improve the functioning of the current system. This is achievable as agencies and ministries are involved in the Alliance on an equal footing to non-state actors, and with a significant degree of commitment, which are crucial preconditions for success. Regarding policy formulation, the Alliance has – to some extent – become a laboratory for new policy approaches that may later be translated into law as it allows actors to debate and consider innovations in broader terms and independent of the legal remit of existing institutions and bodies.

Third, the Alliance helps to improve the alignment of financial incentives. Broadly speaking, the financial incentives for stakeholders in the VET system are already well-aligned in the sense that there is a clear division of labour between employers paying for the firm-based element of training, the state paying for the school-based part, and supporting labour market measures and workers (i.e. unions) accepting a certain degree of wage restraint for apprentices. The Alliance allows actors to engage in a dialogue about the potential necessity to occasionally revise and renegotiate this cost-sharing arrangement to reflect ongoing changes in the socio-economic environment. Furthermore, state actors in the Alliance have committed to back up proposals to introduce new instruments such as assisted apprenticeship training with the required financial resources.

Policy recommendations

Based on the analysis of the strengths and weaknesses of Germany's Alliance for Initial and Further Training, the following section presents a number of policy recommendations specific to the Alliance. More general policy recommendations are developed in the final chapter of this report.

Make better use of the potential of the Alliance to promote innovative skills policies

The Alliance has the potential to devise innovative approaches to the future development of skills policy, and has done so in the past. However, there is also the risk that the work of the Alliance will increasingly get stuck in the details of implementing existing policies and instruments, and shy away from considering the future of skills policy in Germany more broadly. To some extent, this is a consequence of the institutional nature of the German education and training system, but it is also related to the composition of Alliance partners.

Regarding the institutional legacy of the German education system, the Alliance largely remains in the VET domain. An innovative aspect of the Alliance has been the extension of its remit to the further education sector, although this connection might become weaker again due to the enactment of the National Strategy for Further Education. Even more importantly, when considering skills policy in broader terms, it would be necessary to include the higher education sector. Responding to new demands from employers related to technological change and globalisation, the intersection between higher academic and vocational education has become a major source of innovation in the German education system, for example the rise of dual study programmes that combine apprenticeship training with higher education studies. In further iterations, the Alliance should pay more attention to this sector, for example by discussing how and whether joint standards for dual study programmes should be devised, and how young people could be encouraged to pursue this kind of education. The new 2019 Alliance agreement moves in this direction by emphasising the need to invest more in higher VET, including hybrid training programmes that combine VET with higher education studies.

Regarding the composition of Alliance partners, further expanding the range of actors involved might be considered, even though adding further partners could hamper the effectiveness of decision making at some point. Related to the previous paragraph, representatives of the higher education sector could be added as partners, such as the Conference of University Rectors (Hochschulrektorenkonferenz, HRK) or the Science Council (Wissenschaftsrat). Currently, as seen for instance in the debate about the reform of the BBiG, representatives from the higher education sector are reluctant to open up universities to the field of VET. However, involving the higher education sector would signal that the domain of skills policy is not confined to vocational education, but rather encompasses different forms of post-secondary and tertiary education with strong connections to the labour market.

Prevent multiplication of governance bodies

Even though the Alliance has created added value, it is important to prevent the multiplication of governance bodies. The innovative potential of the Alliance lies in the fact that it crosses departmental boundaries as well as levels of government. It would be unfortunate if the establishment of new governance bodies such as the National Strategy for Further Education or the revival of the Education Council (Bildungsrat), which is supposed to improve co-ordination between federal and Länder levels in the field of education, eventually leads to overload of the responsible actors, and overlapping mandates between competing decision-making bodies. Hence, when new co-ordinating governance bodies are established they need to be regularly evaluated against whether or not they still produce added value. This also holds for the Alliance, even though this chapter has argued that it will most likely continue to add value in the future. Such an evaluation could and should be primarily based on feedback from the actors involved, since they know best whether or not the Alliance provides added value. There should, however, also be some form of evaluation of governance structures from the system perspective that involves input from outside observers, experts and academic research.

Link duration of Alliance agreements with election cycles

The temporary nature of the Alliance has advantages and disadvantages. In order to maintain the desired political effect of raising the visibility of skills policy as an important issue on the government's agenda, the Alliance should continue to involve the political heads of the ministerial hierarchies. The mandate (in terms of topics and priorities) of the Alliance should also be renegotiated and adjusted with new agreements on a regular basis. Since the content of the agreements are likely to reflect political context conditions, this process of renewal should be formally connected to the duration of legislative periods, which would also facilitate the implementation of the Alliance's decisions. The 2019 Alliance agreement already points in this direction as it ends in 2021, when the next federal elections are scheduled to take place.

Putting the Alliance on a more permanent basis in terms of funding would allow a further development of its internal governance structure, for example by establishing a more sustainable knowledge base. Given the readily available expertise of the BIBB and the IAB, the Alliance's efforts in this direction would not have to emulate or copy these institutions' research activities, but rather provide a more systemic connection between them. In particular, the Alliance could develop an expertise in studying governance-related aspects of skills policy – an area of research not usually addressed in depth by these institutions. Developing this kind of expertise would also give it a clear mandate.

Allow sufficient time for meaningful stakeholder engagement

Most interview partners expressed concerns that meaningful engagement with stakeholders is difficult when time pressure is high. More concretely, there were three major issues on the agenda in terms of skills policy: the reform of the BBiG, the establishment of the National Strategy for Further Education and the renewal of the Alliance. The federal ministries involved stakeholders in all of these processes, but rather than discussing them together in one forum (e.g. the Alliance), they were treated as separate processes that ran in parallel. Even though the range of actors and stakeholders involved in all three may slightly differ, there is a large overlap in terms of competences and personnel. This arrangement of de facto strong interconnections, but formal separation between the processes, may lead to co-ordination problems and inefficiencies. For instance, negotiations on the renewal of the Alliance were significantly slowed down by uncertainties related to the reform of BBiG. Hence, in order to allow for meaningful stakeholder involvement, stakeholders need to be given sufficient time to develop their proposals. Furthermore, the added value of the Alliance is currently to devise practical solutions to current challenges in the skills system. A vision for its future development is that due to its unique nature as a largely political committee, it could also reflect on and discuss strategic options regarding system-related aspects of governance.

References

Allianz für Aus- und Weiterbildung (2019), *Allianz für Aus- und Weiterbildung 2019-2021 (Alliance for Education and Training 2019-2021).* [25]

Allianz für Aus- und Weiterbildung (2014), *Allianz für Aus- und Weiterbildung 2014-2018 (Alliance for Education and Training 2014-2018).* [22]

Allianz für Aus- und Weiterbildung (2014), *Erklärung der Partner der Allianz für Aus- und Weiterbildung: Gemeinsam für Perspektiven von Flüchtlingen (Declaration by the partners of the Alliance for Education and Training: Together for Perspectives for Refugees).* [24]

Ausbildungspakt (2010), *Nationaler Pakt für Ausbildung und Fachkräftenachwuchs in Deutschland, 2010-2014 (National Pact for Training and Young Professionals in Germany, 2010-2014)*, Bundesregierung, Berlin. [21]

Ausbildungspakt (2007), *Ausbildungspakt verlängert – erfolgreiche Arbeit wird fortgesetzt (Training pact extended - succesful work continues).* [20]

Ausbildungspakt (2004), *Nationaler Pakt für Ausbildung und Fachkräftenachwuchs in Deutschland (National pact for training and young professionals in Germany).* [19]

Baethge, M., H. Solga and M. Wieck (2007), *Berufsbildung im Umbruch: Signale eines überfälligen Aufbruchs (Vocational training in transition: Signal of an overdue departure))*, Friedrich-Ebert-Stiftung, Berlin. [14]

BIBB (2014), *Training regulations and how they come about*, Bundesinstitut für Berufsbildung (BIBB), Bonn, https://www.bibb.de/veroeffentlichungen/de/publication/show/7324. [10]

BMBF (2019), *Berufsbildungsbericht 2019 (Vocational training report 2019)*, Bundesministerium für Bildung und Forschung (BMBF), Bonn, Berlin. [23]

BMBF (2017), *Datenreport zum Berufsbildungsbericht 2017: Informationen und Analysen zur Entwicklung der beruflichen Bildung (Data report on the Vocational Education and Training Report 2017: Information and analyses on the development of VET)*, Bundesministerium für Bildung und Forschung, Bonn, Berlin. [7]

BMBF (2016), *Evaluation des Berufsbildungsgesetzes (BBiG): Evaluierungsbericht (Evaluation of the Vocational Training Act (BBiG); Evaluation Report)*, Bundesministerium für Bildung und Forschung, Bonn, Berlin. [18]

Busemeyer, M. (2015), *Skills and Inequality: The Political Economy of Education and Training Reforms in Western Welfare States*, Cambridge University Press, Cambridge, New York. [3]

Busemeyer, M. (2009), *Wandel trotz Reformstau: Die Politik der beruflichen Bildung seit 1970 (Change despite a backlog of reforms: the policy of vocational training since 1970)*, Campus Verlag, Frankfurt/New York, http://www.mpi-fg-koeln.mpg.de/pu/mpifg_book/mpifg_bd_65.pdf (accessed on 14 January 2019). [11]

Busemeyer, M. and C. Trampusch (2012), *The Political Economy of Collective Skill Formation*, Oxford University Press, Oxford, https://global.oup.com/academic/product/the-political-economy-of-collective-skill-formation-9780199599431?cc=fr&lang=en&# (accessed on 14 January 2019). [2]

Culpepper, P. (1999), “Still a Model for the Industrialized Countries?”, in Culpepper, P. and D. Finegold (eds.), *The German Skills Machine: Sustaining Comparative Advantage in a Global Economy*, Berghahn Books, New York, Oxford. [1]

Estévez-Abe, M., T. Iversen and D. Soskice (2001), “Social Protection and the Formation of Skills: A Reinterpretation of the Welfare State”, in Hall, P. and D. Soskice (eds.), *Varieties of Capitalism*, Oxford University Press, Oxford. [4]

Graf, L. (2018), “Combined modes of gradual change: The case of academic upgrading and declining collectivism in German skill formation”, *Socio-Economic Review*, Vol. 16/1, pp. 185-205. [6]

Greinert, W. (1998), *Das „deutsche System“ der Berufsausbildung: Tradition, Organisation, Funktion (The “German system” of vocational training: Tradition, Organisation, Function)*, Nomos, Baden-Baden. [16]

Keep, E. (2015), “Governance in English VET: On the functioning of a fractured ’system’”, *Research in Comparative & International Education*, Vol. 10/4, pp. 464-475. [12]

Kern, H. and C. Sabel (1994), “Verblaßte Tugenden: Zur Krise des deutschen Produktionsmodells (Faded virtues: On the crisis of the German production model)”, in Beckenbach, N. and W. Van Treeck (eds.), *Umbrüche gesellschaftlicher Arbeit*, Schwartz, Göttingen. [15]

OECD (2015), *Skills for Social Progress: The Power of Social and Emotional Skills*, OECD Skills Studies, OECD, Paris, https://doi.org/10.1787/9789264226159-en. [9]

Powell, J. and H. Solga (2011), “Why are Higher Education Participation Rates in Germany so Low? Institutional Barriers to Higher Education Expansion”, *Journal of Education and Work*, Vol. 24/1-2, pp. 49-68. [5]

Statistisches Bundesamt (2015), *Bildungsfinanzbericht 2015 (Financial education report 2015)*, Statistisches Bundesamt, Wiesbaden. [13]

Streeck, W. (1996), “Lean Production in the German Automobile Industry: A Test Case for Convergence Theory”, in Dore, R. and S. Berger (eds.), *National Diversity and Global Capitalism*, Cornell University Press, Ithaca, London. [8]

Thelen, K. (2007), “Contemporary Challenges to the German Vocational Training System”, *Regulation & Governance*, Vol. 1/3, pp. 247-260. [17]

4 Case study: Lifelong learning in Korea

Lifelong learning becomes ever more important in a fast-changing world. This chapter analyses the lifelong learning system in Korea along three governance dimensions: the promotion of co-ordination across levels of government ("whole-of-government" approach), engaging stakeholders throughout the policy cycle and the alignment of financial incentives. The chapter explains the multi-level governance approach of lifelong learning in Korea and introduces key players and their roles on the different governance levels. The chapter then focuses on the lifelong learning system in Suwon City. The lifelong learning system in Suwon City is characterised by a high density of learning facilities and the participation of a great variety of stakeholders. Based on the analysis, the final part of the chapter develops policy recommendations that address co-operation and co-ordination in the governance of lifelong learning.

Introduction

One of the roles of educational and training systems is to equip learners with the skills required by employers to maintain the competitiveness of the economy. At the same time, educational systems aim to enable citizens to participate in society and social life. In a world characterised by rapid change due to digitisation and the transition towards a global knowledge-based service economy, a key challenge for educational and training systems is to ensure that people can access opportunities to upskill and reskill.

Lifelong learning, which includes informal learning as well as formal and non-formal education over the lifespan, is an important way of meeting this challenge. The governance of lifelong learning is very complex because it requires the engagement of learners, employers and a broad range of stakeholders such as course providers and learning facilities. It also requires the voluntary engagement of participants, meaning that the governance of this sector has to take into account the needs and demands of citizens. At the same time, employment relevant (vocational) lifelong learning is becoming increasingly important as the requirements of the labour market are constantly changing. In order to design employment relevant lifelong learning that successfully increases the employability of participants, it is important to consider business and employee interests in the governance of lifelong learning. Governance also has to ensure that training facilities are provided, that experts develop and update the training content, and that sufficient training spaces are created. This requires the engagement of a broad range of stakeholders.

This case study looks at the lifelong learning system in Suwon City in Korea, a city of 1.2 million inhabitants. Suwon City has managed to successfully establish a dense network of more than 600 lifelong learning facilities that enable citizens to reach a lifelong learning centre within a ten-minute walk. Suwon City received the United Nations Educational, Scientific and Cultural Organization (UNESCO) Learning City award in 2017. The city runs its own lifelong learning centre, and certified lifelong learning educators work in the city's administration to create and strengthen collaboration across the whole government.

With reference to the overall framework of this report, this case study focuses on three of the four dimensions:

- Promoting co-ordination, co-operation and collaboration across the whole of government.
- Engaging stakeholders throughout the policy cycle.
- Aligning and co-ordinating financing arrangements.

The first section introduces Korea's lifelong learning system more generally before the second section describes the lifelong learning system in Suwon City in particular. The third section gives a more detailed analysis of the lifelong learning policies. The analysis is based on document research and 11 semi-structured expert interviews with 18 lifelong learning experts conducted in Seoul, Suwon City and Sejong in April 2019. The fourth section develops policy recommendations and highlights the lessons learned from this case study.

Korea's lifelong learning system

Background

Although education is of very high value in Korea, the focus has traditionally been on university-based higher education (UIL, 2015[1]). After the Korean War in the early 1950s, education policies targeted and expanded primarily basic and higher education (Han, 2008[2]). Today, younger generations in particular have very high educational attainment levels in international comparison: 98% of 25-34 year-olds complete upper secondary education and 70% of 25-34 year-olds complete tertiary education (OECD, 2018[3]). This represents the highest share of young people holding a tertiary degree among all OECD countries.

As well as formal educational attainment, the skill levels of students is above average from an international perspective. The OECD's Programme for International Student Assessment (PISA) shows that Korean students (participants are 15 years old) score is well above the OECD average regarding skills in the field of science, reading and mathematics (Figure 4.1).

Figure 4.1. PISA 2018 scores

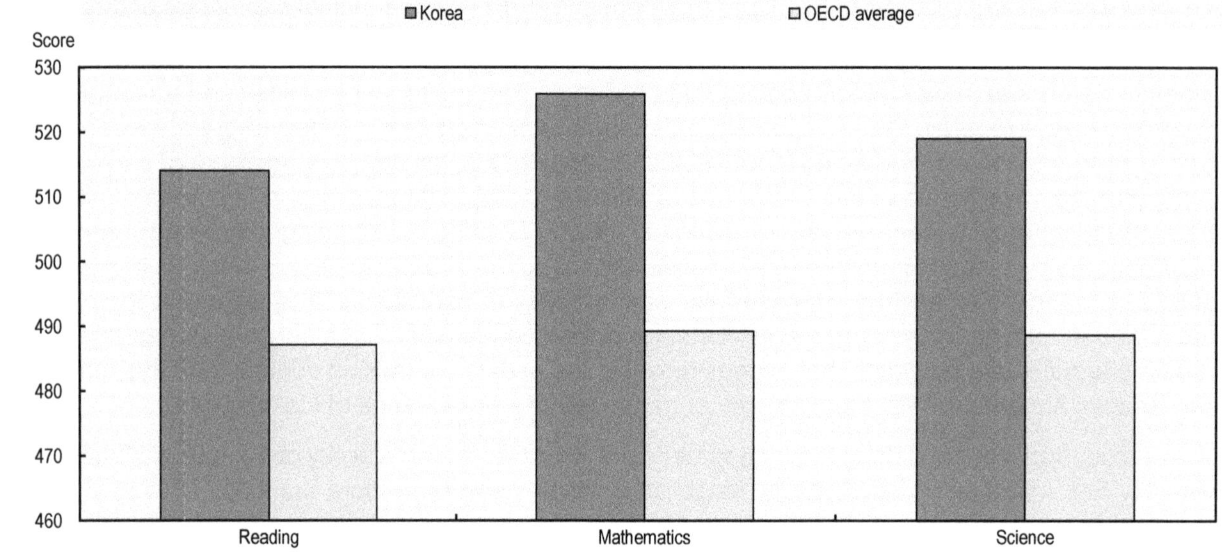

Source: OECD (2019[4]), *PISA 2018 Results (Volume I): What Students Know and Can Do*, https://dx.doi.org/10.1787/5f07c754-en.

StatLink https://doi.org/10.1787/888934112709

However, the Survey of Adult Skills, a product of the Programme for the International Assessment of Adult Competencies (PIAAC), revealed a clear gap between the skills performance of younger and older generations in Korea. Figure 4.2 shows that this gap is also high in comparison with the OECD average.

Figure 4.2. Mean literacy and numeracy skills of adults by age group, Korea and OECD average

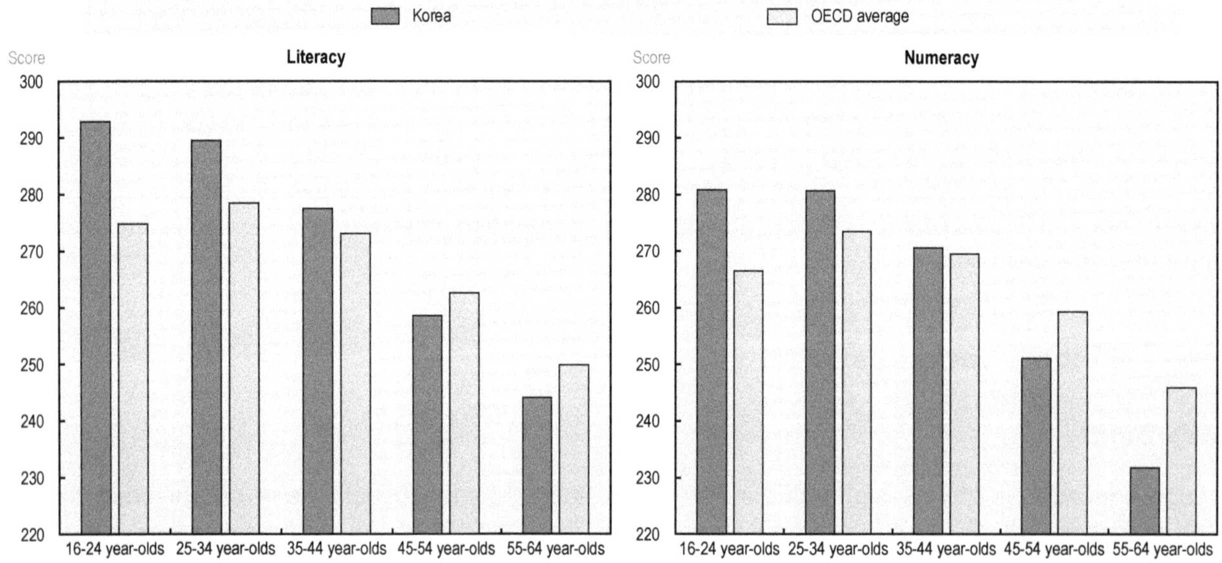

Source: OECD (2016[5]), *Skills Matter: Further Results from the Survey of Adult Skills*, https://dx.doi.org/10.1787/9789264258051-en.

StatLink https://doi.org/10.1787/888934112728

These findings from the Survey of Adult Skills (PIAAC) show that the skills level of young adults is well above that of older generation in Korea (OECD, 2015[6]). When comparing the skills proficiency of 55-65 year-olds, Korea is among the three lowest-performing countries (OECD, 2013[7]). In contrast, 16-24 year-olds in Korea score second after Japan when compared across OECD countries (OECD, 2015[6]). The low levels of basic skills, such as literacy, among the older generations is a serious challenge. Studies have shown that literacy is not only related to employment and income, but also to health and civic engagement (OECD, 2013[7]). In addition, in Korea the relationship between an individual's socio-economic background and skills proficiency is much stronger in the older generation than in younger generations. In fSurvey other words, lower skill levels among the older generation are more strongly related to lower socio-economic status than in the younger generations.

There are challenges in reaching those with low literacy and numeracy skills, as even though they are most in need, they tend to participate less in educational programmes (OECD, 2015[6]). In order to break this vicious circle, educational programmes should target and activate low-skilled and older adults, as identified in the OECD's 2015 diagnostic report on Korea, which said that there was a "need for greater attention to the older cohorts" (OECD, 2015[6]). Differences between age groups are also visible when looking at the employment rate. In 2018, the average employment rate for 15-64 year-olds was roughly 67%, but when broken down by age the rate was 73% for 25-34 year-olds in contrast to 67% for 55-64 year-olds (OECD, 2018[3]). Lifelong learning, upskilling and easy access to education for older generations are important ways of closing the educational gap between generations.

Actors and legal foundations

Korea's lifelong learning system is divided into two pillars, and interviewees highlighted that it is essential to know this fact to understand the system as a whole. The first pillar is governed by the Ministry of Education and focuses on recreational (in the interviews also referred to as "civic" or "life enrichment" education) lifelong learning. Courses do not (necessarily) provide skills that are immediately relevant for employment; instead, the enjoyment and personal development of citizens are the priority. Examples of courses include calligraphy, languages, baking or handicraft. Interviewees explained that many people seek these programmes because they have been deprived of such learning opportunities when they were younger due to earlier economic difficulties in Korea. The national Lifelong Education Act is the legal basis of this pillar.

The second pillar is based on the labour law and is governed by the Ministry of Employment and Labour. This pillar focuses on employment relevant skills. Courses are provided by, for example, polytechnic universities. This case study will focus on the governance of the first pillar but will touch upon the second pillar in order to paint a full picture of the system.

Lifelong learning was not always at the top of the policy agenda in Korea; however, in 1980 Article 31 was added to the constitution which stipulated that "the state is responsible for promoting lifelong education" (UIL, 2015[11]). Interrupted by the Asian currency crisis, it took until the 1990s for the topic of lifelong learning to gain in importance again (Han, 2008[2]).

In 1999, the Lifelong Education Act was enacted, which is the central legal reference for (recreational) lifelong learning at the national level. The act defines lifelong learning as "all types of systematic educational activities other than regular school curriculums, including supplementary education for educational attainment, basic literacy education for adults, occupational ability enhancement education, humanities and liberal education, culture and art education, and citizen's participation education" (UIL, 2013[8]).

The Lifelong Education Act establishes two important lifelong learning instruments at the national level. First, it requires the Ministry of Education to develop a National Lifelong Learning Promotion Plan (NILE, 2018[9]), which sets mid- and long-term goals and identifies challenges. The first plan was launched in 2003 and the ministry has to update the plan every five years. The fourth plan covers the years 2018-2022 and highlights, for example, the equal right to lifelong education of every citizen. It also proposes the creation of an online learning system to make access to lifelong learning easier for employees (NILE, 2018[9]). The National Lifelong Learning Promotion Plan has no binding character but it functions as a guideline for other actors in lifelong learning, such as local and regional governments.

The second instrument established by the Lifelong Education Act is the Lifelong Education Promotion Committee. This committee is chaired by the minister of education who invites a range of vice ministers from different ministries such as the vice minister of culture, sports and tourism, the vice minister for health, welfare and family affairs, the vice minister of environment, and the vice minister of labour. Experts on lifelong learning from academia and the head of the National Institute for Lifelong Education are also members of the committee. The act limits the number of committee members to 20.

The tasks of the committee are only vaguely described in the Lifelong Education Act. Topics to be discussed include the National Lifelong Learning Plan, the evaluation and reformation of the policy system promoting lifelong learning, and co-operation in lifelong learning policies. The committee develops ideas on these issues and its advice should be taken into account by the Ministry of Education when drafting the five-year plan for lifelong learning. However, recommendations are not binding and the act leaves open how detailed and in what way suggestions should be made by the committee. The act also does not specify how often the committee should meet, and currently it does not meet very often. The task of convening the committee is delegated to its chair (the minister of education). As of May 2019 there had not yet been a meeting in 2019.

The Korean Educational Development Institute (KEDI) plays an important role in education research in Korea as the national centre for educational statistics and a think tank involved in educational policy development and implementation (KEDI, 2019[10]). The institute covers all levels and areas in education such as primary education, university-based education and teacher education. However, interviewees expressed concerns that lifelong learning is not of high importance to the institute, and that its research efforts are limited in this regard.

The National Institute for Lifelong Education (NILE), founded in 2008 as part of the Lifelong Education Act, is also an important player in the governance of lifelong learning in Korea. Its role includes the development and implementation of national lifelong education policies (NILE, 2019[11]). NILE supports the Ministry of Education in the drafting of lifelong learning strategies and programmes. Furthermore, NILE developed and manages the Lifelong Learning Educators programme, which is a training programme that provides knowledge on the governance of lifelong learning and deepens the managerial skills of lifelong learning strategies, policies and programmes (NILE, 2017). For example, civil servants can undertake this training in order to become a lifelong learning expert in their department. The certificate, issued by NILE, is nationally standardised, and NILE sets the requirements for attaining the certificate. The training to become a lifelong learning educators is equivalent to at least 50 European Credit Transfer and Accumulation System (ECTS) credits (equivalent to about 1 500 hours of studying) from a university and an internship in the field of lifelong learning. Once training is complete, lifelong learning educators can work in public institutions and design lifelong learning policies, programmes and budgets, as well as manage lifelong learning centres. They can also work for local governments and cities. Their task is to foster and help develop lifelong learning strategies.

NILE also organises one of the central national lifelong learning promotion events: the Lifelong Learning EXPO. Every two years, cities compete to be the host of the Expo, with NILE selecting the successful city. Educational institutions, regions and cities use the Expo to show what they have achieved regarding lifelong learning. It is a very important event not only to present different regional and local approaches to lifelong learning, but also as a place where different stakeholders exchange information, compare their achievements and take new ideas back to their city or region.

Lifelong learning at the local and regional levels

The governance of lifelong learning in Korea is characterised by the idea that planning and implementation is best conducted at the local level (UIL, 2015[1]). Against this backdrop, the Lifelong Education Act requires each of the 17 provinces in Korea to establish a lifelong learning promotion centre. As of 2019, each province had successfully established one of these centres. The centres are financed by the governments of each province and are independent from the Ministry of Education. They conduct research on lifelong learning in their province, develop lifelong learning programmes and offer courses. Interviewees explained that these local lifelong learning centres have a lot of freedom to design their own programmes. The heads of the centres meet three times a year and exchange ideas and discuss challenges with each other. They also travel to other countries to learn about other regional approaches to lifelong learning.

The local/city level also plays an important role in the governance, and especially the implementation, of lifelong learning in Korea. The Lifelong Education Act highlights the importance of the city level by requiring the establishment of city (and district) lifelong education councils. For instance, the head of the city (district) should also be the chairperson of the city's lifelong education council. The chairperson decides on council members, but they should be public officials such as representatives from the city's department of education, specialists in lifelong learning or representatives from lifelong learning institutions. The size of each council is limited to 12 members. These councils, according to the Lifelong Education Act, deal with the implementation of lifelong education projects for local residents and facilitate co-operation between relevant agencies. Thus, the Lifelong Education Act has established a multilevel governance structure for the recreational pillar of lifelong learning, in which province and city level lifelong learning committees play a central role. Figure 4.3 gives an overview over the multilevel governance structure of recreational lifelong learning in Korea.

Figure 4.3. The multilevel governance structure of recreational lifelong learning in Korea

Governance Level	Institution	Role
International Level	UNESCO Institute for Lifelong Learning	Exchange of information
National Level	Ministry of Education	Develops LLL agenda
Regional (Province) Level	Province Lifelong Learning Institute	Research and provision of LLL
City Level	Lifelong Learning Centre	Provide LLL
Citizens Level	Citizens councils	Develop ideas

Lifelong learning for the labour market

The description of actors and governance structures in the previous sections mostly referred to the recreational pillar of lifelong learning; however, the second pillar of lifelong learning in Korea is more relevant to employment. This system is governed by the Ministry of Employment and Labour, and at the centre of this pillar is employment insurance, which is part of Korea's compulsory social insurance system.

The employment insurance scheme was established in 1995, and both employers and employees pay into the insurance fund: employers contribute 0.9-1.5% (depending on the size of the company) and employees contribute 0.65% of their wages. The purpose of the employment insurance is, among others, to improve workers' vocational skills (Article 1 of the Employment Insurance Act). The insurance fund finances vocational training programmes for employees who are currently covered by the insurance or those who are unemployed but were previously covered. Furthermore, it contributes to employers' costs of substituting a worker away for training purposes (UNESCO-UNEVOC, 2018[12]). Interview partners mentioned that even though by law employers are supposed to encourage their employees to take part in training (as stated in the Enforcement Decree of the Employment Insurance Act), in practice employees very rarely make use of this right due to Korean work culture, where employees take as little time off from their work as possible. This means that employees often do not take holidays, and even fewer make use of their right to take paid leave to participate in vocational training programmes during working hours.

The insurance only finances courses offered by training institutions registered with the Human Resource Development Service of Korea (HRD), which is a public institution founded in the 1980s. The Korean Chamber of Commerce (KORCHAM) is a private provider that runs nine centres and offers very similar courses in all its centres. Interviewees explained that the training centres are in contact with local companies to provide more specific skills needed by employers. The courses aim to upskill employees, but are also open to unemployed persons to prepare them for the labour market. An example of a public provider are the 34 (as of 2019) polytechnical colleges. These colleges provide programmes at the post-secondary non-tertiary level and are under the responsibility of the Ministry of Employment and Labour. However, interviewees explained that most providers of employment relevant lifelong learning are small, local private providers.

The employment relevant lifelong learning system is supported through the Tomorrow Learning Card, which represents an individual lifelong learning voucher worth up to KRW 2 million (Korean won) (about EUR 1 500[1]) per year, and up to KRW 3 million (about EUR 2 200) for three years. Every employee covered by employment insurance, as well as unemployed persons, employees whose contract will end soon, or temporary workers can apply for the Tomorrow Learning Card. Applications are made through local employment centres, which check eligibility. When the card is granted by the regional employment centre, the card holder can search a database (HRD-net) run by the HRD to select a training programme. The Tomorrow Learning Card scheme covers up to 100% of the training costs, for example for online courses, or 50% for foreign language courses. Some 469 727 cards were issued in 2016, 518 088 were issued in 2017, and 552 397 were issued in 2018 (these numbers include cards for those who are unemployed and employed) (EIS, 2019[13]).

The Korean Skills Quality Authority (KSQA), founded in 2015 by the minister of employment and labour, is a key mechanism for ensuring training quality. It is responsible for supervising institutions providing vocational training, with a special focus on institutions registered with the HRD database (HRD-net). One of its aims is to identify institutions offering low quality courses, i.e. those that do not increase the employability of participants. For this purpose, the KSQA tries to track the effect of vocational training on employment outcomes. However, this institution appears to play no major role yet in the governance of lifelong learning, as it is rarely mentioned and no further information is available.

Similar to the recreational pillar of lifelong learning, the employment relevant lifelong learning system is characterised by a multilevel governance structure. At the national level, in addition to the Ministry of Employment and Labour, the Korean Research Institute for Vocational Education and Training (KRIVET), established in 1997, and the Korean Labour Institute (KLI), established in 1988, are responsible for conducting VET-related research. Employment centres at the province and city levels are the operating bodies that provide consulting services to citizens with regard to training opportunities.

The lifelong learning system in Suwon City

This case study focuses on a successful example within the recreational pillar of lifelong learning, and sheds light on the governance of the recreational lifelong learning system in Suwon City. The case of Suwon City was chosen because the city has managed to establish and maintain a learning city ecology that includes voluntary participation from citizens, institutes and centres, thus potentially serving as a role model for other attempts to promote lifelong learning. Suwon City governs a very dense network of lifelong learning facilities that allows all citizens to reach a lifelong learning space within five to ten-minute walk from their home (UIL, 2017[14]). Furthermore, Suwon City's government spends more than other cities on lifelong learning, which keeps tuition fees low for participants. This governance strategy leads to a high participation rate, with 39.2% of the population taking part in lifelong learning. Suwon City engages with its citizens in the governance of lifelong learning and thereby tailors the system more to the needs of citizens. In 2017, Suwon City won the UNESCO Learning City Award due to its "outstanding commitment and practice in building a learning city" (UIL, 2019[15]).

Suwon City is located about 40 km south of Seoul in the Gyeonggi Province. It has a population of more than 1.2 million people who live in about 480 000 households (Suwon City, 2017[16]). The average household income per month stood at KRW 3 414 000 (about EUR 2 500) in 2019. Suwon City holds the largest local government in Korea (employing about 3 000 public servants) and is divided into 4 districts and 42 administrative areas, also referred to as neighbourhoods (Suwon City, 2017[16]).

In 2005, the Korean Ministry of Education officially awarded Suwon City the title of Lifelong Learning City. The Korean Ministry of Education has run the Lifelong Learning City project since 2000. In 2019, 160 Korean cities successfully filed their application and became official lifelong learning cities. This makes up about 70% of all Korean cities. The aim of this project is to reward and support cities that are interested in and show motivation to promote and implement lifelong learning. It is a competitive programme, and in order to qualify cities have to go through an evaluation process managed by NILE on behalf of the Ministry of Education. The evaluation looks at different criteria, for instance the existence of a concrete ordinance or law to support the learning city, a designated organisation, and a lifelong learning educator, as well as governance structures that involve residents, experts and local social partners in the decision making and that develop mid- and long-term goals. NILE analyses to what extent the lifelong learning strategy is tailored towards the specific needs of citizens and special local features. In the case of Suwon City, lifelong learning specifically targets elderly and children, which goes along with particular efforts in guaranteeing easy access to lifelong learning.

Once a city is selected as a lifelong learning city, NILE provides information on how to improve and promote lifelong learning, with best-practice examples and specific training about lifelong learning for the city's civil servants offered. Furthermore, the Ministry of Education provides financial support, although this varies greatly depending on the size of the city and its project plan, as described by interviewees. One of the requirements to become a lifelong learning city is that it must have an official lifelong learning educator, who are specifically trained and certified experts in lifelong learning governance. Interviewees explained that two certified lifelong learning educators work in the city government and another seven work in the city for other lifelong learning institutions.

In 2006, Suwon City created a new lifelong learning taskforce and developed a mid- and long-term plan for lifelong learning (Suwon City, 2017[16]). Information on citizen's needs and lifelong learning facilities were collected through a survey in 2007 (Suwon City, 2017[16]). Furthermore, the city organised roundtables for its citizens, which were attended by 100 people, to discuss and collect ideas on lifelong learning in the city. In 2019, there were 11 people working on the governance of lifelong learning in the city of Suwon (which includes the two specifically trained lifelong learning educators).

In 2009, the city created the Suwon Lifelong Learning Council. According to the Lifelong Education Act, these councils at the city level consist of up to 12 members. In Suwon City, city council members, non-governmental organisations (NGOs), private course providers, academics and the heads of welfare centres are part of the Suwon Lifelong Learning Council. The council meets once or twice a year, and the mayor of Suwon City hosts the meetings. The council discusses the overall development of lifelong learning, as well as the challenges it faces. Furthermore, the council can decide top-down on the establishment of new programmes. In early 2019 for example, the council decided to establish an exact vision and define goals for a global learning city, and to invest in artificial intelligence programmes and liberal arts. The council also decides on the distribution of the city's lifelong learning budget. Once the council has taken its decision, it hands over the responsibility of implementation to the working council. The working council consists of managerial level representatives of the different members of the city's lifelong learning council. These include the civil servants of the city and the administrative staff of NGOs and other providers.

One of the key institutions in the development and implementation of lifelong learning in Suwon City is the Suwon Lifelong Learning Centre. The establishment of the centre was initiated in early 2007, and it opened in October 2011 (Suwon City, 2017[16]). It is financed by the city. The centre is responsible for planning and conducting lifelong learning programmes and runs many different courses, including urban gardening (where participants manage their own beehive on the roof), handy craft and literature courses. It also supports clubs and volunteering activities by providing facilities where they can meet. Additionally, the Suwon Lifelong Learning Centre collects and provides comprehensive information on lifelong learning. It advertises its programmes and other lifelong learning opportunities on its website and on printed posters in the centre. The centre's website is visited by an average of more than 1 000 visitors per day (Suwon City, 2017[16]).

Suwon City had established a network of more than 600 learning facilities as of 2019, which are spaces where formal and informal lifelong learning take place. These facilities include community centres (42), libraries (118), child and youth centres (73), cultural and arts centres (20) and a broad range of other lifelong learning facilities (Suwon City, 2017[16]). A variety of private providers are also active in the local lifelong learning market. Learning facilities host all types of lifelong learning activities, and local facilities (such as cafes or welfare centres) can contact the city to become an official lifelong learning space. Civil servants working on lifelong learning in the city government review applications and decide whether to grant the official label to a learning place. The city's label does not come with financial benefits, but allows the learning spaces to officially advertise their membership in the city's lifelong learning network. Interviewees explained that having the label increases the attractiveness of facilities as it has a good reputation among citizens. The extension of this network is important to the city government as it is a key factor in the creation of easily accessible and broad reaching lifelong learning, it also keeps the costs of running facilities low. The city government monitors the density of the network and actively contacts potential providers if an area is missing such facilities.

Some 59 722 lifelong learning programmes were offered from 2011 to mid-2017 (Suwon City, 2017[16]). During this time, almost 4 5 million people participated in these programmes (ibid.). Suwon increased the number of learners from 376 000 in 2011 to more than 790 000 in 2015 (UIL, 2015[1]). Each learner can participate in several programmes, which is why the number of participants is higher than the number of learners.

One of the main priorities of lifelong learning in Suwon City is to increase literacy. Korea faces a considerable generational gap regarding skills levels, with basic literacy competences often lacking among older generations due to the economic difficulties of Korea after the Korean War in the 1950s. Suwon City's lifelong learning strategy specifically addresses this challenge. The city has developed courses designed for older generations, with 17.8% of lifelong learning courses targeting this group (GILL, 2018[17]). Compared to the other 30 cities within Gyeoggi Province, Suwon City offers the third highest number of courses for the age group 65+ (GILL, 2018[17]). However, interviewees also noted that the "new old" generations, now in their 50s and 60s, will have different needs and interests than the current senior generation in their 70s and 80s. For example, illiteracy is less of a problem among younger generations, which means that Suwon City's lifelong learning system will have to prove its flexibility and ability to adjust to new interests and needs in the future (e.g. fewer basic literacy programmes).

In Suwon City, the engagement of and with citizens is a key policy, as underlined by interviewees. For example, the city offers subsidies for lifelong learning projects developed by citizens. Citizens who have an idea for a new lifelong learning programme can develop their own project plan and submit it to the city. The city's civil servants who work on lifelong learning review the project plans and grant funding to those with promise. The city also engages with its citizens through the Urban Policy Citizens' Planning Team, the first of its kind in Korea. Representatives from the 44 neighbourhoods in Suwon City are involved with the aim of integrating citizens into the planning and implementation of city policies. Up to 500 citizens meet in roundtables to present their ideas and opinions on lifelong learning and discuss ways to implement new policies. The results of these roundtable meetings are communicated to the 44 neighbourhoods and taken up by the city government. For the city, these roundtables are an important way of tailoring its lifelong learning programmes to the needs of citizens. NGOs can apply for public subsidies to run lifelong learning programmes. When granted, NGOs are obliged to report on their performance, the outcome of their activities and the use of the budget to the city.

Another important feature of Suwon City's lifelong learning approach is the engagement of its citizens as teachers as well as participants. To become a teacher in Suwon City's lifelong learning system, the applicant has to undertake one year of theoretical and practical training. After this, citizens can become certified "civic lifelong learning teachers". More than 1 000 of these teachers work in Suwon City. Interviewees explained that it is a great opportunity for older generations to actively engage in and contribute to society. Women who have left the labour market often use this opportunity to fill career gaps and start working part time again. Interviewees often described Suwon City's lifelong learning approach as an "ecosystem" of lifelong learning. This term captures the combination of top-down (initiatives by the city) and bottom-up (initiatives by the citizens) policy development.

Although Suwon City applies low-cost solutions in its lifelong learning strategy, such as engaging citizens as teachers and using local facilities as learning spaces, the governance of lifelong learning requires sufficient funding. Interviewees argued that Suwon City spends more on lifelong learning than other cities, and that the budget has increased in recent years. In 2014, the city invested about KRW 2 508 million (EUR 1.9 million) in lifelong learning. In 2016, the budget was about KRW 2 565 (about EUR 1.98 million) and in 2018 it was about KRW 2 772 (about EUR 2.1 million) (Suwon City, 2019[18]).

One interviewee pointed out that the decision to dedicate an increasing amount of resources to lifelong learning is a very conscious decision by the city government, with the dedication of the mayor mentioned as one of the most important factors in developing and supporting lifelong learning investments. Interviewees also highlighted the flexibility of the city budget, which is managed by the city independently to other governance levels.

The vision of Suwon City that drives lifelong learning includes the "pleasure of learning and joy of sharing" (Suwon City, 2017[16]), as well as the "'triple A' approach: learning for Anyone, Anywhere, in an eAsy way" (UIL, 2017[14]). The vision underlines that lifelong learning is a means to strengthen the social cohesion, self-fulfilment and happiness of citizens. Employability and participation in the labour market do not play a large role in Suwon's lifelong learning strategy, but as mentioned, promoting literacy, particularly among older generations, is a central priority. Besides literacy programmes, the School for Anything was founded in 2014 and is specifically designed for older generations. It allows experienced older citizens to share their knowledge with others, especially younger generations. Interviewees explained that courses such as barista courses (the art of making coffee), calligraphy or courses that explain how to use computers, the Internet and smartphones are very popular. Interviewees explained that there is also great interest in programmes on history and cultural heritage because Suwon City is home to Suwon Hwaseong Fortress, a UNESCO world cultural heritage site. Another programme highlighted in one interview, the Every Other

Generation Programme, specifically focuses on closing the intergenerational gap by connecting older and younger generations. It thereby skips one generation to bring the grandparents' and children's generations together. In this programme, senior citizens are paired with students. They meet in parks, cafes or classrooms. In the interviews it became clear that this programme was considered very successful, as young people bonded with older people and formed emotional and social cohesion.

Regarding programmes for children, language courses are popular. For example, The Global Village is a language school with a focus on English, where children learn the language in summer camps. About 32 000 learners participate in 19 different programmes a year. Also popular among families, children and school classes is the city's unique museum, Mr Toilet House, which addresses the human digestive system and the development of toilets in an educational way.

The advertisement and accessibility of information on lifelong learning offers are important to the city government. Interviewees noted that the city and other providers use a variety of channels to reach citizens and inform them of available local lifelong learning opportunities. These channels include websites (for example the Suwon Lifelong Learning Centre website), email newsletters or radio advertisements. Printed programmes and advertisements are posted in public libraries, local community centres, the Suwon Lifelong Learning Centre and in neighbourhoods. Courses are made public so that participants can learn about other programmes and upcoming events.

An important event for the promotion of lifelong learning is Suwon City's annual Lifelong Learning Festival, which brings together citizens and lifelong learning providers. In 2018, 25 000 people attended the public festival. Suwon City engages with many different stakeholders beyond citizens through this festival, such as learning facilities and programme providers. All lifelong learning providers can participate and use the festival to promote their lifelong learning programmes. This motivates stakeholders to take part and helps the city to maintain and even extend its network. Interviewees explained that the two lifelong learning educators organise the festival, which implies that their role in the governance of lifelong learning in Suwon City is important.

Suwon City has been a member of the UNESCO Global Network of Learning Cities (GLNC) since 2016, and in 2017 won the Learning City award. One of the aims of the GLNC is to improve lifelong learning by "promoting policy dialogue and peer learning among member cities" (UIL, 2019[19]). The GNLC consists of 251 cities. Among the 62 members in the Asian Pacific region, 35 are Korean cities, out of which 12 are located in Gyeonggi Province. As one interviewee explained, the mayors of Korean lifelong learning cities regularly participate in international conferences organised by the GLNC. For example, every 12 years the UNESCO Institute for Lifelong Learning holds a conference in collaboration with a lifelong learning city member. The conference focuses on adult learning and brings together representatives from local governments and experts in the field of lifelong learning. It also where the ceremony of awarding the UNESCO Institute for Lifelong Learning Award takes place. Criteria for the award include the creation of co-ordinated structures (e.g. committees), making lifelong learning accessible for all citizens, the organisation of "celebratory events to promote and maintain the process of building the learning city", the establishment of monitoring mechanisms, and documented progress of the city's learning plan (UIL, 2019[20]). Suwon City was one of 16 cities awarded this status in 2017, and interviews showed that the city is very proud of its status. The award (a golden plate) is publicly exhibited in Suwon's Lifelong Learning Centre.

Although Suwon City runs its lifelong learning system independently, the city is embedded in a multilevel lifelong learning governance structure that includes the international level (Suwon City as member of the GLNC), the national level (the Ministry of Education awards Suwon City a lifelong learning city), the regional (province) level (Suwon City's lifelong learning experts participate in the province's lifelong learning council meetings), and the city and citizen level. The Gyeonggi Province, to which Suwon City belongs. It is the most populous province in Korea with about 13 million inhabitants, consisting of 31 cities and counties. Among these, 29 are recognised as official lifelong learning cities, which shows the relevance of lifelong learning throughout the province. The Gyeonggi Province Institute for Lifelong Learning is one of the biggest in Korea regarding budget and personnel. Established in 2011, it employs 200 employees in 6 divisions in 13 different offices and campuses. Interviewees explained that the Gyeonggi Provincial Institute for Lifelong Learning (GILL) develops its own lifelong learning plan, which is inspired by, but not necessarily aligned with, the national Lifelong Learning Promotion Plan. This allows the institute to take regional characteristics into account and tailor the plan to its own goals.

GILL conducts research and surveys, for example on participation in lifelong learning (every two years), on the number and type of lifelong learning institutions, and on barriers to participation in lifelong learning. The centre published 8 reports in 2016, 12 in 2017 and 13 in 2018. The institute also monitors the quality of lifelong learning, which is mainly undertaken through applying a "happiness index" that focuses on participants' subjective perception of lifelong learning. Interviewees explained that the establishment of systematic assessment mechanisms using objective factors is still underway. At the national level, KEDI is in principle responsible for conducting research on lifelong learning. Interviewees explained that GILL and KEDI collaborate to complement each other's data and create a bigger sample that allows for more fine-grained analyses and the development of more specific policy recommendations.

GILL is financed by the Gyeonggi Province government. The institute works closely with the province government, especially with the Gyeonggi Office of Education. For example, it is involved in the establishment and drafting of policies and runs its own policy research department. Furthermore, the institute functions as a hub for exchange of information and best-practice examples among the cities and counties that belong to Gyeonggi Province. The province institute is in daily contact with representatives of the local level, either through formal meetings or informal exchanges via email or telephone. The institute offers counselling and consulting to cities and counties, as well as other organisations.

The heads of the province's lifelong learning centres meet three times a year to exchange ideas, talk about recent developments and, importantly, discuss challenges and problems. The heads of the province centres also meet with NILE at least three times a year, which facilitates the co-ordination of activities across different levels of government. Suwon City's lifelong learning experts participate in the Gyeonggi Lifelong Learning Council, where 65 hands-on officials from the 31 cities and counties meet to discuss pending issues. An important goal of this council is to create a "co-operative system among lifelong learning cities and counties" (UIL, 2017[14]).

Analysis

The following section discusses the strengths and challenges of Suwon's lifelong learning system.

Strengths

High participation and a culture of lifelong learning is fostered by broad access

One of the most important strengths of Suwon City's lifelong learning system is the well-established lifelong learning culture among Suwon's citizens, which goes along with a high participation rate in lifelong learning programmes, a strong willingness of citizens to contribute to their further development, for instance by participating in roundtables, and a strong commitment of citizens to work as lifelong learning teachers. The city managed to increase the number of learners from 376 000 in 2011 to more than 790 000 in 2015 (UIL, 2017[14]), and the literacy rate in the city is moving towards 100% (UIL, 2017[14]). The key factor to achieving this was accessibility.

The city keeps the financial hurdle (i.e. fees) low and guarantees easy physical access to lifelong learning classes. High registration fees might stop interested candidates from signing up for a course. Research by the Gyeonggi Lifelong Learning Institute shows that almost 45% of courses in Suwon City cost less than KRW 40 000 (EUR 30), and fewer than 20% charge more than KRW 50 000 (EUR 38). Furthermore, the dense network of more than 600 learning facilities enables all citizens to reach a learning facility within a ten-minute walk. This is particularly important to enable older citizens to participate. The city government monitors the network of learning facilities to maintain and even extend the network.

The city finances the lifelong learning centre as an infrastructure hub and provides essential personnel, in particular the expertise of the two lifelong learning educators, who are specifically trained to design budgets for lifelong learning and have an overview of the relevant bodies within the government. Korea's approach of offering a specific lifelong learning training programme is an important factor in increasing the capacity of cities, provinces and companies to engage with lifelong learning.

The autonomy of province and city governments helps to design lifelong learning programmes

Although the Korean lifelong learning system is characterised by a multilevel governance structure, it grants considerable autonomy to the different governance levels, such as the province and city level governments. The national lifelong learning plan only offers rough guidelines and does not oblige province and city governments to implement specific lifelong learning programmes. This combination of co-ordination across levels of government with a significant degree of autonomy for lower levels is particularly helpful in ensuring that lifelong learning offers match regionally specific needs.

In the case of Suwon City, the Gyeonggi Province Lifelong Learning Centre conducts province-specific research and develops province-specific recommendations and programmes. Suwon City is free to design its lifelong learning strategy, including how much to invest and which programmes to support, or which new fields of interest, such as artificial intelligence, to explore. This flexibility allows the city to tailor its strategy and programmes to the specific interests of local citizens. At the same time, the city's efforts are embedded in and supported by a comprehensive regional and national framework that promotes lifelong learning.

However, the downside of this autonomy is that local political conditions and the degree of support from a particular government are important background factors. For example, the current mayor of Suwon City is a great supporter of lifelong learning, but there is no guarantee that the successor will put the same emphasis on lifelong learning. Future mayors might have other preferences, and will have the power to change the city's lifelong learning system.

Lifelong learning councils within Suwon City and Gyeonggi Province foster the involvement of stakeholders in policy making

Suwon City's Lifelong Learning Council brings together representatives from the city government, NGOs, heads of local welfare centres and representatives from academia. A similar body exists at the province level, namely the Gyeonggi Province Lifelong Learning Council, which consists of representatives from the province government, training providers and academic experts. These councils represent important bodies that institutionalise the engagement of stakeholders in the governance of lifelong learning, both in terms of monitoring and steering, as well as in the further development of training content. The councils bring together policy makers with institutions in charge of implementing the programmes (such as NGOs and lifelong learning centres). This mutual feedback mechanism ensures that training offers match training needs. Furthermore, the councils foster a culture of collective policy making. However, as remarked by interview partners, the range of institutions represented in the councils could be diversified further in the future. Most importantly, interviewees criticised the fact that employers and employees, as well as citizens, are not represented in the councils (this is further explored below).

The Gyeonggi Provincial Institute for Lifelong Learning (GILL) enables horizontal communication and exchange of data

GILL is a central institution that stimulates the exchange and distribution of information within the province, and connects the province to discourses at the national level. The institute functions like an information hub and is accessible to all cities within the province. GILL is available for cities when they have questions and require information on lifelong learning. Furthermore, it fosters vertical co-operation and networking by bringing together representatives from all 31 cities and counties to discuss current challenges and policy solutions. The process of exchanging ideas is supported with research activities by GILL.

The availability of detailed and high-quality data is a precondition for evidence-based policy making. In Korea, different institutions at the national level conduct research and collect data on lifelong learning. However, the resources of these national research institutions are limited and the data often do not capture regional differences. Institutes at the province level, such as GILL, are crucial to fill the knowledge gap of missing regional data. In this regard, GILL co-operates with KEDI which complements national data sets with local data generated through research projects it has conducted. According to interviewees, 6 out of the 17 Korean provinces have so far followed this example and established vertical co-operation between the provincial institutes and KEDI. This expands the availability of data at the national level. The extent to which these data are used by policy makers, however, could still be improved (see challenges section below).

Challenges

Lack of vertical co-operation

One of the key challenges in Korea's lifelong learning system is the lack of co-operation, both vertical and horizontal. As explained above, Korea's system of lifelong learning has established a range of mechanisms, institutions and bodies to facilitate and ensure co-ordination across different levels of government. However, interviews revealed that when it comes to implementation in practice, the effective degree of co-ordination could be significantly improved.

Regarding vertical co-operation, interview partners stated that the national, province and city level act somewhat independently from each other, rather than tightly co-ordinating their activities. On the one hand, this can be an advantage as it allows the province and city governments to tailor their lifelong education policies to the specific needs of local citizens. On the other hand, however, a lack of co-ordination results in wasted resources when efforts are duplicated, or contradicting strategies when the different levels focus on different priorities. For instance, the provinces do not seem to perceive the five-year lifelong learning plan developed by the Ministry of Education as relevant to them, with GILL and Suwon City both developing their own lifelong learning plans independent from the national plan. This means that the national plan is disconnected from the lower governance levels, which reduces its effectiveness. If no institutions implement the national plan, then it becomes meaningless. More efforts should be undertaken to ensure that regional strategies, while being responsive to local needs, are integrated and embedded in a comprehensive national strategy.

Lack of horizontal co-ordination

Regarding horizontal co-ordination, interviewees underlined the lack of communication and collaboration between the Ministry of Education and the Ministry of Employment and Labour. There are no institutionalised regular meetings between the two ministries, and they only meet "when needed". This gap reflects the detachment of the two lifelong learning pillars as discussed above. Even though the division between recreational lifelong learning and employment relevant lifelong learning might make sense, the disconnection between the two pillars and the ministries is a great challenge. For example, the Ministry of Education develops the overarching lifelong learning plan, but 80% of the budget goes to the Ministry of Employment and Labour.

Greater co-operation and co-ordination between the two ministries and systems would help to overcome system-specific challenges. For example, the employment relevant system suffers from narrow accessibility as access depends on the individual's status regarding the employment insurance. In contrast, ensuring broad access is a strength of the recreational pillar. The recreational system could benefit from opening up towards more employment relevant programmes, thus moving away from its mostly recreational function. Interviewees explained that many citizens are interested in more employment relevant education as part of the easy-to-access recreational system, such as mothers who wish to re-enter the labour market but are not covered by employment insurance. The dense lifelong learning network in Suwon City has the potential to contribute to closing this gap. However, this would require communication and co-operation between provincial employment centres and lifelong learning institutions, as well as city-level employment agencies and lifelong learning centres, which does not take place so far.

Lack of quality control and systematic data collection

Neither national, provincial nor municipal governments have managed to establish an encompassing quality control system. Gyeonggi Province has applied the happiness index, as mentioned above, in an attempt to capture the quality of lifelong learning in the province. However, this index only measures the subjective perception of participants. Objective quality measures such as drop-out or participation rates are not systematically evaluated. In Suwon City, local lifelong learning classes are not systematically monitored. The city focuses on the maintenance and expansion of the network of learning facilities, while potentially losing track of the quality of programmes.

This challenge is closely related to the lack of systematic data on lifelong learning, such as participation rates or number of lifelong learning facilities, which are essential for enabling evidence-based policy making. Although KEDI is responsible for collecting data on lifelong learning at the national level, its capacities are limited and it tends to give priority to other fields in education such as primary or university-based education. Thus, detailed data at the national level for lifelong learning are lacking. Other institutions, such as the Korean Research Institute on Vocational Education and Training, conduct research and collect data, but different data collection efforts are not comprehensively integrated and brought together. GILL collects data on lifelong learning at the regional level, which is an important contribution to developing a more fine-grained understanding of local lifelong learning; however, other provinces do not equip their lifelong learning centres with the resources to conduct research. As a consequence, data availability on lifelong learning resembles a patchwork rather than systematic and all-encompassing approach to data collection.

Narrow target group

Suwon City's system of lifelong learning focuses on children and older generations. One of the reasons why older generations are so relevant for the city, as explained by interviewees, is that they are a big part of the electorate. The city does not systematically take into account the needs of younger citizens interested in developing their career further, those who want to change jobs or those who want to re-enter the labour market but are excluded from the employment insurance. However, interviewees underlined that young people in particular would benefit from lifelong learning programmes that help them find well-paid jobs and enter the labour market. The unemployment rate for those aged under 30 is significantly higher than the average unemployment rate in Gyeonggi Province, but Suwon City's lifelong learning system does not provide (at least not systematically) employment relevant lifelong learning opportunities, with not even 1% of programmes explicitly covering job competences or the topic of employment (GILL, 2018[17]).

Lack of employer and employee involvement

Related to the last point, employers, employer associations and unions are not systematically involved in the governance of lifelong learning in Suwon City, such as the city's lifelong learning council. Interviewees explained that Suwon City maintains close relationships with Samsung because its headquarters are located in Suwon City and it employs about 38 000 employees (Samsung, 2019[21]). However, rather than being involved in the city's lifelong learning programmes, interviewees explained that big companies such as Samsung run their own internal training systems. The lack of employer and union involvement is not unique to lifelong learning governance in Suwon City. Interviewees underlined that employer associations and unions also have little influence on lifelong learning policies at the national level. For example, the national Lifelong Education Promotion Committee only consists of national vice ministers. Even though the horizontal engagement of government stakeholders is encouraged by the committee, there is not a great variety of private actors involved, which means that there is little input from business actors or unions to the development of the national five-year lifelong learning plan.

In order to support the development of a meaningful and relevant national skills strategy, existing governance bodies could facilitate the engagement of private actors and employee representatives in the development of the national learning plan. As some interviewees argued, there is little knowledge about employment relevant training demands (from both employers and employees) among state actors. Giving employers and employees a voice in governance bodies would mediate this lack of knowledge, particularly as high-quality data on training needs are lacking. Involving employers and employees in the design and implementation of the national learning plan also raises the commitment of big business players and multinational corporations to align and co-ordinate their skills strategies with other bodies and institutions.

Summary

The governance of lifelong learning in Suwon City relates to the three dimensions of governance described in the introduction in the following ways. First, in terms of promoting co-ordination across levels of government (the "whole-of-government" approach), GILL acts as a hub for information exchange and brings together representatives from the 31 cities and counties. At the same time, interviewees described governance at the different levels as somewhat independent. For example, the National Lifelong Learning Promotion Plan functions as a guideline, but the provinces and cities also develop their own plans. Taking local requirements into account is an important aspect, but the analysis in this case study revealed room for more intensified co-operation that builds on existing practices and institutions.

Second, regarding engaging stakeholders throughout the policy cycle, the analysis revealed that Suwon City uses its lifelong learning council to engage with lifelong learning providers such as welfare centres and NGOs. Furthermore, it organises roundtables for citizens and takes the results into consideration when designing lifelong learning policies. However, the analysis also revealed a lack of systematic engagement with employers and unions in the governance of lifelong learning. This applies to all governance levels and is related to the institutional separation of the Korean lifelong learning system into two distinct pillars. In the future, this strict separation should be overcome, as the strengths of the different pillars can effectively compensate for the weaknesses.

Third, the analysis revealed two interesting findings in the context of aligning financial incentives. The city government of Suwon City increases its public spending on lifelong learning every year and keeps fees for citizens low to allow easy access to lifelong learning. The city engages with existing facilities such as libraries or welfare centres and helps to host lifelong learning activities, which reduces the costs for the city. However, overall public investments in lifelong learning are somewhat low, which was criticised by interviewees. Although the city is very committed to lifelong learning at the local level, the overall lack of resources is mostly related to the low priority given to lifelong learning at the national level. Hence, more effort can be undertaken to boost the relevance and financial commitment to the development of skills across the life course.

Policy recommendations

Based on the analysis of the strengths and weaknesses of Suwon City's lifelong learning system, the following section presents a number of policy recommendations specific to Korea. More general policy recommendations are developed and presented in the final chapter of this report.

Institutionalise co-operation between the Ministry of Education and the Ministry of Employment and Labour

The unambiguous division of the Korean lifelong learning system into two distinct pillars is rooted in a lack of co-operation and co-ordination between the Ministry of Education and the Ministry of Employment and Labour. As the interviews suggested, contact between the two ministries is irregular and weakly institutionalised. For instance, each ministry develops its own lifelong learning agenda. Establishing more regular and institutionalised means of communication between the two ministries could help to reduce the communication and knowledge gaps between the two pillars. Inter-ministerial conferences aimed at developing a comprehensive national skills strategy should be established to guarantee the exchange of information and allow for the active co-ordination of policy making.

The process to develop the national learning plan is an established mechanism that can form a basis for increased communication and co-operation. For instance, as mentioned the national Lifelong Education Promotion Committee consists of the minister of education and a number of vice ministers. This committee could be a good opportunity to strengthen the whole-of-government approach by facilitating co-operation and communication among different ministries at the national level that have a link to lifelong learning. However, as the activity report of the Ministry of Education shows, this committee rarely meets. The minister of education is responsible for initiating committee meetings, but there are no binding regulations regarding the frequency. Establishing regular meetings and opening them up to other stakeholders, both ministries and non-governmental actors, would increase the relevance of the committee. The committee would also be a contact point for representatives from the provinces to align their lifelong learning plans more with the national strategy, as explained further in the following recommendation.

Strengthen vertical co-ordination

As argued above, the system of lifelong learning is a multilevel governance structure that involves four levels of governance (national, province, city, citizens). The analysis revealed that these different levels are often not well connected, and instead work somewhat independently from each other. In order to strengthen vertical co-ordination across the whole of government, lifelong learning plans at the national, province and city levels should be more synchronised to increase their effectiveness. This requires communication and co-operation along the vertical governance level. One way of increasing co-operation would be to engage with representatives from the provinces when drafting the five-year lifelong learning plan. The relationship between GILL and the cities seems to be well developed, but weakly institutionalised. One way to better connect the province and city level would be to invite province representatives to the city's lifelong learning council meetings as this is the key decision-making body for lifelong learning at the city level.

Establish a comprehensive database on lifelong learning

Many different institutions conduct research on lifelong learning and collect relevant data on, for example, participation, skill levels and employer demands. These institutions include KRIVET, the HRD, NILE, the provinces' lifelong learning promotion centres and the cities. However, data collection efforts appear to be very decentralised and uncoordinated, which means that it is difficult for institutions to access data from each other. The establishment of a comprehensive database that includes all relevant data on skills would be a way to integrate all of the data collected. The case of Estonia's Education Information System (EHIS, Chapter 2) is an example of how data from different sources could be collected in one large comprehensive database accessible not only by the national government, but also by regional governments and even schools. In the case of Korea, such a comprehensive database would increase the transparency and further the development of evidence-based policy making at all governance levels.

Introduce quality control mechanisms

As discussed above, one particular challenge in Korea's otherwise well-developed system of lifelong learning is the lack of systematic quality control. Existing efforts to monitor the quality of courses, such as the GILL happiness index, are focused on subjective assessments of course quality by participants themselves. In addition to measures such as these, objective variables such as drop-out and participation rates, as well as ideally the effect of training on employment outcomes and social cohesion, should be taken into account. This necessitates the collection of data in a comprehensive database (see previous recommendation), as well as political discourse on the criteria for evaluating the quality of lifelong learning offers.

Engage with employers and employees to develop employment relevant lifelong learning

One of the main criticisms raised in the interviews was the lack of employer and employee engagement in the governance structures of lifelong learning. Responding to this criticism, employer and employee representatives should be systematically engaged at all governance levels. The different lifelong learning institutions such as the National Lifelong Learning Promotion Committee and Suwon City's Lifelong Learning Council risk losing track of the needs of employees and the labour market if these important stakeholders are not heard. Systematic research such as surveys among employers might help to understand the skills needed on the labour market, but cannot compensate for the direct involvement of employers in the governance of skills policies. Against the backdrop that unemployment among younger people and those 50+ is higher than average, lifelong learning could be used as a tool to improve employability. Engaging employer and employee representatives in the development of the national five-year lifelong learning plan would be a strong statement. Although the Korean system offers employment relevant training through the employment insurance scheme, this system is not easily accessible for those not covered by the scheme.

Educate employers and employees about the importance of lifelong learning

Enhancing the involvement of employers and employees in lifelong learning should be accompanied with efforts to change the dominant working culture, which, as became clear in interviews, often prevents employees from making full use of existing training opportunities. Although different lifelong learning offers exist, interviewees explained that participation among those working full time is low in Suwon City, as well as in Korea in general. Pressure to perform well at work and to work long hours reduces the time available for lifelong learning. Employers should allow and encourage their employees to participate in lifelong learning activities. For example, if management staff regularly engage in lifelong learning themselves, this might serve a role model for other employees. In the long term, promoting lifelong learning among employees will likely increase their productivity and the overall competitiveness of the company, as well-trained employees can more easily adjust to changing economic circumstances. Small and medium-sized companies may be particularly reluctant to promote lifelong learning among their employees and should therefore be even more encouraged. Employees should be better informed of learning opportunities and encouraged to make use of their existing rights to lifelong learning. A culture of lifelong learning needs to be fostered and strengthened among employees.

References

EIS (2019), *Home*, https://eis.work.go.kr/sys01012.do?tranId=sys01012_00&menuId=081010010&autoRptSrch=Y. [13]

GILL (2018), *GILL's Statistics of Lifelong Education in Gyeonggi-do*, GyenggiDo Provincial Institute for Lifelong Learning, Suwon, https://www.gill.or.kr/. [17]

Han, S. (2008), "The lifelong learning ecosystem in Korea: evolution of learning capitalism?", *International Journal of Lifelong Education*, Vol. 27/5, pp. 517-524, http://dx.doi.org/10.1080/02601370802051637. [2]

KEDI (2019), *Korean Educational Development Institute Mission Statement*, Korean Educational Development Institute, Deoksan-myeon, http://eng.kedi.re.kr/khome/eng/about/vision.do. [10]

NILE (2019), *About NILE Building a Creative Learning Society*, National Institute for Lifelong Education, Seoul, http://nile.or.kr/eng/contents/contents.jsp?bkind=html&bcode=BABAAB&bmode=view&idx=BABAAB&langmode=eng. [11]

NILE (2018), *2018 Lifelong Learning in Korea. National Institute for Lifelong Learning.*, National Institute for Lifelong Education, Seoul, https://d14ujlzb3m57xe.cloudfront.net/sites/default/files/2018_lifelong_learning_in_korea_vol.1.pdf. [9]

OECD (2019), *PISA 2018 Results (Volume I): What Students Know and Can Do*, PISA, OECD Publishing, Paris, https://dx.doi.org/10.1787/5f07c754-en. [4]

OECD (2018), *"Korea" in Education at a Glance 2018 : OECD Indicators*, OECD Publishing, Paris, https://doi.org/10.1787/eag-2018-55-en (accessed on 3 January 2020). [3]

OECD (2016), *Skills Matter: Further Results from the Survey of Adult Skills*, OECD Skills Studies, OECD Publishing, Paris, https://dx.doi.org/10.1787/9789264258051-en. [5]

OECD (2015), *OECD Skills Strategy Diagnostic Report Korea 2015*, http://www.oecd.org/edu/educationtoday (accessed on 7 January 2020). [6]

OECD (2013), *Skilled for Life? Key Findings from the Survey for Adult Skills.* [7]

Samsung (2019), *20 Things You Didn´t Know about Samsung´s Headquater in Swuwon*, https://news.samsung.com/global/purposely-leaked-20-things-about-samsungs-digital-city. [21]

Suwon City (2019), *Expenditure Budget Project Statement (2014-2019).* [18]

Suwon City (2017), *Sustainable Global Lifelong Learning City. UNESCO Institute for Lifelong Learning.*. [16]

UIL (2019), *Learning Cities in Korea: Suwon engages beyond its city borders. UNESCO Institute for Lifelong Learning.*, UNESCO Institute for Lifelong Learning, Hamburg, https://uil.unesco.org/lifelong-learning/learning-cities/learning-cities-korea-suwon-engages-beyond-its-city-borders. [15]

UIL (2019), *The UNESCO Learning City Award 2019 Concept Note*, UNESCO Institute for Lifelong Learning, Hamburg, http://uil.unesco.org/sites/default/files/doc/lifelong-learning/cities/unesco-learning-city-award-2019-concept-note.pdf. [20]

UIL (2019), *UNESCO Global Network of Learning Cities*, UNESCO Institute for Lifelong Learning, Hamburg, http://uil.unesco.org/lifelong-learning/learning-cities. [19]

UIL (2017), *Unlocking the Potential of Urban Communities Volume II Case Studies of Sixteen Learning Cities, UNESCO Institute for Lifelong Learning*, UNESCO Institute for Lifelong Learning, Hamburg. [14]

UIL (2015), *Building a Learning Society in Japan, the Republic of Korea and Singapore UNESCO Institute for Lifelong Learning*, UNESCO Institute for Lifelong Learning, Hamburg, https://unesdoc.unesco.org/in/documentViewer.xhtml?v=2.1.196&id=p::usmarcdef_0000232547&file=/in/rest/annotationSVC/DownloadWatermarkedAttachment/attach_import_c9c19735-7da1-47ed-8bcb-1a3eb2372962%3F_%3D232547eng.pdf&locale=en&multi=true&ark=/ark:/48223/pf0000232547/PDF/232547eng.pdf#UIL_publication_02_RZ_150402_03.indd%3A.45122. [1]

UIL (2013), *Republic of Korea: the 3rd National Lifelong Learning Promotion Plan: 2017*, UNESCO Institute for Lifelong Learning, Hamburg, https://uil.unesco.org/document/republic-korea-3rd-national-lifelong-learning-promotion-plan-2017-issued-2013. [8]

UNESCO-UNEVOC (2018), *TVET Country Profile Republic of Korea*, UNESCO-UNEVOC International Centre for Technical and Vocational Education and Training, Bonn, https://unevoc.unesco.org/wtdb/worldtvetdatabase_kor_en.pdf. [12]

Note

[1] All currency conversions are based on the exchange rate of 29 August, 2019: KRW 1 = EUR 0.000744.

5 Case study: Norway's Skills Policy Council and Future Skills Needs Committee

This chapter discusses Norway's recent efforts in strengthening the governance of its skills system as part of its Strategy for Skills Policy 2017-2021. The focus lies on two new governance arrangements that have been introduced as part of this strategy, the Skills Policy Council and the Future Skills Needs Committee. For the first time, the Skills Policy Council introduced an overarching co-ordination body for the previously fragmented field of skills policy, applying a whole-of-government approach. The council includes not only traditional tripartite partners, but also actors from the third sector. The Future Skills Needs Committee improved information systems by providing political decision-makers with a common data basis and coherent definition of challenges in skills policy that is anchored both in scientific data analysis as well as social partner expertise.

Introduction

Norway is generally regarded as one of the leading countries in terms of how it develops and uses the skills of its people, with most indicators of skills development and use showing above average results for Norway compared to other OECD countries (OECD, 2018[1]; OECD, 2019[2]). Enrolment in pre-primary education is near universal, the scores of Norwegian students in the Programme for International Student Assessment (PISA) are above the OECD average, as is the share of young tertiary graduates, and participation in adult learning is strong. However, similar to other industrialised economies, structural changes put the Norwegian skills system under stress. Rapidly changing technologies and the digitisation of society, increasingly internationalised markets, and a changing workforce due to migration and demographic change create challenges for Norway's skills system, giving rise to new skill demands (Ministry of Education, 2017[3]). In 2014, the *OECD Skills Strategy Diagnostic Report: Norway* highlighted some of the weak points in the Norwegian skills system, and specific challenges that are likely to arise for Norway in the coming years (OECD, 2014[4]). Areas for possible improvements were highlighted in the four categories covered in the report: skills development, the effective use of skills, an active supply of skills and the governance arrangements of Norway's skills system. Governance arrangements have been identified as an "enabling" condition for successfully implementing improvements in the other three areas and will be at the core of this case study.

In order to respond effectively to the identified challenges, and to improve the governance arrangements of Norway's skills system, the Norwegian government, represented by several ministries together with social partners, the voluntary sector and adult learning associations, as well as representatives of the Sami ethnic minority, have committed themselves to implementing the Norwegian Strategy for Skills Policy 2017-2021 (Nasjonal Kompetansepolitisk Strategi) (Ministry of Education, 2017[3]). This strategy prioritises certain issues and policy fields for future skills policy and includes the implementation of two new governance arrangements.

These new governance arrangements, the Skills Policy Council (Kompetansepolitisk råd) and the Future Skills Needs Committee (Kompetansebehovsutvalget), are analysed in greater detail in this case study. This case study is based on document research and semi-structured interviews conducted in April 2019 in Oslo with several representatives from stakeholders such as the respective ministries, public agencies, social partners, learning providers and subnational authorities. It assesses how and to what extent the rearrangement of governance structures contributes to achieving a "whole-of-government approach" to skills policy. While all four dimensions of this approach will be touched on during this case study, the focus is on:

- Promoting co-ordination, co-operation and collaboration across the whole of government.
- Engaging stakeholders throughout the policy cycle.
- Building integrated information systems.

In general, while both the Skills Policy Council and the Future Skills Needs Committee are still relatively new institutions, they already show high potential. Furthermore, they could also act as blueprints for a range of other countries with similar skill regimes. However, this report also shows that certain problems must be tackled in order to further develop the role of these two new institutions and allow them to live up to their full potential.

Norway's education and training system

As mentioned, Norway's skills system is regarded as one of the leading systems among OECD countries, and most indicators show above average results compared to other OECD countries (OECD, 2018[1]). Enrolment in early childhood education is 97% for 3-5 year-olds, and therefore nearly universal. The enrolment rate for 3 year-olds is 20% higher than the OECD average (OECD, 2018[1]). Concerning students' performance in PISA, Norway again ranks above the OECD average by one point in science, 12 points in mathematics and 12 points in reading (OECD, 2019[5]). The share of 25-34 year-olds who have completed tertiary education is more than 48%, compared to an average of 44.5% across OECD countries (OECD, 2020[6]). Norway ranks among the top third of OECD countries regarding coverage in job-related adult learning (participation by individuals and provision by employers), as well as adult learning inclusiveness, flexibility and alignment (OECD, 2019[7]). Norway is also a leader among OECD countries in terms of educational expenses for primary, secondary and post-secondary (non-tertiary) education, with a focus on research and development, and spending on tertiary education is above the OECD average (OECD, 2018[1]).

In the academic literature on skills regimes, the Norwegian case is often described as a hybrid between a "statist" and a "collective" skills regime (Michelsen, Olsen and Høst, 2014[8]; Nyen and Tønder, 2016[9]). In statist systems, the state engages heavily in the provision of vocational education and training (VET) via (full-time) public vocational schools. In collective systems, both employers and the state are collectively responsible for providing VET via apprenticeships at firms and (part-time) vocational schools (Busemeyer and Trampusch, 2012[10]). Norway shows characteristics of both of these systems, with possibilities for individuals to either get vocational qualifications through full-time schools or via dual VET in a system that resembles the apprenticeship model. Similar to other policy areas in Norway, such as labour market policy and wage bargaining, VET is traditionally jointly governed by the state and social partners (i.e. employers' associations and trade unions). As became clear in interviews conducted in this project, the governance reforms at the centre of this case study cannot be understood without keeping in mind the historical legacies of strong social partner co-operation, which can be seen a possible blueprint for the role of the Skills Policy Council and the Future Skills Needs Committee, or as competition.

Common to both statist and collective skills regimes is that in contrast to "liberal" skills systems (for example the United States), VET has an important role in Norway compared to general and academic education, and is in general of high quality and social status. This is visible in the high share of upper secondary students enrolled in VET rather than general education, which is significantly above the OECD average, as can be seen in Figure 5.1. In total, around 16% of upper secondary students are enrolled in combined school- and work-based programmes, i.e. training models that resemble the apprenticeship principle.

Figure 5.1. Share of all upper secondary students in vocational programmes and combined school- and work-based programmes (2015)

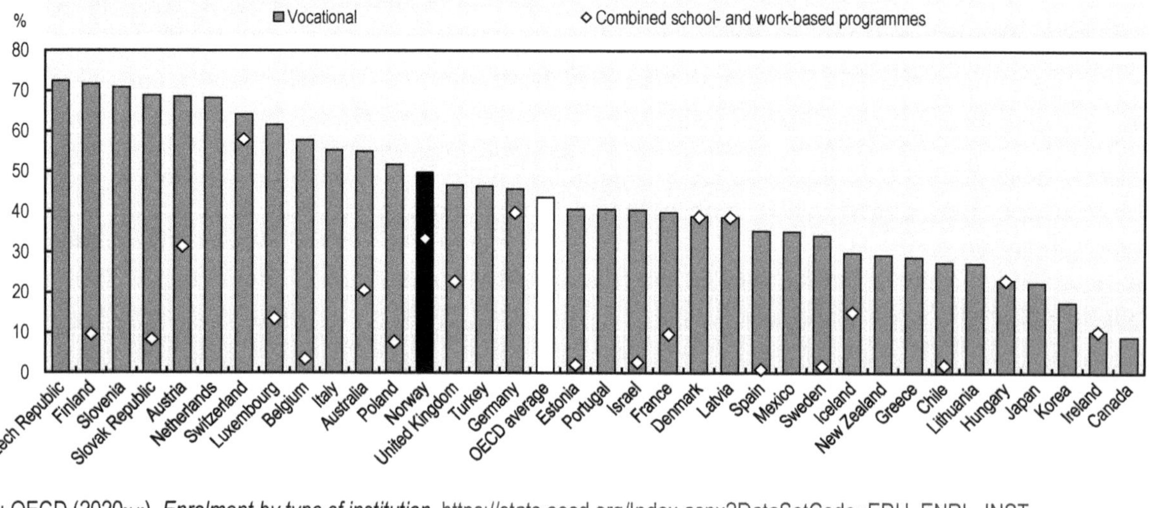

Source: OECD (2020[11]), *Enrolment by type of institution*, https://stats.oecd.org/Index.aspx?DataSetCode=EDU_ENRL_INST.

StatLink https://doi.org/10.1787/888934112747

Apprenticeship models of dual VET have existed in Norway since the first half of the 20th century. The state increasingly took responsibility for VET in the post-war period through the expansion of a school-based training system, although VET remained jointly governed by social partners. In 1994, the dominance of school-based training ended with the introduction of "Reform 94", which was decisive in the development of Norway's skills system towards a hybrid model that combines statist and collective elements (Nyen and Tønder, 2016[9]). The reform fundamentally restructured Norwegian secondary level education by implementing the right for at least three years of secondary education, severely reducing the number of basic courses[1] of study, improving the ability to move from vocational education to other tracks of the educational system and tertiary education, and most importantly introducing the "2+2 model" for VET, which ultimately led to a resurgence of apprenticeships cf. (Bowman, 2005[12]).

Consequently, the Norwegian upper secondary level education system consists of a unitary school system that offers vocational programmes and general academic programmes within the same schools (Nyen and Tønder, 2016[9]), as well as granting opportunities to combine or switch between the different tracks. Students first choose between different broad vocational and general programmes and select specialisations, and then focus on a number of specific trades later on (Michelsen, Olsen and Høst, 2014[8]). Norway's corporatist system of decision making gives tripartite bodies, and therefore social partners, at the national and regional level important advisory and informal decision-making functions in defining the content and structure of VET courses (Nyen and Tønder, 2016[9]).

The hybrid nature of Norway's skills system is also highlighted in the provision of vocational programmes, which can be completed either fully in vocational schools or as part of a firm-based apprenticeship. The "2+2 model" specifies that the first two years of upper secondary education are provided in full-time schools. Students who find a willing firm can then complete a full-time apprenticeship for the subsequent two to three years. Those who do not want to or who are unable to find an apprenticeship place in a firm have the right to complete the programme via a third year in school before taking the final examination.

Over time, and in particular since the "Competence Reforms" (Kompetansereformen) of the late 1990s and early 2000s, continuing and further training, as well as lifelong learning, have become increasingly important in Norway's skills system. The issue was also one of labour's central demands in collective bargaining at that time, especially concerning the financing of further education (Bowman, 2005[12]). Ultimately, the reforms stated that all adults have the statutory right to a primary, lower and upper secondary education,[2] and the right to study leave. Financial assistance and tax incentives were increased, thereby creating a market for continuing education and training. Furthermore, the Norwegian Agency for Lifelong Learning was established (VOX, now called Skills Norway/Kompetanse Norge) (Bowman, 2005[12]). However, no compromise was found concerning the co-financing of further education by employers, unions and the state through a fund. Bowman relates this failure to the lack of an institutional framework of tripartite decision-making bodies within the relatively new realm of continuing training. Consequently, stakeholders were unable to determine which specific training programmes should or should not be supported by the fund.

More recently, structural changes such as rapidly changing technologies, increasingly internationalised markets and a changing workforce due to migration and demographic change have increasingly challenged the Norwegian skills system. The OECD's 2014 Skills Strategy report for Norway highlighted several challenges connected to skills development, skills supply, skills use and the governance of skills (OECD, 2014[4]). For skills development, these challenges included the still comparatively low, but increasing, share of low performers among students, a relatively large share of adults with poor basic skills, falling educational attainment at the upper secondary level, and the lack of career centres in certain counties. Concerning skills supply, the low labour market attachment of people with disabilities and the unused labour market potential of older Norwegians were identified, as well as a lack of focus on helping low-skilled youth. For skills use, a large gap in literacy proficiency between low-skilled and high-skilled occupations, the low access of individuals in low-skilled occupations to employer funded (further) training, a low share of self-employed individuals and business startups, and the large unused potential of overqualified migrants were identified. The report also highlighted that challenges in skills development, supply and use varied substantially at a regional level due to Norway's geography, which is shaped by "long distances, low population density, and small local labour markets with limited possibilities for commuting". Regional variance includes, for example, substantially lower on-time completion of upper secondary school in Finnmark County (55%) than in Sogn og Fjordane County (80%).

The OECD highlighted three key challenges to be addressed regarding the governance of Norway's skills system:

- Limited vertical co-ordination between national, county and municipal levels, and a lack of information on skills for local stakeholders.
- Limited horizontal co-ordination between different ministries (which resemble "silos") to work jointly on common goals.
- Limited co-ordination between (public and private) stakeholders.

The Norwegian Strategy for Skills Policy 2017-2021 tries to tackle these challenges directly. The new government arrangements implemented as part of this strategy can be seen as "enabling conditions" for the design of adequate polices. These are introduced and discussed in the following section.

The Norwegian Strategy for Skills Policy 2017-2021: The Skills Policy Council and the Future Skills Needs Committee

Overview of the strategy

The Norwegian Strategy for Skills Policy 2017-2021 commits the strategy partners to "ensure that individuals and businesses have the skills that give Norway a competitive business sector, an efficient and sound public sector, and an inclusive labour market" (Ministry of Education, 2017[3]). The strategy partners include:

- Public institutions: The Norwegian government represented by the Ministry of Labour and Social Affairs, the Ministry of Local Government and Modernisation, the Ministry of Education and Research,[3] and the Sami Parliament representing the Sami indigenous people in Norway.
- Social partners: Employers represented by the Employers' Association Spekter, the Norwegian Association of Local and Regional Authorities, the Confederation of Norwegian Enterprises (NHO), and the Enterprise Federation of Norway (Virke). Employees are represented by the Federation of Norwegian Professional Associations (Akademikerne), the Norwegian Confederation of Trade Unions (LO), the Confederation of Unions for Professionals (Unio) and the Confederation of Vocational Unions (YS).
- Non-governmental organisations (NGOs) in the field of non-profit adult learning provision are represented by the Norwegian Association for Adult Learning (VOFO).

These strategy partners have agreed on three main objectives:

1. "Contribute to making informed choices for the individual and for society": This mainly includes the creation and improved provision of sufficient information (regionally and nationally) for individuals, educational institutions, and the private and public sector in general, including skills forecasting and career guidance.
2. "Promote learning in the workplace and effective use of skills": This includes the promotion of dual VET, increasing co-ordination between higher education and the labour market, reskilling (especially towards digital skills), and an improved certification of skills acquired in the workplace (and/or abroad).

3. "Enhance skills among adults with weak labour market attachment": This mainly includes increased collaboration between firms, NGOs and private training providers in order to implement adult education measures for specific target groups, such as individuals with poor basic skills, low formal qualifications or those who lack Norwegian skills (i.e. immigrants), or the Sami population.

Two new governance arrangements have been introduced as part of this strategy: the Skills Policy Council and the Future Skills Needs Committee. These governance arrangements aim to facilitate the design and introduction of future substantive policy reforms within the framework of the strategy.

Role of involved stakeholders

The Ministry of Education and Research, and specifically the Department of Skills Policy, fulfils a lead function in co-ordinating skills policy as a whole. It was also mainly responsible for the introduction of the Skills Policy Council and the Future Skills Needs Committee. Furthermore, the Ministry of Education is responsible for the education system ranging from kindergarten, primary and secondary education to vocational and higher education. Within the Ministry of Education and Research, the Department of Integration is involved in skills policies targeting migrants.

Three further ministries are involved in the broader area of skills policies. The Ministry of Labour and Social Affairs is mostly concerned with active labour market policies, as well as formal education and labour market measures in general. The Ministry of Trade is mostly responsible for ensuring that skills policies are in accordance with the needs of the Norwegian economy. The Ministry of Local Government's involvement concerns an ongoing restructuring of Norway's administrative divisions (counties, *Fylke*, currently 19), which involves a reduction in the number of counties and giving regional governments more responsibilities in industrial development and skills policy. For example, counties are involved in the development of regional skills strategies and the evaluation of specific regional skills needs. However, counties are also represented in the Skills Policy Council by one representative of the county council (*Fylkesting*). This representative's role is to report back to all the heads of the county administrations (chief executives).

Skills Norway (Kompetanse Norge), a directorate under the Ministry of Education and Research, is also central to the skills strategy. Previously known as VOX (Norwegian Agency for Lifelong Learning), Skills Norway's main policy goal is to promote lifelong learning, with a particular focus on vulnerable groups such as adults with low skills and education or immigrants. However, its tasks encompass a far wider range of issues, having acted as a main driving force behind the skills strategy in general. Skills Norway acts as the secretariat (with five members) for the Future Skills Needs Committee and a number of additional expert committees. It also funds research in the area of skills more broadly. Most importantly, while decision-making powers reside within the Ministry of Education and Research, Skills Norway advises on future skills policy development in general and is responsible for specific policy implementation. Thereby, it co-ordinates between the main stakeholders of the strategy, including social partners, educational providers and ministries.

Concerning social partners, a wide range of peak-level[4] employer and employee organisations are involved to represent the interests of their members. This includes the NHO and the LO, which were historically often the main social partners driving skills policy in Norway – cf. (Bowman, 2005[12]). As in many other countries with strong social partner organisations, they often supply certain "goods" to their members who are also in the field of skills policy, such as specific further training measures or an educational fund that grants scholarships. Correspondingly, their involvement in the Skills Policy Council aims to better co-ordinate social partners' policy measures with public policy measures.

The Norwegian Association for Adult Learning (VOFO) is an umbrella association that represents exclusively non-profit providers of voluntary formal and informal education and training programmes in the field of adult learning. Such providers range from organisations with connections to political movements such as social-democracy and Christian-democracy, associations representing certain professions (farmers, medical doctors) to religious groups. Programmes are provided in a variety of subjects including basic skills, retraining measures, social skills and cultural education, as well as programmes suited to the needs of certain types of companies.

The Sami Parliament represents the interests of the Sami indigenous people in Norway and is involved in the development of educational programmes involving subjects such as Sami language in primary and secondary education, as well as apprenticeship schemes such as reindeer husbandry.

The relationship between these stakeholders, the Skills Policy Council and the Future Skills Needs Committee is depicted in Figure 5.2.

Figure 5.2. Governance arrangements in Norway's skills system

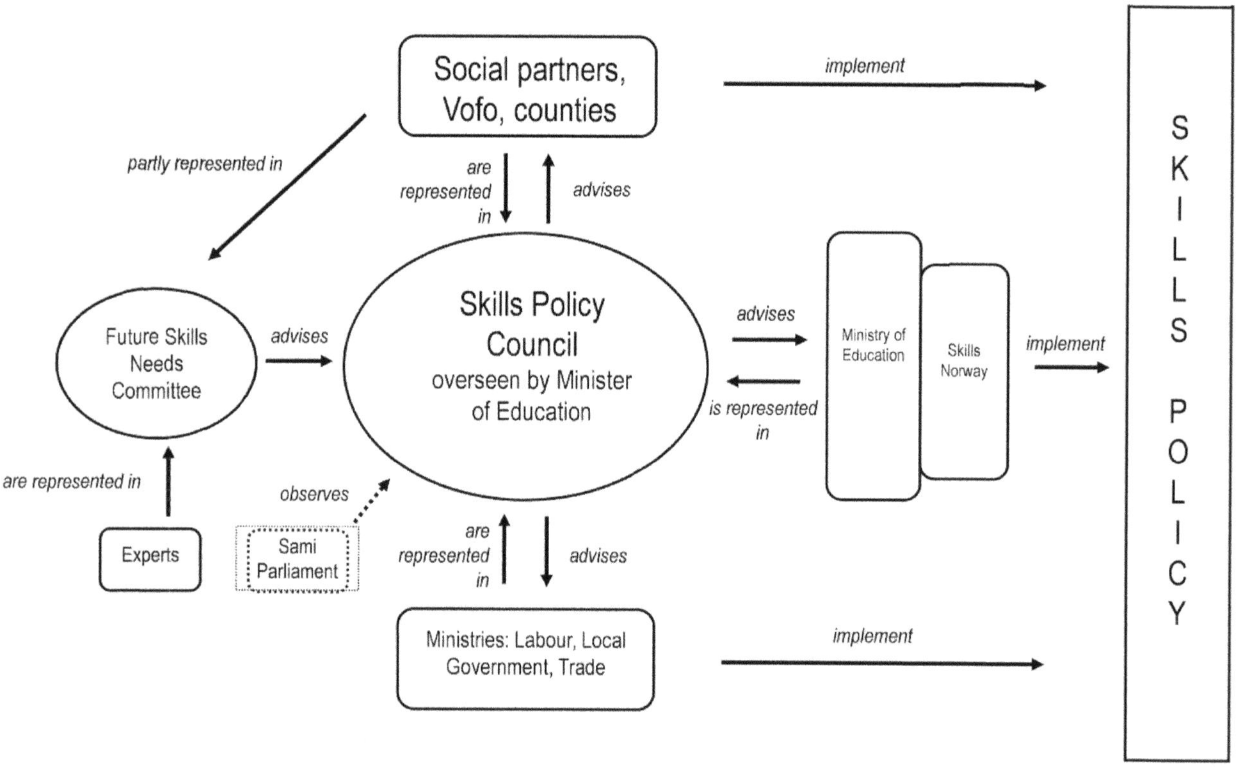

The Skills Policy Council is at the core of the new governance arrangements of the Norwegian Strategy for Skills Policy 2017-2021. According to its mandate (Norwegian Government Security and Service Organisation, 2019[13]), the council's purpose is to "follow-up" on the strategy and to continue to promote co-operation between the involved stakeholders, which should include regular discussions and advice on current skills policy issues, regular reports on the strategy partners' own policy measures to implement the strategy, as well as a potential revision of the strategy if needed. The council has been established only for the period of the current strategy. It is supposed to base its discussions and recommendations on the conclusions of the Future Skills Needs Committee.

In practice, the council acts as a purely advisory body to all stakeholders, with the goal of co-ordinating and improving existing and new policy measures in the field of (public and non-public/social-partner provided) skills policy. The minister of education chairs the council, thereby providing the opportunity for all stakeholders to influence policy making at a very high level. Most importantly, in contrast to other tripartite councils in Norway, the Skill Policy Council does not have a decision or policy-making function, and only gives non-binding advice. This has certain drawbacks, as explored in the analysis section.

All strategy partners[5] plus one representative of the counties have a seat at the Skills Policy Council, as shown in Figure 5.2. The council meets roughly three to four times a year for about two hours. The agenda of the meetings is usually set by the Ministry of Education and Research. Reports from the Future Skills Needs Committee are also presented in the council, with possibilities for members to make comments. Council members present their statements on the agenda topics. Current topics of the Skills Policy Council include a recent regional reform (see above), new findings of the Future Skills Needs Committee (see below), as well as discussions on the future role of the Skills Policy Council itself.

The Future Skills Needs Committee **(Kompetansebehovsutvalget)**

The mandate of the Future Skills Needs Committee is to "provide the best possible evidence-based assessment of Norway's future skills needs, as a basis for national and regional planning, and for strategic decision making of both employers and individuals". This concerns short-, medium- and long-term skills needs (Dalbak, 2018[14]). More specifically, its tasks are to "generate and organise the evidence base" on Norway's future skills needs based on already available data, as well as to "stimulate the development of new evidence". For this purpose, the Future Skills Needs Committee can fund its own research via its own budget financed by the Ministry of Education and Research, which was generally perceived as well-resourced by interviewees.

The committee is expected to co-ordinate and improve existing data creation and utilisation among all involved stakeholders and use a variety of qualitative and quantitative data sources. It is also expected to produce an annual report based on these analyses and assessments, including, for example, current challenges in skills policy and specific regional or sectoral focus points. The committee is appointed for a period of three years, after which its mandate can be extended and adapted and committee members can be changed. The committee meets for around five all-day meetings a year.

Members of the Future Skills Needs Committee are representatives from social partners, the involved ministries, and experts. However, VOFO, the county representative and the Sami parliament are not involved. Participating experts include analysts and researchers from, for example, universities, the Norwegian Labour and Welfare Administration (NAV) and Statistics Norway. In terms of academic disciplines, there is a clear focus on economists, especially among members affiliated to universities.

The secretariat, which is located at Skills Norway and headed by an economist, plays a central role in the Future Skills Needs Committee and oversees the committee's compliance with its mandate. Within the committee, decisions on the content of the reports have so far been made unanimously by all members. Members can collectively and individually give input concerning the agenda of the committee. In the early days of the committee, the secretariat had the most power in agenda-setting and thereby also determined the content (of meetings and consequently reports) to a significant extent before specific decisions by the members were made. As will be outlined later in this case study, measures to resolve such frictions are currently being implemented.

Analysis

This section analyses the functioning of the Skills Policy Council and the Future Skills Needs Committee. It highlights certain characteristics as "best-practice" examples, and identifies possible drawbacks and challenges in both arrangements.

Opportunities and challenges of the Skills Policy Council

Opportunities

In general, all involved stakeholders interviewed for this case study viewed the Skills Policy Council as an improvement to Norway's governance structure within skills policy. They perceived it as a (relatively) successful extension of the existing "Norwegian model" of corporatism and social partnership to the whole field of skills policy, both in terms of an extension across different sub-fields of skills policy and in terms of the actors involved.

The design of the Skills Policy Council builds on similar governance arrangements present in other (sub-) fields as part of the traditional system of tripartite negotiations. These include the tripartite National Council for Vocational Education and Training (Samarbeidsrådet for yrkesopplæring), individual vocational training councils (*Faglig råd*) responsible for individual vocational programmes, county vocational training boards (*Yrkesopplæringsnemnder*), as well as governance arrangements in other policy fields such as labour market policy and wage bargaining. These councils only cover one sub-area of skills policy (for example VET), but often have decision-making functions. This tradition of social partnership acts as an important blueprint for the Skills Policy Council and co-operation between stakeholders, which did not have to be built from scratch as many of the involved stakeholders were already co-operating with each other through existing tripartite bodies.

The Skills Policy Council oversees and applies a holistic approach to a previously very fragmented policy area. While some issue areas such as VET were already covered by previously existing councils, the Skills Policy Council was seen as an improvement by interviewees as it now covers the whole field of skills policy. The other councils only look at skills policy in their own sub-area (for example VET), but do not co-ordinate policy across these different fields.

The Skills Policy Council can therefore identify overarching challenges and consequently help to develop more comprehensive policy solutions instead of addressing only specific parts of the system. Some interviewees also mentioned the benefits of having direct access to high-level government officials, for example the minister of education, which could increase the impact of their recommendations on public policy. Information concerning ongoing political processes is distributed via the council, which opens up the possibility for council members to comment on these issues. Overall, many interviewees (but not all, see further below) believed that they can influence policy making through the Skills Policy Council. At the same time, many stakeholders also perceived the comments of their colleagues within the Skills Policy Council as beneficial to their own work.

Strengthened co-ordination and co-operation is also seen as a main benefit of the Skills Policy Council by interviewed stakeholders. First, it has the potential to improve the quality of policies by strengthening co-ordination between the different measures of stakeholders. Second, it acts as a forum for diffusing expertise within the area of skills policy. Even though there had certainly been co-operation with social partners before the establishment of the Skills Policy Council, it was more infrequent, ad hoc and focused on specific issues, rather than systemic and focused on overarching issues.

Members of the council who are not traditionally part of social partner negotiations (e.g. VOFO, regional representatives) in Norway particularly highlighted the importance of the Skills Policy Council in facilitating co-operation and influencing and developing policies. The council gives these members legitimacy as an important co-operation partner within skills policy, which supports them in reaching out to other stakeholders beyond the formal framework of the council. Thereby, it has served to broaden the engagement of stakeholders. In the words of an interview partner, Norway "cannot afford to miss important contributors to the education system, and that's what we are doing within the council".

Another important contribution of the Skills Policy Council to Norway's governance structure identified by interviewees is its effect on prioritising skills policy among stakeholders. As many interviewees argued, the

Skills Policy Council helps to put skills policy at the top of the agenda of all involved stakeholders, thereby facilitating reforms in this area. Similarly, the Skills Policy Council and the Norwegian Strategy for Skills Policy in general are seen as giving the government legitimacy and capacity to introduce more ambitious and innovative policies.

This effect was not only highlighted by social partners, but also by ministries concerning horizontal co-operation within government. As one interview partner emphasised, the Skills Policy Council “forces ministries out of their silos” to a certain extent and helps to set common goals. It was also highlighted that especially in the long term, building the infrastructure beneficial for co-operation (i.e. the council) may pay off substantially. However, many interviewees also stressed that there are still many issues that have to be improved within the field of horizontal co-operation, as will be shown in the next section.

The positive effect of prioritising skills policy among stakeholders also applies to vertical co-operation between the different levels of government, i.e. the national and county levels. The inclusion of a county representative (one joint representative of all counties) within the Skills Policy Council helps to put skills on the agenda of individual county executives, who often regard other policy areas such as infrastructure as their main priority. Regular meetings between the county representative and the individual county executives facilitate this effect. The high number of counties represented by the single county representative within the council is not seen as a problem regarding possible conflicts of interests between counties.[6] This is connected to the abovementioned fact that in practice, the county representative’s role is to put skills on the agenda of the county executives, rather than reconcile diverging interests.

Vertical co-operation is expected to improve further with the new regional reform (“a real change maker” as one interview partner said), in which the Skills Policy Council was also involved. This reform reduces the number of counties from 19 to 11 and gives the regions more responsibilities in the field of skills policy, thereby possibly leading to a trickling down of the topic of skills to the agenda of local governments. As part of this process, every county is “strongly recommended” to create their own regional skills strategy. The regional reform and the Skills Policy Council have thus triggered governance innovations at the subnational level, including regional skills councils and more targeted skills networks. These innovations were perceived to be beneficial by all interviewees as they can also tackle more specific, hands-on topics.

Interviewees agreed that it is difficult to isolate the effect of the Skills Policy Council on specific policies implemented. In other words, it is hard to say to what extent a specific policy would exist without the new governance arrangements of the Skills Policy Council. As one interview partner admitted, many measures reported by stakeholders within the council might have occurred without the Norwegian Strategy for Skills Policy and its new governance arrangements, but they would have been less co-ordinated with the other strategy partners. Interviewees explicitly mentioned two new policies that they regarded as heavily influenced by the recommendations of the Skills Policy Council:

- Sector/industry programmes for training: This policy involves sector/industry-specific co-operation between government and social partners to design specific further training opportunities for workers affected by digitisation and other factors changing skill demands. Two programmes are currently being designed in the fields of “local care services” and “construction and industry”. Social partners and the government are contributing to programme development and the training provision and recruitment of trainees, while employers have agreed to send employees to training during their paid working time. According to interviewees, the specific idea behind these programmes was recommended directly by stakeholders within the Skills Policy Council.
- Short, flexible courses for advanced digital skills: These further training courses that cover topics such as cyber security, artificial intelligence and the Internet of Things (IoT) are designed in co-operation with businesses and universities. They were implemented as a direct reaction to the skills needs expressed by employer associations within the Skills Policy Council.

Challenges

While all interview partners agreed that the Skills Policy Council is an improvement to Norway's governance structure in skills policy, most also mentioned fundamental challenges that have to be tackled so that the council can live up to its full potential. While interviewed stakeholders sometimes differed in terms of the direction of the council's further development, the challenges cited were remarkably similar.

Most frequently, interviewees argued in favour of a more flexible mode of operation within the meetings that could improve the quality of dialogue. Currently, meetings last for only two hours and are organised so that each stakeholder can comment in turn on the current agenda. This means that members do not have the possibility and time to discuss issues or co-ordinate between council members during the meetings. There are also downsides to the fact that meetings are held and led by high-level political officials, with many interviewees noting that this leads to a prioritisation of politics rather than promoting in-depth debates on specific policies. This can lead to very abstract meetings with "a lot of talking but very little action". As no interactive discussion is possible within the council, there is also no way to negotiate, compromise and reach consensus among the stakeholders; only voicing an opinion is possible. However, measures are currently being implemented to tackle these shortcomings, as mentioned later in this chapter, including providing more time for discussions in the council and reducing the number of agenda items.

The agenda is largely set by the government and the Ministry of Education and Research instead of being decided jointly within the council, although traditional social partners have strong ties with the ministries already due to older tripartite agreements and can use these channels to informally exert influence on the council's agenda. As an interview partner argued, "they will come to us, they are only a phone call away". As well as agenda-setting being dominated by the ministry, there may also be a lack of responsiveness and proactivity on the part of council members. Mechanisms for agenda-setting could thus be improved to ensure sufficient possibilities for stakeholders to influence the agenda, as well as to ensure their commitment.

The challenges mentioned so far are especially detrimental for "new" co-operation partners not represented in traditional tripartite bargaining as they often do not have access to the communication channels established between the traditional tripartite bargaining partners of the Norwegian model of social partnership. This applies to informal connections to the ministries and government, as well as other social partners. Ultimately, these stakeholders lack the informal power of employer associations and labour unions to influence the agenda of council meetings. It is also much harder for them to co-ordinate policy measures with other stakeholders outside meetings of the Skills Policy Council.

Another main issue for the Skills Policy Council is its still unclear role and vague mandate concerning its advisory functions. This is especially problematic concerning its relation to other, older tripartite bodies that have partly overlapping responsibilities, i.e. the Council on Labour Market Issues, the National Council for VET and many other committees involved in education and training policy. No clear rules seem to exist that determine if the Skills Policy Council can actually give recommendations on a certain issue or if they should be subject to other tripartite bodies. This compromises the role of the Skills Policy Council as an overarching body and makes the field of skills policy rather fragmented again.

Similarly, the council's role in policy development is unclear for many strategy partners, which is also an issue of accountability. The Ministry of Education and Research compiles a yearly report of all policy measures implemented by the strategy partners (social partners, ministries, other stakeholders) as part of the Norwegian Strategy for Skills Policy. However, no mechanism exists beyond these yearly reports where strategy partners can assess if the government actually follows up on their specific advice, and vice versa (i.e. if social partners follow up on government advice). Partners do not know what happens with their feedback and cannot see an "end product". The role and responsibilities of the different organisations present in the council also do not seem to be clear to all stakeholders.

All stakeholders interviewed agreed that horizontal co-operation between the different ministries could be improved. It was argued that some ministries only superficially contribute to the strategy without really internalising overarching goals or offering resources for joint projects. Each ministry remains first and foremost dedicated to its own goals, for which it is responsible to parliament. Different priorities are present in the different ministries, for example employment-oriented priorities with large short-term impacts on the unemployed versus long-term priorities concerning economic development or skills needs without immediate payoffs. Agenda-setting was also an issue of horizontal co-operation. Involved ministries, similar to other involved stakeholders, raised concerns that the Ministry of Education and Research primarily sets the agenda within the Skills Policy Council. But again, the underlying issue might not only be the strong agenda-setting power of the Ministry, but also the lack of commitment of other ministries to such issues.

Opportunities and challenges of the Future Skills Needs Committee

Opportunities

Similar to the Skills Policy Council, all interviewed stakeholders agreed that the Future Skills Needs Committee is an improvement to Norway's governance arrangements in the field of skills policy. In addition to being involved in policy making and implementation through the Skills Policy Council, stakeholders are now also engaged in collecting data and creating a common basis for discussion, and can thus jointly identify important issues and challenges ahead. The committee has facilitated the convergence of social partners, government and researchers towards a common, coherent definition and perception of current problems in skills policy. This has been described as essential considering the wide diversity of data and analyses produced by individual organisations and stakeholders in this field, which previously made it hard to look at the policy field in a more holistic way. It was generally perceived as an asset that the committee is relatively protected from direct influence from the political level, and therefore acts as an independent advisory body.

The committee's focus on generating a common foundation of data and evidence helps stakeholders agree on the facts and have a more fruitful dialogue. All interviewees agreed that the joint process of problem definition by stakeholders helps to facilitate and speed-up the work of the Skills Policy Council, as well as the whole policy- and decision-making process of other stakeholders, including ministries and social partners. Research on the process of agenda-setting in public policy research (Kingdon, 2011[15]) shows that problem definition is already an inherently political process. Therefore, involving all relevant stakeholders in the early phases of the policy process can avoid later reform deadlocks. As one interview partner argued, stakeholders now "have a common fundament - that we agree on the statistics. That we do not have to fight about the statistics. That raises the level of the discussions". This holds for social partners, new stakeholders and government ministries (improving horizontal co-operation within government), as all have confirmed to use the committee's reports in their activities. Similarly, the fact that all stakeholders agree on a common problem definition and identify common challenges creates a certain sense of urgency and highlights the importance of skills policy as a policy field in general, thereby potentially putting it to the top of the agenda of all decision makers.

In terms of vertical co-operation between the involved stakeholders, the committee's reports are perceived to have had an increasing impact more recently. In its second report, the committee focused on the regional development of future skills needs, which was seen as especially beneficial by several interviewees as local stakeholders often do not have the resources to effectively use existing data in their decision-making processes. The committee identified future regional challenges in the field of skills policy by combining existing datasets from different data sources and aggregation levels, thereby addressing certain challenges such as demographic change and helping regions to use the new data on skills needs more strategically. The latest report of the committee applied a similar approach to economic sectors and industries. Certain specialised subcommittees have been established within the committee to tackle subtopics (i.e. higher education or work-based learning), which is generally regarded as very promising by committee members. The committee has also identified gaps in the data, for instance regarding regional or sectoral data, in order to put its available research resources to productive use.

In general, all interviewed stakeholders claimed that they can influence the content of the reports, for example by jointly deciding on which data are adequate and reliable. Most importantly, even ideologically opposed social partners seem to be able and willing to compromise about which data to include in the reports. However, as will be visible in the next section, problems connected to agenda-setting and the consequent pre-selection of topics are an issue within the Future Skills Needs Committee.

Challenges

As with the Skills Policy Council, the Future Skills Needs Committee still struggles to identify a clear mandate and an adequate mode of operation. These issues are connected to visible tensions between members of the secretariat and researchers with social partners. Nearly all interviewees admitted certain "communication problems" between these two groups, and the role of the social partners in the committee does not seem to be interpreted by all members in the same way.

Although committee members can decide on the data they acknowledge as adequate and reliable for the report, they cannot influence the wider range of topics considered as fitting for the report. In other words, the agenda of the meetings, and as a result also partly the content of the report, seems to be mostly determined by the secretariat itself, which causes frustration for many committee members. This is particularly problematic as committee members with the most practical experience "on-the-ground", and who are therefore most aware of new socio-economic changes concerning skills, namely the social partners, have problems in putting possible future challenges on the agenda. Many interviewees acknowledged that they expect the situation to improve with new restructuring measures, such as the establishment of subcommittees and workshops. However, these issues also seem to be more fundamentally connected to a focus and preference of the secretariat for more quantitative evidence rather than the more qualitative or anecdotal evidence that social partners can contribute.

The mandate of the committee also seems to be interpreted differently by the secretariat and academics in relation to social partners. The secretariat views the purpose of the committee as gathering and publishing "objective" and purely data-based reports without normative/prescriptive elements, as well as distributing such evidence and funding further research projects. However, the social partners adopt a more holistic perspective, for example arguing that it is not possible to just present "facts" as data always require interpretation, which can never be purely objective and apolitical. As emphasised by interviewees, the choice concerning the type of evidence accepted by the secretariat (quantitative versus qualitative) is not necessarily objective in the first place. As a consequence of these limits, the reports' conclusions are often considered as relatively weak and as "stating the obvious" by many interviewees. The added value of the reports (in terms of content, not necessarily political impact) was often considered as limited by many interviewees, one arguing for example "I could look that up on statistics Norway anytime, so what is new?"

The secretariat seems to have found a compromise position in this regard by agreeing that the committee should highlight commonly identified future "challenges" in the report while not crossing the threshold towards giving policy advice and recommendations. Through specifically highlighting future challenges considered as the most pressing, the secretariat allows for an interpretation of the data – a decision in general welcomed and approved by all stakeholders interviewed. Thereby, the Future Skills Needs Committee raises the level of discussion by providing a common problem definition (i.e. the challenges), while the Skills Policy Council gives political recommendations based on this problem definition. Interviewees agreed that the reports improved year by year, thereby possibly confirming the success of this new compromise.

However, issues concerning the added value of the reports are also partly connected to the committee's policy field, namely forecasting the future skills needs of Norway. Similar to the Skills Policy Council, the concept of the Future Skills Needs Committee has its roots in the Norwegian model of corporatism. The committee is loosely based on the Norwegian Technical Calculation Committee for Wage Settlements (TBU), which provides advice on wage increases based on a variety of available data sources. However, in contrast to the TBU, which bases its decisions on historical data, the Future Skills Needs Committee faces certain challenges unique to the field of skills policy. As many interviewees argued, this involves much more uncertainty than making decisions based on historical data in the TBU, and implies that is difficult to compare the success and performance of the Future Skills Needs Committee to other similar bodies in the Norwegian model of corporatism. In other words, in contrast to the Skills Policy Council, a detailed blueprint is not available for the committee, therefore it is not surprising that it is taking more time for it to find its specific role and mandate.

Interviewees also noted that there is no clear consensus on how to use the funds available to the committee. While the secretariat and researchers want to use the resources for additional research projects, social partners are more in favour of improving the internal processes of the committee. Similar to problems of the Skills Policy Council, social partners want to spend the resources on more and longer meetings and discussions within the committee, thereby improving and fostering its mode of operation and still disputed mandate.

Committee reports so far have clearly focused on facilitating national and regional planning and employers' decision-making processes, while its focus on individuals is still underdeveloped. The clear target group of the committee reports are policy makers rather than individuals seeking advice on acquiring skills (students, unemployed, etc.), and there have been no measures taken to reformulate the reports into a format more comprehensible for young people or their parents. However, many interviewees acknowledged that they were sceptical concerning such a use of the reports, and mentioned limited benefits due to the very general (and system-level) nature of the reports. Furthermore, they highlighted the possible disadvantages of giving overly specific educational advice to individuals in the field of skills policy due to the substantial uncertainties that characterise this policy field.

Summary

The new governance arrangements within the Norwegian Strategy for Skills Policy cover three dimensions of a whole-of-government approach to skills policy. First, the Skills Policy Council mostly tackles the areas of promoting co-ordination, co-operation and collaboration across the whole of government in terms of vertical co-ordination between different levels of government (i.e. counties) and horizontal co-ordination between different ministries and directorates. It also facilitates the engagement of stakeholders throughout the policy cycle by including a range of social partners and NGOs, thereby extending Norway's traditional system of social partnership to new stakeholders. Second, the Future Skills Needs Committee tackles engaging stakeholders throughout the policy cycle and building integrated information systems, as stakeholders themselves are involved in building integrated information systems via the committee. Thereby, the committee creates a common data basis and problem definition in the field of skills policy, which facilitates the work of other governance bodies like the Skills Policy Council.

Policy recommendations

The benefits and challenges of Norway's new governance arrangements identified in the previous section allow for the formulation of a number of policy recommendations, which are the focus of this section.

Give new governance arrangements enough time

In general, decision makers need to be patient when evaluating the impact of the Skills Policy Council or the Future Skills Needs Committee. The broad challenges tackled by the council are unlikely to disappear soon. As some interviewees in Norway argued, similar councils were temporarily established in the past; however, only a permanent council with an established mandate and mode of operation has the potential to fundamentally improve the quality of policies implemented by engaging all relevant stakeholders throughout the policy cycle. Building up a council from scratch only in times of immediate urgency is unlikely to lead to success. Furthermore, the internal governance of councils and similar advisory bodies is likely to improve when interactions are based on mutual trust, which takes time to build. Defining a clear mandate and mode of operation takes time, and is nearly impossible within a short time span. The inclusion of non-traditional stakeholders might also improve over time as informal networks grow between the stakeholders involved within the council. However, this should also be actively facilitated through the council's mode of operation, as discussed further below.

Improve format of meetings and agenda-setting process within the Skills Policy Council

The current format of Skills Policy Council meetings provides insufficient opportunities for discussion and, as a result, does not deepen co-ordination between stakeholders as much as it could. This especially applies to stakeholders who are not part of the traditional system of social partnership in Norway, and therefore lack means of influence outside the format of the council. All interviewees outside of the ministries agreed that space for discussion has to be created to realise the full potential of the council. Some steps are in discussion or are already being implemented to tackle these issues, including a prolongation of meetings and a split between sessions where high-level political decision makers within government are present, and other sessions reserved for discussion between council members. Additional working groups and administrative meetings between official council meetings will also be implemented, and the agenda of meetings will be shortened to free up time for discussion.

These measures could be steps in the right direction; however, additional steps should be taken. For example, the last agenda item of every meeting should give every council member a formal opportunity to influence the agenda of the next council meeting, which is often largely determined by the Ministry of Education and Research, as well as traditional social partners via more informal channels. Improving the format of meetings and giving opportunities to influence the agenda is particularly important to increase the co-operation and co-ordination of "non-traditional" stakeholders outside of tripartite bodies, as they are more dependent on a well-functioning council to interact with other stakeholders.

Improve communication and demonstrate to Skills Policy Council members the impact of their advice

Council members could try to reach common, jointly formulated conclusions and recommendations on certain agenda items/proposed policies. This would also create an opportunity for social partners to reach a compromise between themselves, which is considered impossible within the current format of the meetings, as explained in detail in the previous section. Joint conclusions and recommendations might also help to create a clear added value regarding existing tripartite bodies. Many interviewed council members also noted that they could not see how their recommendations are used, which could be resolved by the obligatory response and feedback of the addressed stakeholder (either ministries or social partners) to recommendations. Such a response would ideally be put into writing to ensure a certain degree of accountability and commitment of the government in relation to stakeholders, and vice versa. Another, more far reaching possibility would be a written agreement between the government/ministry and stakeholders, similar to a coalition agreement, as visible in the case study on the Alliance for Initial and Further Training in Germany (Chapter 3). Furthermore, a written agreement could also be an important step towards jointly making binding decisions within the framework of the council in the future, something seen as potentially beneficial by many interviewed stakeholders. For example, such decisions could be made concerning policies that directly emerged out of the Skills Policy Council.

Clearly define the mandate and reporting line of the Skills Policy Council in relation to other tripartite bodies

As outlined in the last section, the Skills Policy Council struggles to find its role in relation to other, older tripartite bodies in the Norwegian system of corporatism, with the responsibilities of the different bodies not clear to council members. There also seems to be a tension between "new" stakeholders and traditional social partners concerning the mandate of the council. Members not involved in other tripartite bodies particularly emphasise the importance of tackling lower level "on-the-ground" questions, while traditional social partners want the council to stay at a higher level and approach the topic of skills policy in a more holistic manner.

This tension is problematic, as many lower level questions are already tackled by other tripartite bodies in Norway, in particular the National Council for VET. These other bodies only tackle a specific subfield within skills policy, therefore it makes sense to have a more overarching council that co-ordinates between the different subfields (VET, higher education, lifelong learning, etc.) at a higher level. However, clear guidelines should be established concerning which topics can be discussed by the Skills Policy Council at a system level (with lower level questions being addressed in other tripartite bodies, for example the National Council for VET) and which topics can be discussed at a lower level (i.e. where no other lower level tripartite bodies exist). The dense landscape of tripartite bodies might prove to be a benefit for the council in alleviating its workload, therefore making it possible for it to focus on the broader challenges of Norway's skills system.

Some more recent changes to Norway's governance arrangements, such as the planned establishment of regional skills policy councils and regional skills strategies, might partially solve these problems. As one interview partner argued, the "real" practical work happens at the local level. Regional councils could partly tackle such lower level issues. However, the choice of which responsibilities should be delegated to regions in relation to central government is political, and not everything can be decentralised without giving up the uniformity of the educational system. Furthermore, older tripartite bodies often have regional counterparts, for example county vocational training boards that advise county authorities on VET-related matters. Therefore, the mandate of the council (regional and national) has to be clearly defined in relation to other tripartite bodies.

Other suggestions that came up in the interviews should be met with caution. Some interviewees argued that the council could be combined with other tripartite bodies, for example the Council on Labour Market Issues, as there are apparently many intersections between these bodies. However, there is a real danger that such a merged council will become too large, and the issue of skills would become one topic among many. Only a dedicated council can ensure that skills remain at the top of the agenda of all stakeholders. In addition, the inclusion of non-traditional stakeholders such as learning providers only makes sense in a council that is specifically dedicated to skills policy.

Further improve horizontal and vertical co-operation between governance bodies

Some interviewees argued that there are still horizontal co-operation problems between the different ministries. These seem to be highly connected to financing, although this issue is not an explicit part of this case study. In order to facilitate the creation of new policies and ensure the active participation of all ministries, the Ministry of Finance and the government should be open to the idea of a joint budget for measures connected to the Norwegian Strategy for Skills Policy and the Skills Policy Council. However, as one interviewee argued, implementing new policies is not as hard as adapting older policies to new common goals. It could therefore also be an option to shift certain older policies from the individual budgets of single ministries to new joint budgets.

Subnational representation in the council should be monitored and expanded as needed, in the context of Norway's ongoing territorial reforms. As argued before, county-level policy makers are only to a limited extent involved in skills policy, therefore the county representative mostly tries to raise their awareness of the issue. However, the structure with only one representative for a range of counties with possibly different interests could lead to problems regarding the upcoming restructuring and reform of Norway's administrative divisions (counties). As more and more tasks are delegated to regional governments, conflicts of interest between the regions may become increasingly predominant, and a joint representative for all counties may then no longer suffice to represent their interests in a body such as the Skills Policy Council. This possible source of conflict should be monitored considering its potentially negative effects on the power dynamics within the council, even if there is currently no evidence to suggest such a scenario. Similar problems may also be more predominant in other countries where subnational units have more autonomy in skills policy. Conflict might also arise vertically concerning the co-ordination and division of responsibilities, budgets and tasks that could be delegated from ministries to regions. In this respect again, relying on only one county representative within the Skills Policy Council could be problematic.

Use full potential of social partners' expertise in the Future Skills Needs Committee

Social partners within the committee expressed concern that their expertise in the world of work is not fully valued by all committee members. There are organisational and more fundamental reasons for this. First, similar to the Skills Policy Council, social partner members of the committee were dissatisfied with the format of meetings as it does not fully enable the committee to make use of the social partners' expertise, and interviewees preferred more time and resources for discussions. Furthermore, interviewees were dissatisfied with their low degree of influence on the agenda of the committee, which they perceived as being mainly steered by the secretariat.

However, as many interview partners mentioned, steps in the right direction have already been taken or will soon be implemented, for example more meetings in plenum, multi-day seminars and workshops. Interviewees also highlighted that they expect to have more influence on the agenda within the several subcommittees and working groups (for example on the health sector) that will begin soon within the committee. Such specialisation could de facto lead to more decentralised decisions in the new subcommittees and working groups, and detach agenda-setting in these bodies from the secretariat. Nonetheless, the committee's mode of operation in its "main assembly" should also be "de jure" reformed so that committee members, not just the secretariat, jointly decide on an agenda.

Second, making full use of social partners' potential might also be complicated by the relatively strong concentration of one academic discipline, economics, within the committee, with most researchers on the committee economists. Economics as a discipline has a strong focus on quantitative evidence, whereas social partners can be a rich source of qualitative evidence. It might therefore be beneficial to increase the diversity of academic disciplines within the committee and include those that place a greater focus on processing qualitative evidence, including sociologists or political scientists. Such an interdisciplinary approach might substantially increase the benefits of having social partners within the committee. Furthermore, insights of social partners could inform the choice of future research areas and projects funded by the committee as they can point towards important issues not yet reflected in quantitative evidence, thereby highlighting where future research might prove especially beneficial.

Refine the mandate of the Future Skills Needs Committee concerning targeting individuals

The Future Skills Needs Committee has so far focused on facilitating national and regional planning and employers' decision-making processes, but its role in assessing Norway's future skills needs for individuals is not yet fully developed. A brainstorming process is underway within the committee on how to best distribute committee findings to the wider public, thereby focusing on supporting individuals in their educational choices. Proposals include podcasts or smaller leaflets that summarise the committee's reports in an understandable manner. The secretariat has written two web articles directed at individuals, and the manuscripts have been circulated among members of the committee for comments and input. In addition, a survey assessing information sources, opinion formation and the educational choices of upper secondary students is currently being commissioned.

However, it also has to be considered to what extent individuals should actually be a direct target group of the Future Skills Needs Committee, or if the mandate should be limited to the target groups of (political or firm-level) decision makers, and thereby on facilitating national and regional planning and employer support. The target group of individuals is also problematic concerning the committee's mandate, as understood by many members, that specific recommendations are not allowed. As mentioned, many interviewees acknowledged that they are sceptical of targeting individuals due to the very general (and system-level) nature of the reports, as well as the possible disadvantages of giving overly specific educational advice to individuals due to the substantial uncertainties that shape this policy field. Furthermore, a variety of websites already seem to exist that specifically target individuals concerning their educational choices, and it is questionable to what extent the committee could produce added value at the individual level compared to existing offers. However, the existing websites and offers that target individuals could themselves be informed and advised of decisions in the Future Skills Needs Committee, thereby adding the perspective of social partners to existing offers.

References

Bowman, J. (2005), "Employers and the Politics of Skill Formation in a Coordinated Market Economy: Collective Action and Class Conflict in Norway", *Politics & Society*, Vol. 33/4, pp. 567-594, http://dx.doi.org/10.1177/0032329205280925. [12]

Busemeyer, M. and C. Trampusch (2012), *The Political Economy of Collective Skill Formation*, Oxford University Press, Oxford, New York. [10]

Dalbak, K. (2018), *Norwegian Committee on Skill Needs*, https://kompetansebehovsutvalget.no/mandate-of-official-norwegian-committee-on-skill-needs/ (accessed on 6 January 2020). [14]

Kingdon, J. (2011), *Agendas, alternatives, and public policies*, Pearson, London. [15]

Michelsen, S., O. Olsen and H. Høst (2014), *Nord-VET-The future of VET in the Nordic Countries Origins and development of VET 1850-2008-an investigation into the Norwegian case*, http://www.nordforsk.org/en (accessed on 6 January 2020). [8]

Ministry of Education (2017), *Norwegian Strategy for Skills Policy 2017-2021*. [3]

Norwegian Government Security and Service Organisation (2019), *Kompetansepolitisk råd (Skills Policy Council)*. [13]

Nyen, T. and A. Tønder (2016), *Cooperation and Reform in Vocational Education and Training*. [9]

OECD (2020), *Enrolment by type of institution*, https://stats.oecd.org/Index.aspx?DataSetCode=EDU_ENRL_INST (accessed on 6 March 2020). [11]

OECD (2020), *Population with tertiary education* (indicator), https://dx.doi.org/10.1787/0b8f90e9-en (accessed on 30 January 2020). [6]

OECD (2019), *Getting Skills Right: Future-Ready Adult Learning Systems*, Getting Skills Right, OECD Publishing, Paris, https://dx.doi.org/10.1787/9789264311756-en. [7]

OECD (2019), *OECD Skills Strategy 2019: Skills to Shape a Better Future*, OECD Publishing, Paris, https://dx.doi.org/10.1787/9789264313835-en. [2]

OECD (2019), *PISA 2018 Results (Volume I): What Students Know and Can Do*, PISA, OECD Publishing, Paris, https://dx.doi.org/10.1787/5f07c754-en. [5]

OECD (2018), *"Norway" in Education at a Glance 2018: OECD Indicators*, OECD Publishing, Paris, https://dx.doi.org/10.1787/eag-2018-en. [1]

OECD (2014), *OECD Skills Strategy Diagnostic Report: Norway 2014*, OECD Skills Studies, OECD Publishing, Paris, https://dx.doi.org/10.1787/9789264298781-en. [4]

Notes

[1] Basic courses of study are broad general or vocational programmes in the first upper secondary school year (for example in "health", "construction", etc.).

[2] I.e. those adults who have never attended primary or secondary education before, for example migrants.

[3] The Ministry of Justice and Public Security was also involved until 2018, when the department of immigration was transferred to the Ministry of Education and Research as part of an organisational restructuring.

[4] Meaning the highest hierarchical level of unions and associations, i.e. country-wide organisations that might encompass several sector-level and regional organisations.

[5] Except the Sami parliament, which has an observer status.

[6] For example, one could expect that a single representative might not be able to reconcile the diverging interests (due to size, location, economic structure, etc.) between a large number of counties.

6 Case study: Portugal's National Agency for Qualification and Vocational Education and Training (ANQEP)

Having one of the lowest educational attainment rates among European countries, in 2007 Portugal implemented a major reform in order to promote vocational education and training and to increase participation in upper secondary education. This chapter introduces the National Agency of Qualification and Vocational Education and Training (ANQEP, Agência Nacional para a Qualificação e o Ensino Profissional) that was established in the course of the 2007 reform. ANQEP is responsible for the overall co-ordination of the National Qualifications System. Thereby, it fulfils the difficult task of bringing different ministries, agencies and stakeholders engaged in the provision of skills formation together. This chapter presents the responsibilities and organisfation of ANQEP within Portugal's skills formation system and discusses how it contributes to implementing the "whole-of-government approach" in Portugal.

Introduction

In the last two decades, Portugal has made impressive progress regarding the provision of skills and qualifications to its people. Although strongly affected by the economic and financial crisis, it has managed to greatly improve the educational attainment of its population in recent years. For instance, between 2000 and 2013, the upper secondary attainment rate of 25-34 year-olds doubled, as did the proportion of 25-64 year-olds who had completed tertiary education (OECD, 2014[1]; OECD, 2015[2]). Nevertheless, Portugal still has one of the lowest educational attainment rates among European countries (OECD, 2018[3]).

In the early 2000s, the Portuguese government identified vocational education and training (VET) as a central instrument to address the issue of educational attainment, with a focus on adults in particular. Although some progress has been made, there are still currently about 70% of 55-64 year-olds and about 60% of 45-54 year-olds who have not completed upper secondary education. The government aimed to provide pathways to qualifications for adults by establishing a system for the recognition of prior learning and by offering modularised courses leading to certification at the upper secondary level. With the adoption of the VET reform in December 2007, Portugal established a comprehensive National Qualifications System (Sistema Nacional de Qualificações, SNQ) that included all VET qualifications – for adults as well as youth. The legal framework of the SNQ was updated in 2017 (decree law no. 14/2017).

The focus of this case study is the National Agency for Qualification and Vocational Education and Training (Agência Nacional para a Qualificação e o Ensino Profissional, ANQEP), formerly the National Agency for Qualification (Agência Nacional para a Qualificação, ANQ). ANQEP was established in 2007 (decree law no. 276-C/2007) to co-ordinate the SNQ. It is jointly supervised by the Ministry of Education and the Ministry of Labour, Solidarity and Social Security. There are also several governance bodies within ANQEP that involve stakeholders from different parts of the economy and other government bodies. Therefore, ANQEP is a prime example of how inter-ministerial co-ordination between different governmental departments can be combined with efforts to improve collaboration between governmental actors and stakeholders, in line with a whole-of-government approach to skills policy. Based on document research and numerous interviews with representatives from public authorities and social partners, which were conducted in Lisbon in April 2019, this case study describes how co-ordination, co-operation and collaboration across the whole of government can be achieved. It demonstrates how stakeholders can be meaningfully engaged and how financing mechanisms can become well aligned. In this respect, ANQEP has introduced great advances in the Portuguese VET and adult education system. While highlighting positive aspects, this case study will also point out the challenges and problems that ANQEP has encountered in recent years. Most importantly, although its competences are clearly defined in law, ANQEP still struggles with finding its role in Portugal's VET system, which may not be surprising given that it is a relatively new agency. Nevertheless, the case of ANQEP provides valuable insights for other VET systems that aim to adopt a whole-of-government approach.

With reference to the overall framework of this report, this case study focuses on three of the four dimensions:

- Promoting co-ordination, co-operation and collaboration across the whole of government.
- Engaging stakeholders throughout the policy cycle.
- Aligning and co-ordinating financing arrangements.

Portugal's education and training system

After a period of considerable financial constraints and high unemployment rates between 2008 and 2012, Portugal has successfully undergone a demanding adjustment programme designed to promote growth and social well-being. As part of this programme, several reforms and initiatives relating to skills have been implemented in recent years, as skills policies have become a top priority for policy makers. Portugal has already made substantial progress in raising the educational attainment of its population: the share of young people aged 20 to 24 with at least upper secondary education increased from 49.4% in 2005 to 77.5% in 2016 (OECD, 2018[4]). Similarly, the number of early leavers from education and training decreased dramatically from 38.3% in 2005 to 11.8% in 2018, now slightly above European Union EU-28 average (Eurostat, 2019[5]).[1]

Despite these improvements, Portugal still faces significant challenges: Educational success is strongly dependent on student's socio-economic background, the share of long-term unemployed is comparatively high, and educational attainment rates are still below the OECD average (OECD, 2015[2]), and are particularly low for adults. About 73% of 55 to 64 year-olds have not reached upper secondary education, compared to about 28.5% of 25 to 34 year-olds. At the same time, as shown in Figure 6.1, the latter share is also greater than the OECD average of 15%. Similarly, the share of Portuguese 25 to 34 year-olds with completed upper secondary education (about 36%) lags behind the OECD average by approximately 5% (Figure 6.1).

Figure 6.1. Educational attainment of 25-34 year-olds

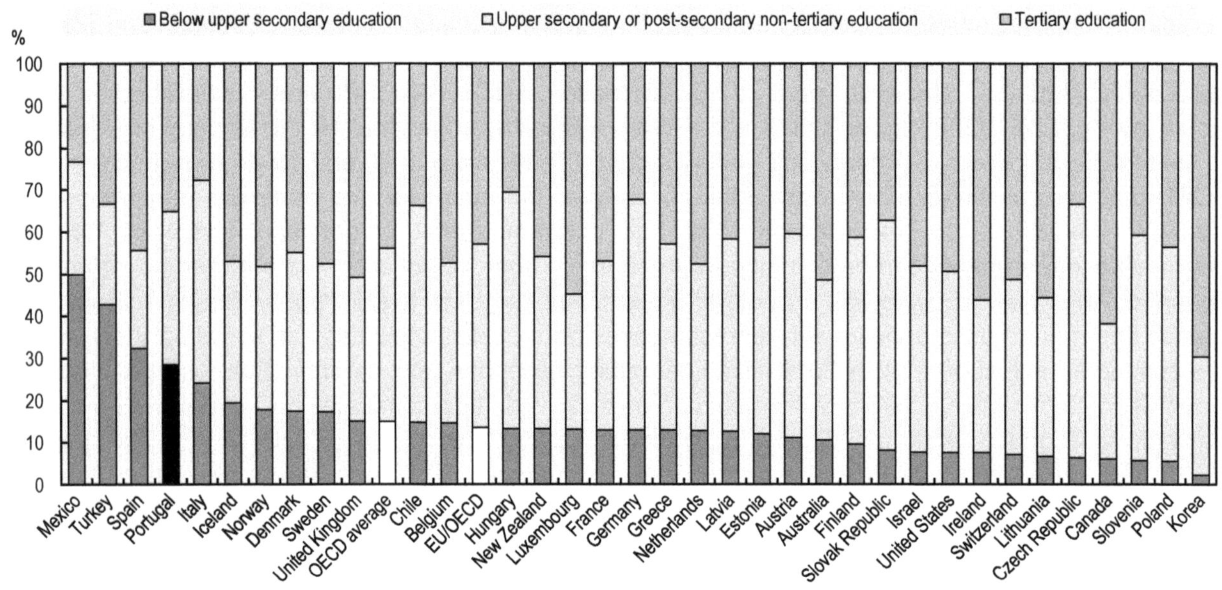

Source: OECD (2020[6]), *Educational attainment and labour-force status*, https://stats.oecd.org/Index.aspx?DataSetCode=EAG_NEAC.

StatLink https://doi.org/10.1787/888934112766

Promoting opportunities in VET can help Portugal to tackle these problems. The current VET system in Portugal is the result of a large-scale reform adopted in December 2007 and implemented in 2008 (decree law no. 396/2007). Before this point, the main public provider of VET was the Institute for Employment and Vocational Training (Instituto do Emprego e Formação Profissional, IEFP). Other training providers included firms, VET schools (*escolas profissionais*) and VET courses (*cursos profissionais*) at public secondary schools. However, VET training was not well regulated, and standardisation at the national level, when existent, was not integrated between the different governmental departments. The only common factor among VET providers was that they mainly viewed VET as a pathway for low-performing students into the labour market. As a consequence, VET suffered from low prestige.

Today, VET is the joint responsibility of several ministries, including the Ministry of Education, the Ministry of Labour, Solidarity and Social Security, and the Ministry of Economy. Besides ANQEP, several other public agencies are responsible for the implementation of VET policies, for example the IEFP. In addition, the VET law describes several ways in which stakeholders can participate in decision making.

With the 2007 reform, the government decided to prioritise VET to address the problems of low educational attainment, especially for adults (Figure 6.1), and of high numbers of early school drop-outs. It drew up plans to bring the different parts of the VET system together into a single national framework under the joint supervision of the Ministry of Education, the Ministry of Labour, Solidarity and Social Security, and the Ministry of Economy. The law created common objectives, tools and structures to ensure that VET qualifications better match labour market needs and to reinforce the recognition, validation and certification of competences. It entailed two major innovations: the establishment of a comprehensive National Qualifications System (SNQ) to create common national standards for VET courses, regardless of the provider; and the creation of a new public agency (ANQEP) to co-ordinate the SNQ, among other roles (OECD, 2015[2]).

The SNQ includes the following tools:

- National Qualifications Framework (Quadro Nacional de Qualificações, QNQ), designed in line with the European Qualifications Framework.
- National Catalogue of Qualifications (Catálogo Nacional de Qualificações, CNQ).
- Qualification Needs Anticipation System (Sistema de Antecipação de Necessidades de Qualificações, SANQ).
- National Credit System for VET (Sistema National de Créditos do EFP).
- An online tool for the guidance and qualifications record of individual learners (Qualifica Passport).

The National Catalogue of Qualifications currently consists of more than 300 qualifications in 43 sectoral areas of education and training (Área de Educação e Formação). VET thus takes place in a large number of very different economic areas, including tourism, information and communication technology (ICT), social welfare, and commerce (DGEEC, 2020[7]). In order to regularly update the qualifications catalogue, there are 16 sectoral Qualifications councils under the ANQEP umbrella, in which various stakeholders, such as firms, employers' associations, trade unions and training providers, discuss the creation of new and the updating or abolition of existing qualifications. They are supported by specialised ANQEP staff that provide administrative and financial support.

Portugal's VET system consists of different types of programmes, which all need to be consistent with the qualifications defined in the National Qualifications Catalogue (Table 6.1). At the upper secondary level, most VET students attend professional courses (80%) or apprenticeship courses (15%), which both rank at ISCED level 3 (ANQEP, 2020[8]). Professional courses last 3 years, and apprenticeship courses last from 2.5 to 3 years, with both awarding a vocational certificate and a diploma attesting the completion of the 12th year of schooling (DGERT, 2016[9]). The courses differ, however, regarding the type of provider and the extent of firm-based learning. In apprenticeship courses (*Cursos de Aprendizagem*), work-based learning is very important, and students spend 40% of their time in workplace training. Providers are either IEFP training centres, training centres of social partners or private for-profit centres. All providers are under the supervision of the IEFP. In contrast, in professional courses (*Cursos Profissionais*) only about 19-27% of students' time is spent in workplace training. Providers are mainly public or private schools under the supervision of the Ministry of Education that engage with employers to establish partnerships for workplace training and the technical components of the curriculum (DGERT, 2016[9]). Other programmes at the lower and upper secondary level include specialised art programmes (*Cursos Artísticos Especializados*) and education and training programmes for young people (*Cursos de Educação e Formação de Jovens*) (DGERT, 2016[9]; OECD, 2015[2]); however, as the number of participants is very small in these programmes, the remainder of the case study focuses on professional and apprenticeship courses.

Table 6.1. VET programmes at the upper secondary level

Programme	Age	ISCED levels	Training providers	Share of work-based learning
Professional courses	15-18	354	Schools (public and private)	19-27%
Apprenticeship courses	18-24	354	IEFP, social partners, for-profit institutions	40%
Specialised art programmes	15-18	344, 354	Schools (public and private)	4-13%
Education and training programmes for young people	15-18	354	Schools (public and private)	n/a
Vocational programmes at the upper secondary level	15-18	N.A.	Schools (public and private)	Determined individually by the providers

Portugal has taken a number of measures to encourage greater participation in adult learning and increase the educational attainment of adults. The Qualifica Programme, launched in 2017, formulates three goals to be reached by 2020: 1) 50% of the population to have finished upper secondary education; 2) 15% of adults to have taken part in lifelong learning activities; and 3) 40% of 30-34 year-olds to have obtained a higher education certificate (ANQEP et al., 2020[10]). In order to achieve these goals, around 300 Qualifica centres have been established across the country to provide information and guidance and to refer adults (18+) to education and training pathways. These centres are also responsible for the certification of prior learning acquired in formal, non-formal and informal contexts. The process of prior learning recognition is simplified by an online tool, the Qualifica passport, which allows adults to record their qualifications and skills and identify further learning pathways (ANQEP et al., 2020[11]). The Qualifica programme has also established a national credit system in line with some principles of the European Credit System for Vocational Education and Training (ECVET).

The second main innovation of the 2007 VET law was the establishment of the National Agency for Qualification (ANQ), later renamed the National Agency for Qualification and Vocational Education and Training (ANQEP). A public institute that reports to both the Ministry of Education and the Ministry of Labour, Solidarity and Social Security, ANQEP is an important example of a whole-of-government approach to skills issues. It will be the focus of the analysis in the next sections.

The role of ANQEP in Portugal's education and training system

ANQEP's predecessor – the National Agency for Qualification (ANQ) – was created in 2007 as the main co-ordinating body of the National Qualifications System. With the creation of the ANQ, the government wanted to better align the supply of skills produced by the education system with the demands of the labour market. In 2012, after the economic crisis, ANQ was renamed ANQEP – the National Agency for Qualification and Vocational Education and Training – although its mission remained the same.

ANQEP is an agency under the supervision of three ministries – the Ministry of Education, the Ministry of Labour, Solidarity and Social Security, and the Ministry of Economy (although the latter has less influence than the former two ministries). Stakeholders are part of the oversight board and have a key role in the definition of ANQEP's general lines of action. It is an important example of a whole-of-government approach whereby different types and levels of government work closely with stakeholders to improve and strengthen the governance of the skills system.

ANQEP reports to the Ministry of Education and the Ministry of Labour, Solidarity and Social Security (Figure 6.2). Both ministries finance the personnel and administrative expenses of the agency. The Ministry of Economy has policy responsibilities in VET and adult learning, but these responsibilities are determined by government decisions and are thus not static. The ministers of education and labour appoint the president and the two vice presidents of ANQEP, within a mandatory public recruitment policy in which candidates for public administration positions have to apply. Although supervised by the two ministries, as a public institute, ANQEP has administrative and financial autonomy, thus has more autonomy than other government bodies, such as a directorate general. However, ANQEP does not have autonomy to set its own policy goals and instruments, but instead decides on the implementation of the instruments set by the government.

ANQEP's work is monitored by its General Board, which evaluates ANQEP's yearly programme and discusses its achievements. As defined in the law, the board comprises a maximum of 25 members that represent the social partners, the Ministry of Education and the Ministry of Labour, Solidarity and Social Security, the IEFP, other stakeholders such as the National Association of Professional Schools, and independent experts. The members of the General Board are proposed by the president of ANQEP to the Secretary of State of Education and the Secretary of State of Employment, who are responsible for their nomination. The General Board meets at least twice a year.

The sectoral councils, which are made up of several important stakeholders, define and update qualifications based on the technical and methodological orientations of ANQEP. ANQEP also provides administrative support to the work of the sectoral councils such as sending out invitations to meetings, setting the agenda for the updating process and chairing council meetings. ANQEP financial resources may be used to hire external experts with expertise in updating processes, if needed. The members of the sectoral councils are nominated by ANQEP and work voluntarily.

Figure 6.2. Governance arrangements of ANQEP

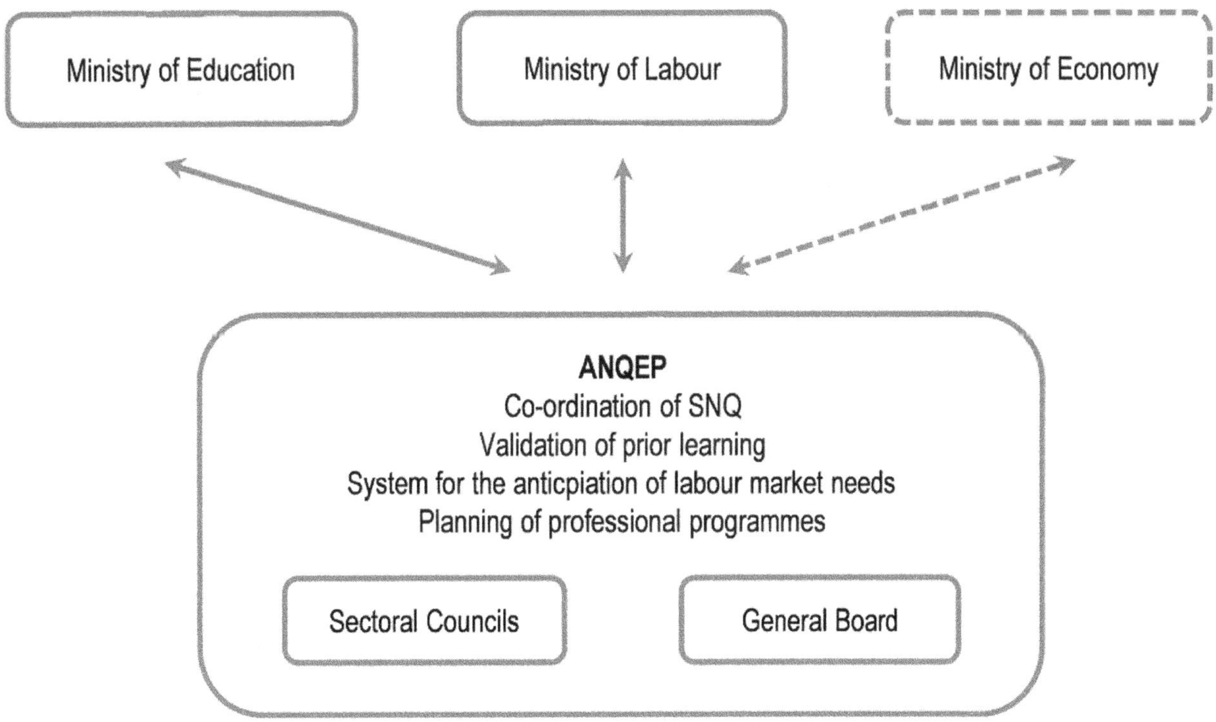

ANQEP's main task is to co-ordinate the SNQ, which involves a number of different elements. First, ANQEP co-ordinates the continuous updating of the National Catalogue of Qualifications, with the involvement of the sectoral councils. While ANQEP is not directly responsible for the updating process (this is done by sectoral councils), it provides the necessary administrative and financial support. Considering that the members of the councils are volunteers delegated from other organisations, the role of ANQEP in these processes should not be underestimated.

Second, ANQEP is responsible for developing and managing the national system for the recognition, validation and certification of competences. As such, it oversees around 300 Qualifica centres, whose main task is the certification of prior learning experience. In order to ensure that the same standards apply across the whole country, ANQEP provides training to Qualifica centre staff and oversees the National Credit System for Vocational Education and Training. In addition, it manages the Qualifica Passport, which records the qualifications and skills acquired by individuals.

Third, ANQEP has established the Qualification Needs Anticipation System (SANQ) to evaluate which qualifications are needed in the labour market. SANQ uses a variety of data sources and indicators to rank qualifications according to priority levels from one to ten. Typically, the process of anticipating labour market needs involves several aspects. Firstly, ANQEP uses statistical data about recent employment dynamics and conducts a survey to identify the short- to medium-term skills needs of employers. Secondly, the European Centre for the Development of Vocational Training (Cedefop) provides projections for the future development of skills demand in Portugal. Thirdly, the IEFP provides SANQ with data about job vacancies at the regional and occupational level. Finally, to evaluate the quality of the various training providers, SANQ considers the total number of students, the share of students who received certification and data on the transition of students into the labour market. Since most data are available at the regional level (NUT II), SANQ can determine the demand for each qualification in the National Catalogue of Qualifications at that level. All these data are integrated to generate a regional vision, which allows inter-municipalities to deepen their analysis at the subregional (NUT III) level.

The final task of ANQEP in co-ordinating the SNQ is its important role in planning the supply of professional programmes. ANQEP identifies the number of placements in the different courses needed at national and inter-municipality levels with the help of SANQ and – together with the inter-municipal communities – determines which courses are offered to meet local labour market demand. Importantly, there are separate systems for the planning of professional and apprenticeship courses. While ANQEP and the Ministry of Education are responsible for professional courses, the IEFP is responsible for apprenticeship courses, as well as for supervising apprenticeship training providers. To determine priority levels, the IEFP developed its own anticipation system before SANQ was developed, and now uses SANQ data to complement their own information.

ANQEP is publicly financed. Compared to other OECD countries, the share of public funding for VET in Portugal is above average (OECD, 2018[4]). ANQEP's administrative and personnel expenses and activities are financed by the general state budget, as well as the budgets of the Ministry of Education and of the Ministry of Labour, Solidarity and Social Security.

European Union (EU) funds make up a large part of the overall funding of the different VET programmes, especially for professional courses. The Human Capital Operational Programme of the European Union (POCH, *Programa Operacional Capital Humano)* contributes significantly to the direct financing of the different VET programmes and of the Qualifica centres (DGERT, 2016[9]). In addition, parts of the EU Operational Programme for Social Inclusion and Employment (POISE, Programa Operacional Inclusão Social e Emprego) support activities that promote the development of skills of vulnerable groups to integrate those not in employment, education or training (NEET) into the labour market (DGERT, 2016[9]). The programmes financed by European funds are co-funded by Portugal's national budget.

Private funding is more important for apprenticeship courses. Here, the courses are co-funded by EU structural funds and the IEFP, whose budget is mostly made up of social security contributions paid by employers. Thus, through this mechanism, the private sector also participates in the financing of VET. Other sources of private funding do not exist at the level of upper secondary education as students do not pay tuition fees.

Analysis

A whole-of-government approach aims to improve co-operation and co-ordination across horizontal and vertical levels of government, as well as between public and private actors. In doing so, coherent and mutually reinforcing institutions are established that are flexible enough to respond to regional demands and new socio-economic challenges. This analysis will explore how ANQEP contributes to strengthening the governance of Portugal's skills system. The analysis is based on a detailed review of national and international reports on Portugal's skills system and ten interviews with experts and representatives from various institutions involved in the governance of ANQEP. Nine interviews were conducted in April 2019 in Lisbon, one interview was conducted via phone.

Opportunities and challenges in the governance framework of ANQEP

Effective skills policies require close co-ordination, co-operation and collaboration between a large number of public agencies at the national and subnational level. ANQEP is the result of such cross-government co-ordination as its predecessor, the ANQ, was created by an agreement between the minister of education and the minister of labour.[2] ANQEP reports to the Ministry of Education, the Ministry of Labour, Solidarity and Social Security and the Ministry of Economy. The former two ministries formally supervise ANQEP, appoint its management team and the General Board, and finance ANQEP's administrative and personnel expenses and activities. ANQEP co-ordinates the National Qualifications System and the actors involved. These include government agencies such as the IEFP, the Agency for Development and Cohesion, and the Directorate-General for Education; VET schools; and apprenticeship providers. Consequently, ANQEP faces two challenges: it needs to bring all involved institutions at various levels of government together; and it has to perform its tasks in agreement with the Ministry of Education, the Ministry of Labour, Solidarity and Social Security and the Ministry of Economy.

Within the current government, co-operation between the Ministry of Education and the Ministry of Labour, Solidarity and Social Security works well. As a high-level official in one of the ministries stated: "We don't take a step without involving the other. It is a very dynamic process". All interview partners confirmed that a large amount of co-ordination takes place. Apparently, officials in the ministries have worked together for several years already and know and trust each other, which fosters collaboration.

However, these ministries have not always worked together in such a productive way, and there were often conflicts when the development of the skills system was not a top priority for the government. In 2011 and 2012, Portugal experienced major debates about the future of ANQ, with the newly elected government questioning the mission and effectiveness of the agency. Nevertheless, the ANQ was not abolished. Rather, the government modified its mission and put stronger emphasis on VET at the upper secondary level, symbolically expressed in the renaming of ANQ to ANQEP. According to several interview partners, the agency was preserved because it was supported by stakeholders and because the low educational attainment rates in the Portuguese population was highly debated in public. To abolish the ANQ would have been a sign that the government did not value the issue enough. The debate about the future of the ANQ in 2011 shows that the continued survival of the agency depends strongly on the government's commitment to skills policy. If the development of the skills system is very important to the leadership of the government, co-ordination across the whole-of-government is easier to facilitate.

Collaboration in the Portuguese skills system also takes place between the national and the subnational levels. Although Portugal is a non-federalist state with a strong central government, ANQEP promotes co-ordination with the subnational level to allocate resources as efficiently and effectively as possible. An important step to reach this goal was the creation of SANQ in 2014. With this instrument, ANQEP can define skills priorities at the subnational level as SANQ offers regional level data on placements by courses, success rates of training providers and future labour market needs. Based on these skills priorities, ANQEP, the Ministry of Education and other state authorities indicate which programmes are more relevant and identify potential providers. To align these programmes to local labour market needs, the government has encouraged inter-municipalities to invest in joint efforts regarding skills policies.

Overall, Portugal has made impressive progress in creating a high degree of collaboration across the different stakeholders; however, there are still different priorities and perspectives. First, as mentioned by interviewed stakeholder representatives, the priorities of the Ministry of Education and the Ministry of Labour, Solidarity and Social security may differ. The Ministry of Education is obviously closely connected to schools and therefore emphasises school-based VET programmes. In contrast, for the Ministry of Labour, Solidarity and Social Security and the IEFP, as the agency most involved in skills policies, VET is viewed as an instrument to integrate (young) people into the labour market, and they consequently foster VET programmes with a high share of workplace learning and employer engagement. However, the different perspectives do not appear to form an obstacle to ANQEP's work, which is helped by the management team being appointed by the Secretary of State for Education and the Secretary of State for Employment.

Second, the relationship between ANQEP and the IEFP is challenging. The IEFP is an agency of the Ministry of Labour, Solidarity and Social Security and is one of the biggest providers of apprenticeship programmes. It also supervises other apprenticeship providers and is responsible for planning a large number of apprenticeship courses across the country. By contrast, the Ministry of Education supervises professional programme providers and plans programmes together with ANQEP. ANQEP oversees the National Catalogue of Qualifications that is obligatory for both types of programmes. Because of this arrangement, ANQEP is much more involved in the provision of professional courses than apprenticeship courses. At the same time, the different providers compete for the same students – and this competition is getting fiercer because of demographic changes resulting in shrinking cohort sizes.

In this context, the IEFP and apprenticeship course providers – often trade unions or business associations – express concerns that professional programmes have an advantage for two reasons. First, the schools that offer professional programmes are also often lower secondary schools, and students prefer to stay at the same school rather than change to a training centre that they do not know. Second, the IEFP and apprenticeship providers argue that professional programmes receive more political support than apprenticeship programmes. The fact that the IEFP established itself as the major VET provider before the 2007 reform increases the competitive situation between the two agencies and makes it difficult for ANQEP to influence apprenticeship programmes in the same way as professional programmes. There is still competition between ANQEP and the IEFP. For example, the IEFP uses a different system of labour market anticipation needs to ANQEP, even though SANQ has been developed within the framework of the National Qualifications System. However, interviews also showed that ANQEP and the IEFP are aware of these challenges and willing to work together to develop a more coherent skills system.

Opportunities and challenges to involving stakeholders

The 2007 VET law was negotiated during a time when tripartite arrangements played an important role in Portugal's policy making. Between 2005 and 2009, co-ordination among social partners and the state was at its peak in Portugal (European Commission, 2016[12]). In this context, the new VET law was discussed and agreed on between employers, trade unions and the national government before being adopted by parliament. The law prescribes the engagement of social partners and stakeholders, such as training providers, regional representatives and other experts, as well as trade unions and employers' representatives, more generally in ANQEP's various governance bodies. Stakeholders are responsible for monitoring the work of the agency through the General Board and for the definition of qualification standards via the sectoral councils.

Representatives of the various stakeholders take part in the General Board of ANQEP, which monitors the agency's work. It discusses ANQEP's yearly programme and evaluates its achievements. Interview partners did not perceive the General Board to have an influential role in Portugal's skills system as conflictual discussions usually do not take place during these meetings. Although not obliged to, the board has always agreed on the yearly programme of ANQEP in the last few years. Regular meetings between the most important stakeholders are essential for developing trust within the skills system. As has been shown in the literature, networks and informal agreements play an important role in VET policies (Culpepper, 2007[13]; Emmenegger, Graf and Trampusch, 2018[14]). The meetings of the General Board create these networks as stakeholder representatives can meet and have the opportunity to exchange their views about priorities and goals. Thus, it provides stakeholders with the opportunity to find common solutions for shared challenges.

At the sectoral level, stakeholders meet regularly in the sectoral councils. Again, these meetings are a good opportunity to connect with other stakeholders at the industry level. Sectoral councils have more responsibilities than the General Board, for example they are responsible for the definition of qualification standards and thus define which qualifications are part of the National Qualifications Catalogue. This is a difficult endeavour in a number of ways, for example the sectoral council members work voluntarily and are not paid. They are often employed in the field of skills development, for example a school principal or head of a training centre, and are delegated by their institution to the respective sectoral council. Importantly, all members are training experts, but not necessarily experts in updating qualifications, which requires a different type of expertise. Therefore, it is a major challenge for sectoral council members to update qualification standards regularly, especially when considering that labour market demands change frequently and that the 16 sectoral councils are co-responsible for more than 300 qualifications in the National Catalogue of Qualifications. ANQEP has recognised this problem and provides various measures of support, including technical and methodological support, and makes financial resources available to pay for experts in the updating processes.

There are challenges to involving stakeholders in the governance of ANQEP. First, the feeling of ownership for their work in sectoral councils is decreasing as ANQEP is taking over an increasing amount of competences. As a consequence, council members are increasingly withdrawing from their responsibilities. This is a self-reinforcing pattern: the more stakeholders withdraw, the more ANQEP assumes responsibilities as it has a strong interest in ensuring that qualification standards are updated regularly. One interview partner confirmed that the work of the sectoral councils is too dependent on ANQEP: "They [the sectoral councils] should be more responsible to take initiative, more aware of their important role in reviewing the catalogue and the provision of skills." This is identified as a major problem for the innovative capacity of Portugal's skills system: "We need to put more energy in them [the sectoral councils]". ANQEP is currently working on solutions to tackle this problem, but these solutions need to be agreed on with the stakeholders to ensure that they are also taken on board.

The second challenge to involving stakeholders in the governance of ANQEP regards the integration of business into the skills system. A large body of literature has shown that small firms are much more cost-sensitive than large firms (Culpepper, 2007[13]; Culpepper and Thelen, 2008[15]). Portugal's economy is characterised by a large number of very small firms: micro (up to 9 employees) and small (10-49 employees) businesses employ more than 60% of the working population, which is 10 percentage points above the EU-28 average (Eurostat, 2016[16]). These businesses often lack the financial and administrative resources to invest in the skills of their employees compared to large firms. Because of the difficulty of engaging with micro and small firms, ANQEP concentrates on establishing close ties with medium-sized and large firms, as well as with specific employers' associations, to increase firm participation in training. For example, ANQEP has reached partnership agreements with some sectors, such as the tourism and hospitality sector and the metal sector, to demonstrate to firms that VET provides a solution to their specific skills needs. Thereby, Portugal is making some progress regarding getting firms to participate in VET. Nevertheless, the commitment of individual firms and whole economic sectors differs significantly. Here again, trust and personal ties play an important role: if business representatives personally know representatives from ANQEP or the IEFP, they are more likely to see the value of participating in the training of young people.

To sum up, the 2007 VET reform formally established the participation of stakeholders in the work of ANQEP, namely in the definition of qualification standards. They thus have considerable responsibility for the development of the National Qualifications System. This comes with great opportunities, but also with significant challenges.

Summary

The ANQ was established with the explicit aim of bringing education and the labour market closer together. According to interview partners, political leadership by the two ministers in charge at the time – the minister of labour and the minister of education – was essential in order to put political weight behind the development of the 2007 VET law. The ministers brought the prime minister and other cabinet members on board, as well as key social partners.

However, explicit political support is not the only condition necessary for the implementation of a whole-of-government approach. For example, in 2012, political priorities shifted to other policy fields as a consequence of changes in the composition of government. During the 2011 election campaign, the ANQ's existence was even questioned. In the end the ANQ survived because it had the support of the social partners and other stakeholders, and because tackling low educational attainment was still an important topic. The newly elected government eventually decided to continue prioritising VET at the upper secondary level, as well as ANQEP as the central agency for the future development of skills policies. Hence, the case of ANQEP shows that to establish a sustainable new institution it needs to be supported both by political actors and by stakeholders such as training providers, employers' associations and trade unions. It also needs a clear purpose and the means to tackle important societal challenges.

ANQEP is also a good example of stakeholder engagement. The 2007 VET law was part of a tripartite agreement that prescribed the participation of stakeholders in two governance bodies: the General Board, which supervises the work of ANQEP, and the 16 sectoral councils, which develop the qualifications in the National Catalogue of Qualifications. The governance of ANQEP therefore involves a broad range of stakeholders, including business associations, trade unions, firms, public and private schools, apprenticeship providers, and representatives from other government bodies. These bodies not only provide an opportunity to influence VET policies, but are a place where different actors get to know each other and can build trust and informal networks. It is important that the General Board and the sectoral councils are embodied in the law so that they are less vulnerable to changes in political priorities.

Through SANQ, which helps to identify and quantify the demand for qualifications at the sectoral and subnational levels, ANQEP contributes to ensuring that students develop the skills that are important for their future career prospects. ANQEP defines the criteria regarding the planning of VET course network. According to these criteria, the General Directorate of Schools Establishments and inter-municipalities negotiate the options with school networks at the subregional level. ANQEP also supports sectoral councils, which define the qualifications that need to be updated, abolished or newly included in the National Catalogue of Qualifications.

Since 2007, Portugal has established a coherent VET system in which different stakeholders – public and private – collaborate extensively. In this, ANQEP plays a major role. The agency has withstood a difficult financial situation as well as political uncertainty, but it can provide valuable insights for other VET systems regarding implementing a whole-of-government approach to ensuring that the labour market has the skills it needs, as well as involving stakeholders in the governance of skills systems. These insights are summarised below:

- **Bringing together two ministries with different priorities and perspectives**: Currently, the Ministry of Education and the Ministry of Labour, Solidarity and Social Security work closely with ANQEP to develop Portugal's skills system. The officials working on skills policies in both ministries know and trust each other. In addition, skills policies are a priority of the current government and ANQEP receives the necessary political support to fulfil its tasks.

The disadvantage with this is that as ANQEP depends a lot on the government's priorities it could be less supported if government composition changes.

- **Co-ordinating with VET providers**: Portugal's VET system at the upper secondary level is characterised by the distinction between professional programmes, provided by public and private schools, and apprenticeship programmes, provided by specific training providers. These programmes are monitored by different institutions (the IEFP and the Ministry of Labour, Solidarity and Social Security for apprenticeship programmes, and the Ministry of Education for professional programmes). This creates tension between education and labour side providers and leads to competition for students, financial resources and influence. These tensions are likely to intensify due to the declining number of students. Nevertheless, all interviewed partners expressed concern about the current situation and a strong willingness to improve co-operation.
- **Fostering co-ordination with the subnational level**: Portugal has achieved major progress in this regard. Despite its centralised state structure, the Ministry of Education has promoted a local co-ordination process for the provision of VET courses according to subnational labour market needs, engaging with the inter-municipal communities. The establishment of SANQ was a major step to involve the subnational level in the governance of Portugal's skills system.
- **Planning training during uncertainty**: EU structural funds make up a high share of the budget of Portugal's VET system. These funds are disbursed for a specific period (normally seven years), which makes the planning of courses difficult, especially towards the end of a funding period. Furthermore, the heavy reliance on EU funding creates a strong dependency of Portuguese skills policies on priorities in the EU's budget process, constituting another source of uncertainty.
- **Allocating resources effectively and efficiently**: Despite the difficult financial situation, Portugal has the means to allocate resources effectively and efficiently. For this, SANQ is a decisive instrument as it helps policy makers to channel fiscal resources to areas with the largest expected impact.
- **Coping with changing political priorities**: ANQEP and the VET system have to be prepared that political priorities can shift the government's focus to other policy areas. Although the cuts in the budget can largely be explained by the difficult economic situation in recent years, Portugal is missing a reliable and stable funding mechanism for its skills policies – on this, see also OECD (2018[3]).
- **Building the commitment of certain stakeholders**: A large group of different stakeholders – such as training providers, public authorities and social partners – send representatives to the General Board and the sectoral councils. However, commitment to skills policies varies greatly between stakeholders. While education and training providers have a natural interest because VET is their main business, the commitment of social partners is less immediate. Engagement also differs greatly between economic sectors. In order to tackle this problem, ANQEP has tried to establish close ties with business associations and develop solutions that meet the needs of the different industries more flexibly, for example the partnership agreements with the tourism and hospitality sector and the metal sector.
- **Engaging stakeholders through formal and informal means**: Regular meetings among public actors and involved stakeholders aim to develop better skills policies by giving everyone affected by policy decisions a say. However, the informal nature of policy making in VET should not be underestimated. The General Board and the sectoral councils offer the opportunity to network and build trust among stakeholders.
- **Balancing stakeholder responsibilities and skills system efficiency**: As VET is closely connected to labour market needs, it is an advantage that stakeholders define qualification standards in Portugal. However, updating qualifications is very demanding work that requires specific competences and strong stakeholder participation. Although ANQEP provides sectoral councils with the adequate resources, it has been forced to assume more and more responsibilities, which has led to a decrease in the feeling of ownership on the part of stakeholders.

Policy recommendations

For decades, Portugal has lagged behind other countries within the European Union in the educational attainment rates of its population. In addition, it has been one of the EU countries hit hardest by the financial and economic crisis between 2009 and 2012, which led to high unemployment rates (especially among youth), serious financial constraints and large cutbacks in the public sector. The country has not yet fully recovered from these years; however, it has successfully undertaken a large adjustment programme to re-establish economic growth and social well-being. Within this programme, skills policies have played an important role. Today, Portugal is catching up with the other European countries in many regards, for example by increasing the share of people with upper secondary or tertiary education, by combatting early school leaving successfully, and by achieving better results in the Programme for International Student Assessment (PISA). The creation of a unified and standardised VET system has contributed greatly to this success, and ANQEP has had a major role to play.

While the example of ANQEP gives valuable insights into how a whole-of-government approach can be implemented in VET policies, the agency also faces a number of challenges. Portugal's new VET system was only established in 2008, and the financial crisis has stalled innovative reforms for several years. Overall, the skills system of Portugal is still evolving, as is ANQEP. Interviews showed that there are open questions regarding the competences and the governance structure of ANQEP within Portugal's VET system. The following policy recommendations follow from this analysis.

Stabilise ANQEP's role in the Portuguese skills system

ANQEP is highly dependent on political priorities. Many of the problems described in this chapter, such as the lack of stable funding sources or insufficient personnel resources, are related to this problem. It is also the reason why ANQEP's role in the co-ordination of the National Qualifications System is still contested, especially regarding apprenticeship courses. On the one hand, ANQEP is responsible for the overall development of the VET system in Portugal. On the other hand, different VET programmes are administered by different agencies: ANQEP is responsible for professional programmes and uses SANQ to determine labour market needs, while the IEFP administers apprenticeship courses and uses a different system for the anticipation of labour market demands. Depending on the government's priorities at the time, either ANQEP or the IEFP are equipped with more resources and receive more control over the skills system.

As a national agency, ANQEP's responsibility is to implement government (or parliamentary) decisions. Therefore, its work will always depend on political priorities. Nevertheless, Portugal's government could try to stabilise ANQEP's role in the national skills system by, for example, clarifying its responsibilities compared to the responsibilities of the IEFP. For the sake of efficiency and effectiveness, consideration should be given to abolishing parallel structures in these two institutions. This concerns first and foremost the divided responsibilities for professional courses (ANQEP and the Ministry of Education) and apprenticeship courses (the IEFP and Minister of Labour, Solidarity and Social Security). Harmonisation should also be pursued regarding the different systems for the anticipation of labour market needs.

Stabilise the financial basis of the Portuguese VET system

Efforts should be made to stabilise the funding and broaden funding sources for the VET system in general and for ANQEP specifically. ANQEP's funding is very dependent on political priorities and the overall economic situation of Portugal, which makes it very difficult for ANQEP to make long-term plans. In addition, many programmes in Portugal's VET system are mostly financed by EU structural funds. This constitutes another source of insecurity, as these funds need to be renegotiated every seven years. With 90 employees, ANQEP is relatively understaffed, especially in comparison to other public agencies such as the IEFP and the Directorate-General for Education. It is therefore necessary to broaden and stabilise the financial basis of ANQEP, for example by increasing the share of private funding sources or holding firms accountable financially. ANQEP needs to have sufficient financial and personnel resources to fulfil its tasks. The latest recruitment of new staff is a first step in the right direction.

Engage the General Board in a meaningful way

Formally, stakeholders are highly involved in the development of the National Qualifications System. However, in practice stakeholder engagement is a significant challenge for ANQEP. The role of the General Board is not perceived to be influential by stakeholders, even those who are members. For many, it is only a symbolic body that agrees on the annual programme of ANQEP without having a say in its work. However, the General Board could play a major role in fostering and improving Portugal's skills system as a large number of different actors – such as employers, schools, trade unions and inter-municipalities – are involved in its governance. The General Board could be used as a place where these different actors formulate their expectations and discuss politically how to promote the system. However, for this, board members would need the legitimation by their organisation to discuss issues openly. The weak role of the General Board might be a consequence of the fact that intermediary associations are generally weak in Portugal. In this case, how to promote the capacities of these associations might need to be considered.

Support the sectoral councils so that they can meet their duties

The VET law gives responsibilities to sectoral councils that are unable to be met. Members of sectoral councils work voluntarily and are often experts in skills policies; however, they lack expertise in the development of qualifications. Despite this, they face an enormous catalogue of qualifications that they are required to regularly update. This task is particularly demanding given that they do not receive financial nor pedagogical support. As a result, stakeholders increasingly withdraw from their responsibilities in sectoral councils. In order to ensure that qualification standards are updated and meet the demands of the labour market, ANQEP increasingly takes over tasks, while the participation of stakeholders decreases. This, however, runs counter to the law's intention that skills are to be developed by experts from the field.

In order to solve these problems and stimulate ownership by stakeholders, ANQEP should focus on building the capacities of sectoral council members. One way to do this could be to equip the councils with more expertise regarding the work of updating qualifications. For example, ANQEP could develop a framework that describes the updating process step by step. All sectoral councils could be obliged to follow this framework when new qualification demands are identified. The implementation of the framework in each sectoral council could be supported by third-party experts. In addition, ANQEP could prescribe that qualifications within the National Catalogue of Qualifications need to be revised regularly. In Switzerland, for example, the new VET law requires revisions of training regulations every five years.

Regarding the relationship between ANQEP and sectoral council members, ANQEP could put more trust in the work of stakeholders. Consideration should be given to restricting ANQEP's role to providing administrative support to the councils and giving members of the sectoral councils sole responsibility for updating qualifications. To help councils better fulfil their role they should be provided with more support by third-party experts, as described above. In exchange, stakeholders would need to understand that participation in decision making comes with responsibilities. Stakeholders should (re-)develop a sense of ownership for VET and confidently fulfil their important role in sectoral councils and the General Board.

References

ANQEP (2020), *Catálogo Nacional de Qualificações (National Catalogue of Qualifications)*, http://www.catalogo.anqep.gov.pt/ (accessed on 4 February 2020). [8]

ANQEP et al. (2020), *Passaporte Qualifica (Qualifica Passport)*, https://www.passaportequalifica.gov.pt/cicLogin.xhtml (accessed on 4 February 2020). [11]

ANQEP et al. (2020), *Qualifica*, https://www.qualifica.gov.pt/#/ (accessed on 4 February 2020). [10]

Culpepper, P. (2007), "Small states and skill specificity: Austria, Switzerland, and interemployer cleavages in coordinated capitalism", *Comparative Political Studies*, Vol. 40/6, pp. 611-637. [13]

Culpepper, P. and K. Thelen (2008), "Institutions and collective actors in the provision of training", in Mayer, K. and H. Solga (eds.), *Skill formation: Interdisciplinary and cross-national perspectives*, Cambridge University Press, New York. [15]

DGEEC (2020), *Estatísticas da Educação 2017/2018 (Education Statistics 2017/2018)*, http://www.dgeec.mec.pt/np4/96/ (accessed on 5 February 2020). [7]

DGERT (2016), "Vocational education and training in Europe: Portugal", *Cedefop REferNet VET in Europe Reports*. [9]

Emmenegger, P., L. Graf and C. Trampusch (2018), "The governance of decentralized cooperation in collective training systems: A review and conceptualisation", *Journal of Vocational Education & Training*, Vol. online first. [14]

European Commission (2016), *The Role of Social Partners in the Design and Implementation of Policies and Reforms*, European Commission, Brussels. [12]

Eurostat (2019), *Education and training outcomes*. [5]

Eurostat (2016), *Structural Business Statistics Database*, https://ec.europa.eu/eurostat/web/structural-business-statistics/data/database. [16]

OECD (2020), *Educational attainment and labour-force status*, OECD Publishing, Paris, https://stats.oecd.org/Index.aspx?DataSetCode=EAG_NEAC (accessed on 4 February 2020). [6]

OECD (2018), *Education at a Glance 2018: OECD Indicators*, OECD Publishing, Paris, https://doi.org/10.1787/eag-2018-en. [4]

OECD (2018), *Skills Strategy Implementation Guidance for Portugal: Strengthening the Adult-Learning System*, OECD Skills Studies, OECD Publishing, Paris, https://dx.doi.org/10.1787/9789264298705-en. [3]

OECD (2015), *OECD Skills Strategy Diagnostic Report: Portugal 2015*, OECD Skills Studies, OECD Publishing, Paris, https://dx.doi.org/10.1787/9789264300279-en. [2]

OECD (2014), *Education at a Glance 2014: OECD Indicators*, OECD Publishing, Paris, https://dx.doi.org/10.1787/eag-2014-en. [1]

Notes

[1] Early leavers from education and training include all persons who have attained at most lower secondary level education (ISCED level 2) and who are currently not in education and training.

[2] The social partners were also part of this agreement. More on this is elaborated in the next section.

7 Case study: Massachusetts' (United States) Early Warning Indicator System (EWIS)

This chapter focuses on the role of integrated information systems in the public school system of the United States. In the United States, the education system is regulated at the state level. However, an accountability system exists between the state and the federal level based on education data, which makes sure that standards are achieved nation-wide. The case study looks at the Early Warning Indicator System (EWIS) in the state of Massachusetts. Based on various data sources, EWIS calculates individual probability levels of meeting certain predefined academic milestones for students from first to twelfth grade. The schools can use this information to direct specific support measures to the students at risk. This chapter introduces the technical details and distribution of responsibilities in the use of EWIS. Furthermore, it discusses how co-ordination across different levels of government can be achieved when establishing integrated information systems.

Introduction

The state of Massachusetts is widely regarded as having the best public school system in the United States of America, scoring first in national student assessment tests. Massachusetts' students also rank among the top internationally in reading, science and mathematics (OECD, 2016[1]). The media and public perception is that the success of Massachusetts' education system is largely attributed to a significant educational reform in 1993, the Massachusetts Education Reform Act (MERA) (Rowe, 2016[2]; Baker, 2019[3]). However, the academic debate is more ambiguous about the effect of MERA on educational outcomes (Dee and Levine, 2004[4]; Guryan, 2001[5]; McDermott, 2004[6]). While Massachusetts' schools are still predominantly controlled by local school districts, the reform redefined the partnership between districts and the state, and formally put the state government in charge of ensuring the equity and quality of education in Massachusetts' schools. Today, schools are closely monitored by the state, especially those with significant opportunity and achievement gaps.

The educational reform resulted in a major increase in state funding for public schools, especially in low-spending districts, where total per-pupil revenues increased by 7% between 1993 and 1996 (Dee and Levine, 2004[4]). Additional state funding was particularly directed at schools in poorer areas to increase equality of opportunity among students. In exchange for receiving funding, schools were required to align their curricula to state-wide standards and to participate in a student assessment system, the Massachusetts Comprehensive Assessment System (MCAS). MERA also introduced an accountability system for school districts and schools. Low-performing schools are subject to state intervention and need to implement various measures to meet state standards. If their performance does not improve, they can be closed down by the state administration. Massachusetts' accountability system is based on various data collection exercises that help assess the quality of schools, including MCAS results as well as other indicators, such as high school graduation rates and absenteeism. Over the years, Massachusetts has built a comprehensive information management system to assess students, schools and school districts.

This case study focuses on the Massachusetts' Early Warning Indicator System (EWIS), which is part of the state's information management system, although it is not used for accountability purposes. EWIS builds on existing state-wide data collection and uses statistical models to calculate the probability that a student will meet a predefined academic milestone. It assigns students a risk level according to these probabilities. EWIS gives information on the risk level for every student in Massachusetts from 1st to 12th grade. It helps schools and school districts identify students at risk of not meeting academic milestones so that they can provide them with additional support to meet these milestones. EWIS data are provided and administered by the Department of Elementary and Secondary Education (DESE). Schools and districts have access to the data, and using the data as part of an implementation cycle (Figure 7.3) is their responsibility.

The use of EWIS is not obligatory for districts and schools, which is a challenge. Schools and districts need to be made aware of EWIS and be given the knowledge to use the data. They also need financial and personnel support to implement the data effectively. In order to achieve these goals, DESE and the school districts work together to enhance data literacy among schools and help them establish support systems based on early warning indicators. Therefore, with reference to the overall framework of this report, this case study focuses on two of the four dimensions:

- Promoting co-ordination, co-operation and collaboration across the whole of government.
- Building integrated information systems.

The following section provides a short introduction to the technical details of EWIS and the involved actors at the federal, state and local level. The analysis that follows is based on the insights from interviews with stakeholder representatives and experts conducted in September 2019 in Massachusetts. The case study closes with a number of policy recommendations for the future development of governance regarding EWIS.

Massachusetts' education and training system

Massachusetts' school system is widely regarded as the best public school system in the United States. Since 2005, the state has scored first in National Assessment of Educational Progress (NAEP) tests, a US-wide and representative academic achievement test, in 4th and 8th grade reading and mathematics (Commonwealth of Massachusetts, 2020[7]). Massachusetts was among the three US states, along with Connecticut and Florida, that asked the OECD for results at the state level in the 2015 Programme for International Student Assessment (PISA) and scored well above US and international averages, ranking 2nd in reading (along with Canada and Hong Kong), 6th in science (equal with Macau, China) and 20th in mathematics out of 72 countries (OECD, 2016[1]). In the US 2019 Best High Schools Ranking, Massachusetts was the state with the highest percentage of top-ranked public high schools in the United States (U.S. News, 2020[8]). Other education indicators also show that Massachusetts is among the top performing states within the United States. With a high school graduation rate of 88%, it ranks 12th among the 51 states and federal districts, above the US average of 85%. The school drop-out rate among 16 to 24 year-olds is 3.6% (US average 5.4%; 7th rank), the pupil-teacher ratio is 13.3 (US average 16.0; 11th rank) and the state spends USD 16 986 (US dollars) per pupil (US average USD 11 841; 7th rank) (National Center for Education Statistics, 2018[9]).

Despite this overall strong performance, a more detailed analysis of the data reveals striking differences between subgroups of students. Differentiating students by race and ethnicity shows that students of colour and students of Hispanic origin have much lower 8th grade NAEP results in mathematics than white students or students of Asian origin (Figure 7.1). Similarly, students from low-income families, students whose first language is not English and students with disabilities perform worse than students from high-income families, those without disabilities or those with English as their mother tongue (Figure 7.2). Similar results can be observed when comparing 4th grade reading performance on NAEP, PISA scores and MCAS scores by student group (Massachusetts Education Equity Partnership, 2018[10]). Race and ethnicity also determine the likelihood of graduating from high school. While the high school graduation rate of white students is 93%, only 80% of African American students and 74% of Hispanic students graduate from high school. Compared to other US states, Massachusetts performs below average in this regard. When comparing the graduation rates of students of different races across the 51 states and federal districts, Massachusetts ranks 7th for white students, 21st for African American students and 38th for Hispanic students (National Center for Education Statistics, 2018[9]).

Figure 7.1. Massachusetts 8th grade mathematics performance in NAEP, by race/ethnicity

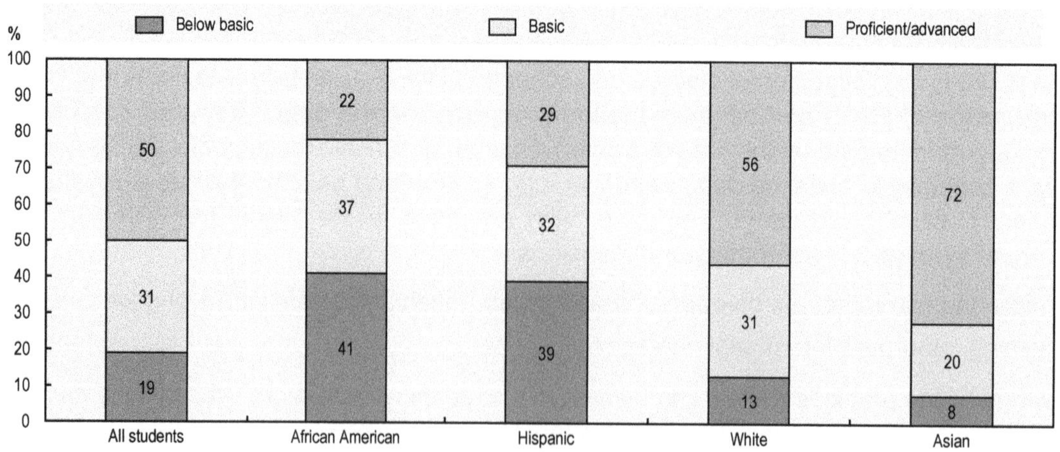

Source: Massachusetts Education Equity Partnership (2018[10]), *Number One for Some: Opportunity and Achievement in Massachusetts*, https://number1forsome.org/wp-content/uploads/sites/16/2018/09/Number-1-for-Some-9.25-18.pdf.

StatLink https://doi.org/10.1787/888934112785

Figure 7.2. Massachusetts 8th grade mathematics performance in NAEP, by socio-economic background

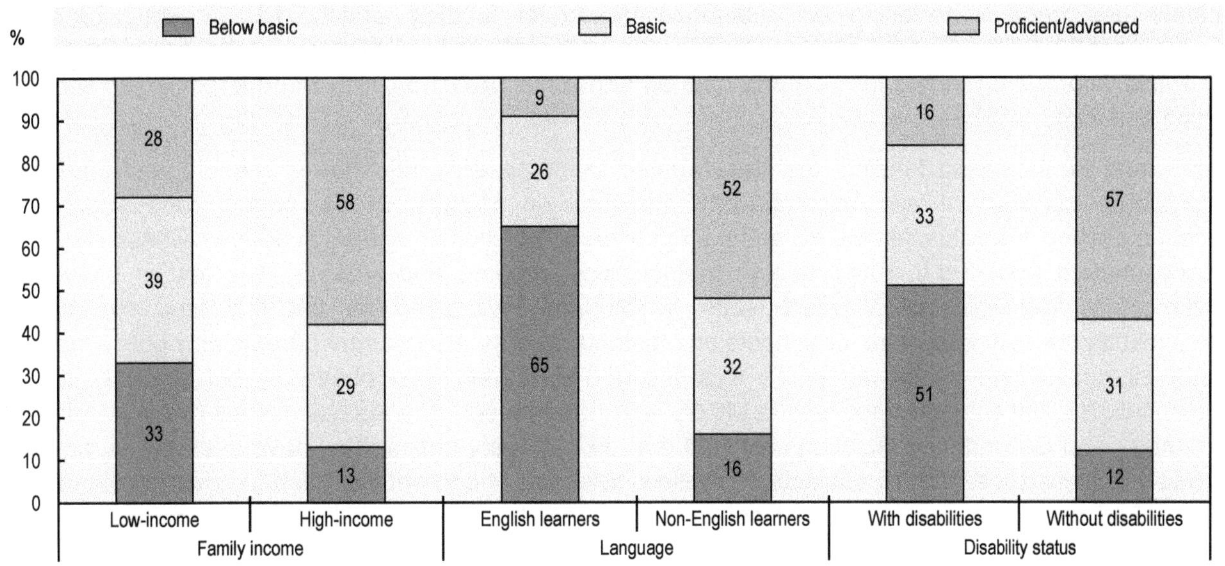

Source: Massachusetts Education Equity Partnership (2018[10]), *Number One for Some: Opportunity and Achievement in Massachusetts*, https://number1forsome.org/wp-content/uploads/sites/16/2018/09/Number-1-for-Some-9.25-18.pdf.

StatLink https://doi.org/10.1787/888934112804

Equity between students, as well as school districts, is a big concern in the education system of Massachusetts. In the United States, every public school belongs to a school district, which is an independent local administration responsible for various issues concerning primary and secondary education.[1] In Massachusetts, there are 1 850 public schools in 525 school districts. School politics first and foremost takes place at the district level. Among other things, districts are responsible for the maintenance of school buildings, the selection of curricula materials (e.g. books), and for ensuring that schools comply with federal and state law. School districts also provide a large share of public school financing and collect property taxes for this purpose. In Massachusetts, 57% of public school revenue comes from local (school district) sources (US average 44.9%) while only 38.7% comes from the state (US average 47.1%) and 4.3% from the federal budget (US average 8%) (US Census Bureau, 2018[11]). The heavy reliance on local taxes creates inequalities, as richer districts generate higher tax revenues than poorer districts.

Massachusetts started to tackle the problem of inequalities in 1993 with MERA, through which the state government took responsibility for establishing and ensuring a minimum level of educational spending for all districts (the so-called "foundation budget") for the first time. The foundation budget is determined in three steps. First, it is calculated how much money each school district needs, which depends on the number of pupils (including kindergarten), the number of students who are economically or socially disadvantaged, and a price differential that accounts for regional differences in cost of living. Second, depending on property values, each district's local contribution is determined. Third, state aid is calculated by adding the funding needs of all schools within a district derived from the needs-based formula in step one and subtracting this sum from the district's local contribution calculated in step two. The state pays the difference between the need and the local contribution. State aid can never be lower than in the previous year (Lee and Blagg, 2018[12]), and districts can contribute more than the foundation budget without losing state aid. On average, districts' school spending is 26% above the foundation budget, and in some districts is more than 300% of what has been calculated in the formula (Lee and Blagg, 2018[12]).

Because only wealthy districts can afford to spend more than expected by the formula, this funding formula has increasingly been criticised by policy makers and stakeholders for privileging wealthy districts over disadvantaged districts that have many economically disadvantaged students. As a consequence, the state has been undertaking an evaluation of school funding since 2015 (Chester, 2014[13]). In September 2019, the Senate and the House of Representatives of Massachusetts announced that they would reform the funding formula and give an additional USD 1.5 billion to underprivileged schools (Vazins and Stout, 2019[14]).

In exchange for increased funding, the state wanted to increase its influence in schools, and therefore implemented assessment and accountability measures in Massachusetts' primary and secondary education system. It established MCAS at the student level, which is an annual academic assessment test of each student from 3rd to 10th grade in mathematics, reading and science. The test is based on the curriculum framework of Massachusetts, which was introduced for the first time by MERA. MCAS results are very important for schools and districts as they are used by parents and policy makers to monitor quality and performance. As a consequence, it has been observed that schools narrow the curriculum to the subjects assessed in MCAS. In a recent report, the Massachusetts Commissioner of Elementary and Secondary Education criticised that "in too many cases, they have seen the curriculum narrowed to focus on assessed subjects or shallow coverage of content in a rush to cover all standards before MCAS testing. They also reported instances of too much time spent drilling students on tested skills, divorced from a cumulative, meaningful learning context" (Riley, 2019[15]).

In addition to the assessment of students, MERA established an accountability and assessment system for schools and districts. Based on various indicators such as MCAS results, high school completion rate and the percentage of chronic absenteeism, it provides information on how each school is doing compared to other schools, and on progress towards meeting certain targets. Each school is assigned to one of six groups, ranging from "needs broad comprehensive support" to "schools of recognition" (DESE, 2020[16]).Together with the district, the state intervenes in every school that belongs to one of the two lowest performing groups. Examples for interventions are the expansion of the school day to increase the number of school lessons, the replacement of the curriculum to improve teaching content, and the suspension of collective bargaining agreements to push back the influence of teacher unions (DESE, 2011[17]). In very rare cases, schools are closed.

Massachusetts' accountability system is data driven. DESE reports on data collected by the state and school districts through a variety of tools and reports. The DESE website lists 11 data reports created from various data collections which cover drop-out rates, teacher assessment data, enrolment data, enrolment in institutions of higher education, grade retention reports, graduation rates, MCAS results, mobility rates, per pupil expenditure reports, plans of high school graduates and student growth percentile. Districts and schools also often compile additional local data that are not reported to the state.

The reforms of Massachusetts' education system following MERA must be understood within a broader nationwide debate on the US education system. Ten years before MERA, a federal commission published the report *A Nation at Risk* that described the failure of American public schools and demanded higher academic standards. The report was followed by considerable discussions on the public education system, resulting in the 2001 No Child Left Behind Act (NCLB). This act expanded the federal role in public education, in particular by establishing a comprehensive assessment and accountability system in exchange for additional funding from the federal level. States that wanted to receive federal money were obliged to implement state-wide academic assessment tests and to control school quality. The 2015 Every Student Succeeds Act (ESSA) relieves the states from such strict control of the federal level. However, states are still required to implement student assessment tests and to evaluate the quality of schools using quantitative indicators.

With the NCLB, the United States underwent a policy shift towards federal involvement in public schools. This was possible because the position of Democrats and Republicans on education policies converged in the 1990s. While Republicans abandoned their opposition to a federal role in education, Democrats' focus shifted from input and equity concerns to standards and accountability (McGuinn, 2005[18]). As a consequence, the NCLB established greater federal investment in exchange for school and state accountability based on quantitative data assessments. Thus, the NCLB and ESSA had a profound impact on the US public education system, and introduced data-driven assessment and accountability systems in the majority of states for the first time. However, for Massachusetts these systems were not new, as they had been already implemented with MERA. Nevertheless, the federal educational reforms intensified the role that accountability measures played in Massachusetts and accelerated the development of information management systems.

The Early Warning Indicator System

Massachusetts' Early Warning Indicator System (EWIS) was established in 2011 to help identify students at risk of not meeting certain academic milestones from 1st to 12th grade. It was established after Massachusetts received a federal grant as part of the Statewide Longitudinal Data Systems (SLDS) grant programme. The SLDS programme was one response to the accountability provisions of the 2001 NCLB and was authorised by the Educational Technical Assistance Act of 2002. It awards grants to states to enable them to adequately collect, manage and use educational data. Massachusetts' application for the 2009 SLDS grant included the expansion of its existing Early Warning Indicator Index (EWII), which evaluated the probability of students entering 9th grade, which is the first grade in high school in the United States, not graduating high school on time. EWII was criticised for its limited methodology and scope: "The current methodology was developed by DESE using a limited set of criteria and a methodology that is not as research based as it needs to be. In addition, the current reports do not go beyond grade nine or identify students that are primed for additional academic opportunities" (US Department of Education, 2009[19]). This was criticised by school districts, which argued that schools were receiving information about at-risk students too late.

In order to improve its early warning indicator system, Massachusetts wanted to use the SLDS grant to establish a broad data information system that predicts the likelihood of all students in every grade meeting certain key academic milestones, such as graduating from high school. The grant enabled the state to collaborate with the American Institutes for Research (AIR), a non-profit behavioural and social science research association, in developing EWIS. AIR and DESE began by conducting a literature review on early warning indicators and observing early warning systems in other states and districts in the United States. They compared the findings with the indicators used in EWII and suggested a design for EWIS. Following this, a series of multilevel models were tested to identify the variables that best predict the likelihood of students failing key academic benchmarks (American Institutes for Research, 2020[20]). In summer 2012, DESE provided risk data to the districts for the first time. While some aspects of the model on which EWIS is based have been updated since its development, and the data in the model are updated annually, the main statistical assumptions have stayed the same. Following a second SLDS grant, EWIS has been expanded to post-secondary education, with risk levels predicting post-secondary outcomes first available for districts in 2016. The establishment and development of EWIS in Massachusetts was solely financed by federal money received through the SLDS grants in 2010 and 2015.

Massachusetts decided to base its early warning system on data-based indicators rather than on more qualitative sources such as teachers' knowledge about their students for two main reasons: first, SLDS grant holders are required to establish and use data-based information systems, and second, Massachusetts did not wish to introduce new data collection exercises (and corresponding burdens) to schools and districts, and local teacher level knowledge did not exist within the state data system. With this decision, Massachusetts also complied with education policy decisions related to MERA regarding the importance of quantitative accountability indicators, as well as the focus of federal education policies on data-based information management systems since the NCLB. Despite this, since EWIS was established there have been discussed regarding how it adds value compared to the knowledge teachers have of their students. This will be further discussed later on in the case study.

Technical details

EWIS predicts the risk of individual students failing to meet relevant academic milestones without additional support. There are three risk levels: low, moderate and high (Table 7.1). These risk levels indicate "whether a student is currently on track to reach the upcoming academic milestone" (DESE and AIR, 2014[21]). EWIS uses data from the previous school year to determine the risk levels. The risk levels do not represent a relative measure but are calculated based on the individual student's performance. It is thus possible that all students in a specific grade or even school are in the low-risk category.

Table 7.1. Student risk levels

Low risk	Likely to reach the upcoming academic milestone. Approximately 90% of students who are at low risk will meet this academic milestone within each age group.
Moderate risk	Moderately at risk for not reaching the upcoming academic milestone. Approximately 60% of students at moderate risk will meet this academic milestone within each age group.
High risk	At risk for not reaching the upcoming academic milestone. Approximately 25% of students at high risk will meet this academic milestone within each age group.

Source: Massachusetts Department of Elementary and Secondary Education and American Institutes for Research (2014[21]), *Early Warning Implementation Guide: Using the Massachusetts Early Warning Indicator System (EWIS) and Local Data to Identify, Diagnose, Support, and Monitor Students in Grades 1-12*, www.doe.mass.eduhttp://www.earlywarningsystems.org.

EWIS organises student risk by four grade level groupings: early elementary (grade levels 1-3), late elementary (grade levels 4-6), middle grades (grade levels 7-9) and high school (grade levels 10-12). The grade levels come with different academic milestones (Table 7.2). For example, in the early elementary age group, students need to meet requirements in English language reading and understanding, whereas students in the late elementary group also need to meet certain standards in mathematics. The standards are related to MCAS. High school students are evaluated on four academic milestones: high school graduation, college enrolment, academic readiness and college persistence, with the last three indicators measuring the college and career readiness of students (post-secondary level). It is therefore possible that high school students have different risk levels. For example, an 11th grade student could have a low risk of missing high school graduation, but a moderate risk of missing college enrolment.

EWIS risk levels are calculated by a regression model using different indicators that are validated and updated annually. The risk model was originally developed by AIR and DESE and is continuously updated by data experts at DESE. According to interview partners at DESE, the indicators need to fulfil certain preconditions. First, they need to fulfil the requirements of a rigorous statistical model. For this, researchers from inside and outside DESE regularly assess the validity, goodness of fit and specificity of the updated EWIS models. Second, for each indicator the data must be available for every student. Third, EWIS demands that no new data need to be produced, but that existing state-wide data collections are used. Data sources include the Student Information Management System (SIMS), the Student Course Schedule (SCS) (courses taken by students), the School Safety Discipline Report (SSDR) (criminal offences and discipline actions at schools), data from MCAS and English language proficiency tests (DESE and AIR, 2014[21]).

Table 7.2. Age groups, grade levels, and academic milestones

	Age group	Grade levels	Academic milestones
K12	Early elementary	1-3	Reading by the end of grade 3. Meeting or exceeding expectations on the grade 3 English language arts (ELA) state assessment.
	Late elementary	4-6	Middle school ready. Meeting or exceeding expectations on the grade 6 ELA and mathematics state assessment.
	Middle grades	7-9	High school ready. Passing grades on all grade 9 courses.
	High school	10-12	High school graduation. Completing high school graduation requirements in four years.
Post-secondary			College enrolment. Enrolling in post-secondary education.
			Academic readiness. Enrolling in credit-bearing courses without developmental education.
			College persistence. Enrolling in a second year of post-secondary education.

Source: DESE and AIR (2014[21]), *Early Warning Implementation Guide: Using the Massachusetts Early Warning Indicator System (EWIS) and Local Data to Identify, Diagnose, Support, and Monitor Students in Grades 1-12*, www.doe.mass.eduhttp://www.earlywarningsystems.org.

The indicators EWIS use include information about the school-student relationship, for example attendance rate, suspensions or school moves; biographical information on the student, for example gender or need for special education; and the results of state-wide assessment tests for different academic subjects. As EWIS risk levels depend on the age group, different indicators are used for different age groups (Table 7.2). For example, to assess the college and career readiness of a high school student (post-secondary level), SAT (Scholastic Assessment Test) and AP (Advanced Placement) scores are included, as well as if a student learns a foreign language at school (DESE and AIR, 2014[21]). Similar to other education data reports, EWIS data are published on an online secure data platform called Edwin Analytics (or Edwin), where reports can be accessed by authorised users at the school, district and state level.

There is no mandatory way of how schools and districts should implement EWIS locally. However, DESE suggests that EWIS is implemented in a six-step process over the school year (Figure 7.3). In this process, schools are advised to start with putting a team together (step 1) and reviewing EWIS data (step 2) at the beginning of the school year. In the third step, information provided by EWIS data and the experience and knowledge of educators are combined to explore underlying causes for the poor performance of a student (step 3). The school should then implement additional support measures for the specific student (step 4), which are to be evaluated (step 5). These steps three to five are to be repeated throughout the school year. At the end of the school year, DESE advises schools to use the insights they have gained throughout the school year to summarise the successes and challenges of the early warning process and refine the process (step 6). Thus, reflecting and revising is an important part of the early warning implementation cycle.

Figure 7.3. The early warning implementation cycle

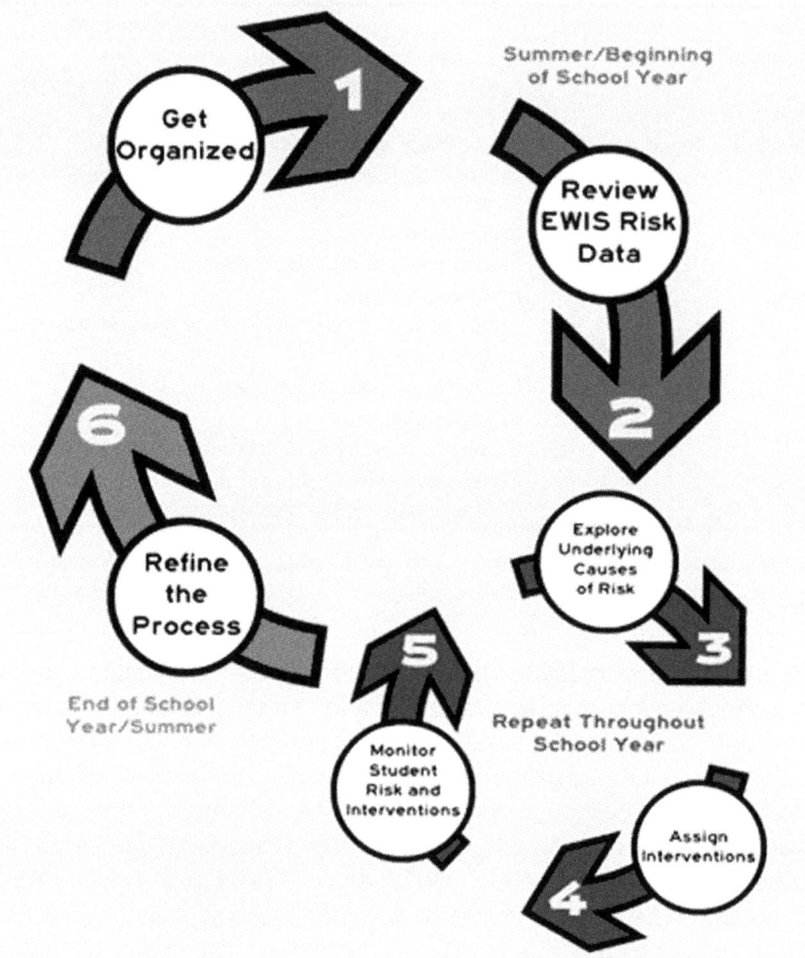

Source: DESE (2020[22]), *Early Warning Implementation Cycle*, http://www.doe.mass.edu/ccte/ccr/rlo/ewis/story_html5.html.

Responsibilities

Different levels of government have been or still are involved in the establishment, administration and implementation of EWIS (Table 7.3). In order to establish and further develop EWIS, Massachusetts successfully participated in two rounds of the federal SLDS grant programme. This programme, established in 2005, is a competitive programme that is used as a means to help states develop, improve and efficiently use data management systems to improve student learning and outcomes and to facilitate research on student achievement. Out of the six grant rounds since 2005, Massachusetts has been successful three times. The establishment of EWIS was part of the 2009 grant round that awarded nearly USD 13 million to Massachusetts. EWIS is listed as one of six measures in Massachusetts financed by the SLDS grant: "A more robust and nuanced risk and opportunity identification methodology is implemented by DEEC (Department of Early Education and Care) and DESE that starts at birth and continues through high school that more precisely identifies students at risk of dropping out and students who are ready for more rigorous academic course work" (US Department of Education, 2009[19]). In 2015, Massachusetts received another SLDS grant of around USD 7 million. Parts of this grant were used to expand EWIS to predict readiness for post-secondary education: "As a result of this grant, Massachusetts school districts will know which of their students are on track for success in post-secondary education in time to intervene if needed" (DESE, 2015[23]).

Table 7.3. Distribution of responsibilities at different levels of government

Federal	Institute of Education Sciences	Awards SLDS grants
State	Department of Elementary and Secondary Education	Collects data Develops model Engages in public relations Provides technical assistance
Substate	School districts Schools	Decides on data access (districts) Implements early warning cycle (districts/schools)

The implementation of the SLDS grant is the responsibility of the state government, although it must report annually to the federal level. As described earlier, Massachusetts co-operated with AIR in the establishment and administration of EWIS; however, AIR is no longer involved. DESE annually updates the model on which EWIS is based, publishes the results on Edwin Analytics, works to make EWIS known to school districts, and provides technical assistance in school districts that use EWIS data.

Massachusetts has not received SLDS funds since September 2019, and the state now finances EWIS solely by its own resources. The number of staff responsible for EWIS-related activities has decreased considerably. According to interview partners at DESE, data analysts update the data and the model itself annually and publish the results on Edwin. In addition, DESE still provides school districts with a contact person if there are questions on the usage of EWIS. The amount of work for these tasks differ across the year. For example, requests from districts mostly arise in August and September when new data have been released. Interview partners at DESE estimated that the number of DESE employees working on EWIS equals about one to two full-time equivalents on average across the year.

DESE provides access to students' individual EWIS data for public school districts. However, it is the decision of the districts if and how they use the data, and who has access within the district. According to interview partners at DESE, about 80% of districts accessed EWIS data on Edwin in the school year 2018/2019. It can be assumed, though, that the number of districts that have really used the data – for example to get an overview on school performance or to provide data for individual schools – is significantly smaller. DESE does not control data usage by the districts; however, during the field research for this case study the impression was gained that most educators and school officials do not know about EWIS. DESE is aware of this problem and has implemented several measures to increase knowledge of EWIS:

- Created a website (DESE, 2020[24]) that offers information about what EWIS is and resources on how the data can be accessed and used. In addition, the website provides hands-on reports of districts and schools that use EWIS.
- Publishes a monthly email newsletter with news about EWIS as well as other data-related state resources (DESE, 2019[25]).
- Offers training on EWIS. Annually, there is one large event where districts and schools can learn about EWIS, as well as several smaller events and webinars.
- Works with the Massachusetts School Counsellors Association (MASCA), which offers professional development training to educators, to offer a series of courses on EWIS. Participants can receive professional development points, which they need for licensing in Massachusetts.
- Given Early Warning Implementation Grants to ten schools and school districts to enhance data use throughout the school year. Grant holders received additional support in order to implement the early warning implementation cycle (Figure 7.3) at their schools. Grant holders met several times to exchange their experiences of EWIS.

Interviews with various holders of the Early Warning Implementation Grant show that there is a high interest in early warning indicators as it helps districts and schools identify students at risk using reliable quantitative data. However, during interviews it became apparent that districts and schools use EWIS in very different ways. One of the interviewed schools uses EWIS to learn about the educational biography and risk levels of students who were not pupils at the school in the previous year. Since EWIS provides longitudinal information about individuals, it is a very good source of information for this purpose. Other interview partners use the grant to implement the early warning implementation cycle (Figure 7.3) and to establish a team that works on their own early warning indicators. Thereby, they add school-related data such as school assessment tests (besides MCAS) and missed classes (instead of missing school days) to EWIS to account for more local needs. Interviewed grant holders appeared to have the impression that EWIS supports and even assists this flexible usage of the grant, as long as schools and districts use data-based systems to identify students at risk and direct additional support measures to them: "DESE was pretty explicit that there are multiple ways you could use the data".

Analysis

Opportunities for innovative governance reforms

Data-based information systems have the potential to inform policy makers, schools, students and parents about educational and labour market trajectories. Massachusetts has recognised the potential of information systems and collects a large variety of data-based indicators on schools' and students' performance and behaviour in different databases. EWIS does not generate new data but builds on this existing data. The added value of EWIS therefore needs to be discussed, and it is important to know what state authorities, districts and schools learn from EWIS that they do not already know from other data sources or their personal experiences with students.

There are several ways in which EWIS adds value. First, it is the only data-based information system that uses a model that calculates students' individual risk level of failing to meet a predefined academic standard. It is a very comprehensive system as it collects longitudinal data for every student in Massachusetts from 1st to 12th grade, and makes predictions regarding the college and career readiness of high school students. EWIS is sensitive to the age groups of students and uses different indicators and predefined academic milestones for four age groups. The data are updated annually, and DESE regularly evaluates the statistical fit of the model with the help of internal and external experts, and updates it if needed. During the interview with a responsible for the statistical model, it was noted that DESE pays particular attention to the way in which the indicators are used. Overall, DESE has developed a comprehensive, age-sensitive statistical model that rather accurately predicts the likelihood of students meeting or failing to meet academic goals. This is confirmed by representatives of the schools and districts interviewed who said that the students they perceive as having difficulties at school are the same identified as being high risk in EWIS. Thus, theoretically EWIS should allow teachers, principals and career counsellors to be able to tell easily if and in what area a student needs additional support. There will be further discussion on how practitioners use the data later on in the chapter. EWIS users can access information on all indicators that are part of the risk model such as the students' results in state assessment tests or their attendance rates. Therefore, schools and districts will not only be able to identify students at risk, but they will also be able to assess the reasons for potential academic failure.

Second, EWIS builds on the personal interaction between students and schools. Data-based information systems are often criticised because they only consider students' academic performance and can thereby lead to a biased assessment of students by educators. The early warning implementation cycle used by Massachusetts shows, however, that EWIS very much takes into account students' personal circumstances, for example if parents get divorced. EWIS provides schools with an overview of where their students perform well academically and where they do not. It is for the schools to decide on support measures that increase the academic performance of students based on their personal situations. Thus, when identified as being at high risk by EWIS, educators, counsellors, the student and sometimes even the parents discuss together which support measures are needed to improve the student's performance. The personal relationship between students and educators and the background information educators have on their students are therefore an important part of the data cycle.

Given that the risk levels EWIS predicts correspond with the perceptions of schools regarding which of their students are high risk, it may be questioned how EWIS can add to the knowledge schools have obtained in their day-to-day interactions with students. However, schools do not know their students to an equal degree. As one interview partner emphasised: "Easy kids are those who misbehave. Everyone knows them. The kids who are hard to assess are the quiet ones." The data EWIS provides help schools to have better knowledge of those students who are not disruptive in class but who nevertheless have (academic) problems. Through EWIS, schools can also receive longitudinal information on new students who have moved from one school in Massachusetts to another. For one of the schools visited as part of this case study, this was the main application of EWIS. EWIS data are also very valuable for school districts. Instead of having to look at different databases to assess school performance in, for example, state-wide assessment tests and missed lessons, EWIS provides a broad overview of the performance of students in different schools.

Third, how EWIS is administered contributes to how it adds value. EWIS is based on existing state-wide data collections and does not require new data to be collected. This makes the administration of the system much easier – for DESE as well as for the districts that provide data to the state. In addition, the fact that data management is done within the state's administration allows for quick reactions to changing demands to the model. DESE can easily update the statistical model as well as the data because the expertise to do so is in-house. One interview partner noted that Massachusetts is an exception in this regard, as responsibilities for the statistical model of education data information systems in most other US states are usually outsourced to for-profit organisations. Furthermore, the provision of EWIS data does not consume considerable financial and human resources at DESE, which is important as the federal SLDS grant expired in 2019. The comparatively inexpensive management of EWIS ensures that the early warning system will continue after 2019.

Fourth, the voluntary nature of EWIS can be seen as an advantage. DESE provides EWIS data to every district, but districts and schools are not forced to use the data in their work. As interview partners confirmed, there are some challenges regarding the relationship between DESE and school districts, as although districts enjoy autonomy in many regards, their performance is observed and assessed by DESE. In the case of EWIS, though, DESE is perceived by the interviewed districts and schools as a partner in supporting students to maximise their educational potential. Interview partners confirmed that they could contact the responsible persons at DESE if questions arose, and that they were very helpful and gave a lot of advice – not only on the use of EWIS but also on other data-related questions, such as the implementation of data cycles on the ground or the establishment of school- or district-specific databases. The provision of a large number of information resources on an EWIS-specific website, the launch of the EWIS newsletter, collaboration with MASCA and the offer of training show that DESE wants to raise awareness among districts of the early warning system. DESE is very open to various types of data usage as long as districts and schools build up an effective system that helps to identify and support weaker students. Thus, in the case of EWIS all public authorities in Massachusetts' education system work together as partners to the benefit of the students in the state.

To sum up, EWIS is a very helpful tool to identify students that need extra support to reach academic success. It provides a very simple outcome variable – the probability that a student will meet a certain predefined academic goal – but also includes information on a large variety of indicators that can explain this outcome. In addition, EWIS is administered in an efficient and (cost-) effective way as it is done in-house and does not require new data collections. It can therefore be regarded as sustainable in terms of resources, even after the initial SLDS grant expired. Nevertheless, there are several challenges related to EWIS, which are detailed in the next section.

Ongoing challenges

The biggest challenge Massachusetts faces is to increase the number of EWIS users among districts and schools. It is not possible to indicate how many districts and schools use EWIS in their work besides the ten grant receivers because DESE does not collect this information. As described in the section on EWIS, DESE has launched several initiatives to increase the number of districts and schools that use EWIS: the website and newsletter aim to increase general knowledge about EWIS, the collaboration with MASCA offers training events to train people in actually using EWIS, and the grants bring a broader perspective on data cycles to the grant receivers and help them connect with each other. Nevertheless, in terms of data usage by districts and schools, further improvements could still be made. One of the key questions is why EWIS is still receiving little attention in some districts and schools seven years after the first data round was released.

There are several potential reasons for this. First, the information DESE provides on EWIS is not targeted to users. The website contains a large number of support resources, but the sheer number could create confusion and make it difficult for users to find what they need. In addition, the needs of the users differ largely. Some districts and schools have been using the data implementation cycle before EWIS and only need information on specific technical issues, which is hard to find online. Others have never used data information systems before and are overwhelmed by the wealth of information on the website or in the newsletters. DESE tries to better target the information by offering substantial individual support. This is helpful for those districts and schools that already use EWIS, but it makes it more difficult to reach out to other potential users.

Second, EWIS suffers from a certain lack of knowledge in districts and schools on how data information systems can help educators, counsellors and districts to improve the academic performance of students. According to DESE, EWIS should be used to identify students at risk and provide them with support measures so that they meet their academic milestones. It is therefore not enough to have a quick view of the data. Rather, EWIS data are displayed in a large excel sheet with several columns that give information about students' results in the various indicators. It takes time and knowledge to process and find ways to deal with this information. In order to use EWIS effectively, staff in schools, for example principals or career counsellors, are needed to implement the early warning implementation cycle on site, i.e. to identify students at risk, explore the underlying causes, and assign and evaluate interventions. This process is time consuming, and these staff members will have a number of other obligations that they need to fulfil. Therefore, schools might see EWIS as a nice add-on to their regular work, but it might not be their priority. This is especially the case if schools are not familiar with or know how to use data. Newsletters that provide information on EWIS do not reach these schools.

It can be argued that it is the task of school districts to reach out to the schools and let them know about EWIS. The Early Warning Implementation Grants were directed to districts rather than individual schools, and access to data in Edwin is determined at the district level. However, EWIS is a non-coercive initiative and the districts cannot be forced to use it. If districts know about the value of information systems to their work, and if they are familiar with the usage of data, they will be more likely to embrace a system such as EWIS than districts not used to information systems. The competitive early implementation grants of DESE have enforced inequality between school districts regarding the usage of EWIS: the interviews conducted by the OECD team showed that the successful districts had prior knowledge about and experience in information management systems, for example because they have used other data systems before or because individual district employees are data specialists. Districts that do not have this knowledge have probably not taken notice of the grant call and have not applied.

Thus, schools and districts with a prior data usage culture are significantly more likely to use EWIS because they recognise its value for their work. For DESE (i.e. the state government), the challenge is to devise policies that encourage schools that use EWIS to use the system more effectively, as well as expand the number of schools that use EWIS in the first place.

As mentioned previously, during interviews it became clear that even districts and schools that implement EWIS and the early warning implementation cycle use do so in very different ways. According to these users, this is because the data EWIS contain are – naturally – limited. EWIS uses data from various state-wide databases, but these data are not always tailored to the needs of the schools. For example, an interview was conducted with a school which realised that to determine students at risk it was not the number of missed school days (EWIS data) that was decisive, but the number of missed classes. In addition, DESE releases the EWIS data annually in August, whereas schools collect data on their students throughout the year. As a consequence, several schools and districts have established their own data information systems with indicators more targeted to local needs.

DESE does not know how districts and schools use EWIS data because there has been no evaluation conducted. This is part of a larger problem. Since the end of the federal SLDS grant in 2019, EWIS has had to cope with very limited financial resources. Interview partners confirmed that the state spends enough money on EWIS to keep it running, with sufficient resources for the provision of data, annual updates of the model and to provide some support to districts and schools, such as training and webinars. However, more expensive activities to increase the number of users, such as a second round of early implementation grants or improving the quality of EWIS through comprehensive evaluation, cannot be financed through the state funds provided for EWIS.

The final main challenge of EWIS concerns data privacy. EWIS data are available at the individual student level, which increases the importance of complying with data privacy rules. DESE ensures that the servers on which data are stored are safe from external attacks. However, its decentralised set-up makes EWIS prone to internal violations of data privacy rules. DESE can only partly control who has access to the data because school districts decide on this issue. Therefore, compliance with data privacy rules is difficult for DESE to control. The risk that data privacy is (unintentionally) violated is increased by the fact that the experience of EWIS users with data information systems varies significantly. Interestingly, compliance with data privacy rules was not perceived as a big issue during interviews, perhaps because data privacy plays a less important role in the United States than in Europe (Heisenberg, 2005[26]).

Summary

To sum up, EWIS relates to two dimensions of governance: co-ordination across levels of government and building integrated information systems. EWIS was developed through the support of a federal grant (the SLDS grant programme). It is administered by DESE and implemented in the 525 public school districts and their schools in Massachusetts at the local level. EWIS is a non-coercive measure, which means that districts and schools are not required to use it. The advantage of this is that DESE and the districts act as partners to boost the educational performance of students. However, it also requires DESE to invest in the training of district administrators and educators so that they can effectively and efficiently use the data EWIS provides to improve the academic performance of Massachusetts' students. This includes various aspects, such as the implementation of the data cycle and compliance with data privacy rules.

EWIS is also an example of how to build integrated information systems. It provides a statistical model that calculates the individual risk level of students from 1st to 12th grade in meeting certain predefined academic milestones. It also offers insights into factors that could potentially explain why students fail to meet these milestones. EWIS relies on multiple quantitative data sources from existing state-wide collections. As a consequence, the administration of EWIS is comparatively easy as no new data need to be collected. The responsibilities between the various actors engaged in EWIS, most importantly DESE and districts and schools, are clearly defined. However, EWIS still struggles with the fact that the needs and demands of its users differ.

Policy recommendations

Based on the analysis of the strengths and weaknesses of Massachusetts' EWIS, this section presents a number of policy recommendations specific to Massachusetts' early warning system. In order for schools to use EWIS, the following three conditions must be met: 1) schools and districts must be aware of the advantages that the system can bring into their work; 2) schools and districts must have the knowledge to work with data; and 3) schools and districts must have financial and personnel resources to use EWIS. The following policy recommendations for the future of EWIS follow from this analysis. More general policy recommendations are developed and presented in the final chapter of this report.

Establish a monitoring system to constantly evaluate EWIS

EWIS is a complex system that entails several elements: a statistical model that calculates risk levels for every student in Massachusetts, a variety of indicators compiled from different state-wide data collections, and the early warning implementation cycle that makes suggestions on how to use the information provided by EWIS in schools. EWIS involves different levels of government. While the division of responsibilities between the federal Institute of Education Sciences that awarded the two SLDS grants to Massachusetts and the state's DESE is clear, this is not necessarily the case for interactions between DESE and districts and schools due to the decentralised nature of EWIS. EWIS is a non-coercive measure that supports districts and schools to identify and support academically weak students. But its use cannot be enforced by DESE.

Since its establishment in 2012, the statistical model on which EWIS is built has been evaluated and updated several times. However, no monitoring takes place on the usage of EWIS. DESE can keep track of the number of downloads of EWIS data from the data platform Edwin. However, EWIS is much more than a spreadsheet of data: the data need to be interpreted, and consequences for academically weak students need to be implemented and evaluated. Unfortunately, DESE currently does not know how many districts and schools implement EWIS and for which purpose the districts and schools use the data. To ensure that EWIS contributes to its original goal, namely supporting students at risk of not meeting age-related academic goals, Massachusetts should implement a monitoring system that regularly evaluates the use of EWIS by districts and schools, for example the number of schools that use the early warning implementation cycle every year.

Empower schools and districts to work with information management systems

Although there is no reliable information on the districts and schools that use EWIS, it can be assumed that the number is not very high. DESE has tried to raise awareness about the advantages of EWIS through various initiatives, including a website, newsletters and several events throughout the year for districts and schools. Through the early implementation grant, DESE supported ten districts and schools that were keen to implement the data cycle EWIS builds on. However, EWIS suffers from the fundamental problem that many potential users lack the knowledge and skills of how to appropriately use the available data. Data need to be interpreted and analysed, which means that users have to know how the data has been generated and processed. Users also need to possess at least some skills in working with information systems. However, data literacy is lacking in many of Massachusetts' districts and schools.

It is therefore not enough to provide specific information resources on EWIS. Rather, potential users of EWIS need to be enabled and empowered to use data information systems in an efficient and effective way. The collaboration between DESE and the Massachusetts Schools Counsellors Association is a first step towards reaching this goal. Together, they offer courses on how to use EWIS in schools and award professional development points that school counsellors in Massachusetts need for licensing. Similar initiatives could be established with other stakeholders such as the Massachusetts School Administrators' Association or teacher unions. Additionally, Massachusetts could make data literacy a mandatory aspect of the curricula of prospective teachers and student career counsellors. For this, more resources will be needed, for example for additional early implementation grants or the training of prospective users. Districts must also ensure that schools are adequately staffed with people who have the time and knowledge to use EWIS, for example guidance counsellors or school psychologists.

Improve the usability of EWIS

Even if users have the knowledge and skills to use data information systems, they might have problems using EWIS because its usability is limited. EWIS data come in a large spreadsheet with the columns showing the risk levels, the indicators on which the risk model builds and additional socio-economic variables; and the rows listing the values of each student in every variable. The dataset can be found at Edwin and downloaded as an Excel file for further analysis. However, for inexperienced users the huge dataset is not easy to handle. DESE and policy makers could consider how to improve usability, for instance by developing transparent and easy-to-use tools for the Edwin website that allow for simple analyses of the data.

The information resources that DESE provides to users are also not very targeted. The website contains a large number of links and a great deal of information. A cleaner design that guides users directly to the resources they need could help considerably. The newsletter could also be better used, for example, instead of announcing that a new round of EWIS data has been released, DESE could promote that it has released new data that help to improve students' academic performance. The new strategy of DESE to let users of EWIS report on their experiences is another way to improve its public relations activities.

References

American Institutes for Research (2020), *Massachusetts Early Warning Indicator System*, American Institutes for Research, Washington, DC, https://www.air.org/project/massachusetts-early-warning-indicator-system (accessed on 9 February 2020). [20]

Baker, C. (2019), *An Education Promise We Can Keep*, Boston Globe, Boston. [3]

Chester, M. (2014), *Building on 20 Years of Massachusetts Education Reform*, Massachusetts Department of Elementary and Secondary Education, Malden, MA. [13]

Commonwealth of Massachusetts (2020), *Massachusetts NAEP Results Lead Nation for 12th Year | Mass.gov*, https://www.mass.gov/news/massachusetts-naep-results-lead-nation-for-12th-year (accessed on 9 February 2020). [7]

Dee, T. and J. Levine (2004), "The fate of new funding: Evidence from Massachusetts' education finance reforms", *Educational Evaluation and Policy Analysis*, Vol. 26/3, pp. 199-215. [4]

DESE (2020), *District and School Accountability Systems*, Massachusetts Department of Elementary and Secondary Education, Malden, MA, http://www.doe.mass.edu/accountability/ (accessed on 9 February 2020). [16]

DESE (2020), *Early Warning Implementation Cycle*, Massachusetts Department of Elementary and Secondary Education, Malden, MA, http://www.doe.mass.edu/ccte/ccr/rlo/ewis/story_html5.html (accessed on 9 February 2020). [22]

DESE (2020), *Early Warning Indicator System (EWIS)*, Massachusetts Department of Elementary and Secondary Education, Malden, MA, http://www.doe.mass.edu/ccte/ccr/ewis/ (accessed on 9 February 2020). [24]

DESE (2019), *EWIS Distribution List*, Massachusetts Department of Elementary and Secondary Education, Malden, MA, https://us14.campaign-archive.com/home/?u=d8f37d1a90dacd97f207f0b4a&id=95b57784c7 (accessed on 9 February 2020). [25]

DESE (2015), *2015 Massachusetts SLDS Grant Application*, Massachusetts Department of Elementary and Secondary Education, Malden, MA. [23]

DESE (2011), *Description of M.G.L. Ch 69, Section 1J: An Act Relative to the Achievement Gap Process for "Underperforming" Schools*, Massachusetts Department of Elementary and Secondary Education, Malden, MA, http://www.doe.mass.edu/turnaround/level4/level-4-legislation.pdf (accessed on 21 February 2020). [17]

DESE and AIR (2014), *Early Warning Implementation Guide: Using the Massachusetts Early Warning Indicator System (EWIS) and Local Data to Identify, Diagnose, Support, and Monitor Students in Grades 1-12*, Massachusetts Department of Elementary and Secondary Education; American Institutes for Research, Malden, MA, http://www.doe.mass.eduhttp://www.earlywarningsystems.org. (accessed on 9 February 2020). [21]

Guryan, J. (2001), "Does money matter? Regression-discontinuity estimates from education finance reform in Massachusetts", *National Bureau of Economic Research* NBER Working Paper No. 8269, http://dx.doi.org/10.3386/w8269. [5]

Heisenberg, D. (2005), *Negotiating privacy : the European Union, the United States, and personal data protection*, Lynne Rienner Publishers, Boulder, Colorado. [26]

Lee, V. and K. Blagg (2018), *School District Funding in Massachusetts: Computing the Effects of Changes to the Chapter 70 Funding Formula*, Urban Institute, Washington DC. [12]

Massachusetts Education Equity Partnership (2018), *Number One for Some: Opportunity and Achievement in Massachusetts*, Massachusetts Education Equity Partnership, Massachusetts. [10]

McDermott, K. (2004), "Incentives, capacity, and implementation: Evidence from Massachusetts education reform", *Journal of Public Administration Research and Theory*, Vol. 16/1, pp. 45-65. [6]

McGuinn, P. (2005), "The national schoolmarm: No Child Left Behind and the new educational federalism", *Publius: The Journal of Federalism*, Vol. 35/1, pp. 41-68. [18]

National Center for Education Statistics (2018), *Digest of Education Statistics-Most Current Digest Tables*, U.S. Department of Education - National Center for Education Statistics, Washington, DC, https://nces.ed.gov/programs/digest/current_tables.asp (accessed on 9 February 2020). [9]

OECD (2016), *PISA 2015 Results (Volume I): Excellence and Equity in Education*, PISA, OECD Publishing, Paris, https://dx.doi.org/10.1787/9789264266490-en. [1]

Riley, J. (2019), *The Commissioner's report to the Board: Our way forward for Massachusetts K-12 public education*, Department of Elementary and Secondary Education, Malden. [15]

Rowe, C. (2016), *Massachusetts is a lot like us, so why are its schools so much better?*, The Seattle Times, Seattle. [2]

U.S. News (2020), *Best High Schools in the U.S.*, https://www.usnews.com/education/best-high-schools (accessed on 9 February 2020). [8]

US Census Bureau (2018), *2017 public elementary-secondary education finance data*, US Census Bureau, Suitland, MD. [11]

US Department of Education (2009), *Application for grants under the Statewide Longitudinal Data System Recovery Act grants: PR/award R384A100044*, US Census Bureau, Suitland, MD. [19]

Vazins, J. and M. Stout (2019), *After Years of Debate, Top Mass. Lawmakers Unveil School Funding Plan*, Boston Globe, Boston. [14]

Note

[1] The exception is the state of Hawaii, which only has one school district.

8 Conclusion and general policy recommendations

The concluding chapter of this study broadly summarises the main findings and takeaways from the set of case studies discussed in previous chapters, building on the analytical framework developed in the introductory chapter. It also develops a set of policy recommendations that aim at strengthening the governance of skills policy across OECD countries. More specifically, it recommends to establish co-ordinating committees with a meaningful mandate and clear internal governance structures, to promote the involvement of non-governmental stakeholders while managing the risk of undue influence of special interests, to support the establishment of information management systems that provide usable and relevant information to stakeholders, and to invest and commit diversified fiscal resources needed to strengthen skills policies.

Overview and introduction

This report has provided a comprehensive analysis of the governance of skills policies in selected OECD countries. The introductory chapter laid out a general theoretical framework, including a set of preliminary policy recommendations developed in the context of the *OECD Skills Strategy 2019* (OECD, 2019[1]). The purpose of this final concluding chapter is to reflect on the validity of these policy recommendations given the insights from the detailed case studies of Estonia, Germany, Korea, Norway, Portugal and the United States that make up the main part of this report. It brings together the most important insights from these case studies, and considers how they help fine tune and further develop the preliminary policy recommendations from the introductory chapter of this report. The concrete policy recommendations from each case study are used to develop broader and more general policy recommendations that hold across country cases, building on the positive experiences of these countries in pursuing new approaches to skills policy.

In order to facilitate the practical application of the learnings contained in this report, a self-assessment tool for policy makers and stakeholders is provided in Annex A. Based on a number of "yes/no" questions informed by the recommendations presented in this chapter, the tool enables all interested parties to explore the capacity of a particular country to strengthen the governance of its skills policy regime.

It is important to highlight that this report does not aim to highlight or promote a single "best practice" model of how the governance of skills policies should be organised, as each country case has idiosyncratic characteristics such as particular economic and welfare state institutions, particular traditions of engaging and interacting with non-governmental stakeholders, different approaches to the co-ordination of activities across levels of government and, more generally, different policy-making practices and cultures.

Given these idiosyncrasies, simply transferring "best practice" models from one country context to another is not always advisable or feasible. Still, despite these differences, in many cases mutual learning is possible, and good governance practices in one country can be transferred to others (sometimes in a modified form), especially when countries share similar traditions and institutions.

The introductory chapter identified four challenges that need to be met to strengthen the governance of skills systems, which have served as the conceptual backbone for the case studies:

- Promoting co-ordination, co-operation and collaboration across the whole of government.
- Engaging with stakeholders throughout the policy cycle.
- Building integrated information systems.
- Aligning and co-ordinating financing arrangements.

Instead of simply revisiting these challenges, which were already discussed extensively in the introductory chapter, this concluding chapter first reflects on how they played out in the concrete case studies, and which additional insights can be gained. Subsequently, it presents a set of general policy recommendations that directly refer to the four dimensions of governance. They should be regarded as refined, empirically enriched and contextualised further developments of the initial policy recommendations presented in the introductory chapter.

Challenges in the governance of skills systems: Insights from the case studies

Promoting co-ordination, co-operation and collaboration across the whole of government

The promotion of co-ordinated policies across levels of government, as well as across different ministries, is crucial to strengthen the governance of skills systems. Different government agencies, ministries and organisations need to send out a coherent message to stakeholders and the broader society to facilitate sustainable and reliable stakeholder engagement. Achieving such a whole-of-government approach may sound simple as, formally speaking, different levels of government and ministries within government are located in a pre-defined hierarchy of authority and accountability. In practice, however, as the case studies have shown, central governments often face numerous challenges in the implementation process.

A first example of these complexities is ultimately a consequence of the inherently limited extent to which the central and/or top levels of government can control the actions of sublevel agencies and ministries. Controlling every action of sub-agencies is simply not feasible and would lead to information and management overload at the higher levels of government. Although the establishment of data-based information management systems (see below) may mitigate this problem to some extent, there is still an inherent limitation regarding how much information can be processed at the top level. Furthermore, subnational governments, particularly in decentralised countries, have a significant degree of autonomy in setting their own priorities and agendas because their political legitimation is independent from the central government. Governmental agencies and ministries are also partly autonomous in setting their agendas as a consequence of particular kinds of expertise they have developed within the general government's division of labour.

Hence, from the perspective of the central government, the crucial question is how to achieve a coherent strategy that respects the partial autonomy of subnational governments and sublevel agencies, and mobilises and contributes to their particular expertise, as well as ensuring that policies are coherent and co-ordinated across the whole of government. As discussed in the introductory chapter, this challenge is particularly pronounced for skills policies compared to other policy areas, as education and training policy-making competences are typically in the hands of lower levels of government, particularly in decentralised, federalist countries. Furthermore, skills policy cuts across traditional domains of government ministries, most importantly ministries of education on the one hand and ministries of labour and social affairs on the other.

As the case studies have shown, there are no easy solutions. One strategy might be to strengthen hierarchical governance modes, i.e. by simply committing lower levels of government and ministries to comply with a national strategy set at the top level. The obvious downside of this strategy is that lower levels of government are likely to voice open opposition to such a hierarchical strategy if they are not involved in its design. They might even make use of their partial autonomy and undermine its implementation. To a significant extent, these actions of local governments are related to the fact that they usually have better access to local knowledge and regional needs than central governments. Eventually, a hierarchical strategy of policy co-ordination is likely to fail as government agencies and subnational governments "dig themselves in", and are more likely to engage in "turf wars" with their counterparts rather than implementing the overall strategy.

Against this background, the strategy that most governments in the cases studies choose is one that combines hierarchical modes of steering with engagement of a range of governmental stakeholders (see further below for a discussion of the involvement of non-governmental stakeholders). For example, the Norwegian Skills Policy Council includes representatives from different ministries and local governments (counties). The Alliance for Initial and Further Training in Germany (Chapter 3) brings together different federal ministries (education, labour) with representatives of the equivalent ministries from subnational governments (*Länder*). ANQEP, the Portuguese National Agency for Qualification and Vocational Education and Training (Chapter 6) pursues a similar approach.

Setting up new committees to co-ordinate and implement a whole-of-government-approach to skills policy is an obvious response to the abovementioned challenges. The risk of such a strategy, however, is that committee structures proliferate and become overly complex. In the worst case, this may lead either to gridlock or ineffective co-ordination, when newly established structures are regarded as "talking shops" rather than effective decision-making bodies. Hence, the challenge for pursuing a whole-of-government-approach through the establishment of new governance structures is to find the right balance between hierarchical steering, which is needed to some extent to further the development of a joint strategy and – if needed – to break potential gridlock in committees, and collaborative decision making.

A second challenge related to the implementation of a whole-of-government-approach in skills policy is to keep skills policy at the top of the government's agenda. Arguably, this is more of a challenge for the experts and stakeholders involved in skills policy rather than the top level of central government itself, since the latter is ultimately in charge of setting the national agenda. Broadly speaking, the case studies revealed a particular dynamic regarding the timing of skills policy becoming top of the government's agenda: when governments face a real or perceived crisis (e.g. low educational achievements among adults in Portugal or among the elderly in Korea, high levels of youth unemployment in Germany) they are more likely to prioritise skills policies, compared to when there are few problems.

The issue with this problem-driven approach to skills policy is that the associated policy responses are likely to be less comprehensive and more selective, responding to particular issues at a certain point in time rather than promoting a more encompassing skills policy agenda. The crisis-driven approach to skills policy is also likely to affect the degree of involvement and commitment of governmental and non-governmental stakeholders. During crisis periods, commitment is likely to be higher, related to and driven by the central government's efforts to put this issue at the top of the agenda. However, once the immediate crisis is over, joint commitment is likely to reduce.

The crisis-driven approach is likely to be counterproductive and ineffective in the long term. If governments prioritise skills policy at times of crises, when resources are scarce, policy responses are likely to focus only on the most pressing short-term problems, thus neglecting structural and long-term challenges to the skills system. The question for the top level of governments is how to avoid falling into the crisis-driven policy response mode, and instead to prioritise skills policy when times are good. When resources are less scarce, governments have more leeway to adopt and pursue long-term strategies that tackle structural issues in the skills system, such as lifelong learning or the integration of disadvantaged youth who face problems accessing the skills system even in good economic times.

Engaging with stakeholders throughout the policy cycle

Governments strive to reach out and involve non-governmental stakeholders throughout the policy cycle, i.e. from policy development to implementation. As discussed in greater detail in the introductory chapter of this report, the involvement of non-governmental stakeholders has many advantages: most importantly, it promotes a sense of ownership among stakeholders, which eases potential problems during the implementation stage of policies. Non-governmental stakeholders also bring particular kinds of expertise to the table, which would be otherwise difficult for governmental actors to access and use. This broadening of the information base of policy decisions is useful to design more effective and legitimate policies.

However, there are also several challenges to engaging with stakeholders. One of them, as mentioned in the introduction of this report, is to identify and map out the relevant stakeholders in a given skills system. The case studies have shown that policy makers generally have a comprehensive overview of the different actors involved in the skills system, in particular regarding organisational representatives of labour market interests, such as employers' associations, trade unions or other professional associations. What can be more of an issue is how to distinguish between relevant and less relevant actors, which is – to some extent – also a decision that depends on the prevailing political context.

There are certain trade-offs to be considered in this regard. A voluntaristic "laissez-faire" strategy would consist of government actors simply extending an invitation to all stakeholders that wish to contribute and get involved. This strategy has the advantage of being inclusive in the sense that government actors do not make preliminary judgements on which stakeholders should or should not get a voice at the table.

The case of lifelong learning in the Korean city of Suwon (Chapter 4) is a good example of such an approach. In this case, numerous local stakeholders and interested individuals are involved in the further development and design of lifelong learning programmes.

The other cases studied in this report represented a different approach more rooted in the "corporatist" tradition of interest mediation (Schmitter, 1979[2]; Streeck and Schmitter, 1985[3]). According to this model, stakeholder involvement is more selective in the sense that its goal is not to maximise the number of stakeholders involved in decision making, but rather to reach out and include those stakeholders that can legitimately speak and represent different functional interests in society. Thus, the various councils and committees analysed in the case studies of this report usually include representatives from peak organisations of business and labour, as well as some selected other societal stakeholders (e.g. independent experts or school representatives). However, in some cases such as the Norwegian Skills Policy Council (Chapter 5), policy makers involve strategically selected stakeholders that are traditionally not part of the corporatist system in order to tackle new questions.

The notion of corporatism entails the idea that all relevant sectors of society are represented and that decisions are made by consensus. However, the political context in which new committees and councils are established is also important. In the case of Germany, for instance, the first National Pact for Vocational Training and Qualification of Skilled Workers – a predecessor of the Alliance for Initial and Further Training, which is the focus of the German case study – only included representatives from government and business. Union leaders refrained from participating due to a previous government decision to not introduce a training levy. This example shows the challenge of how to convince non-governmental stakeholders to contribute to and participate in joint decision making independent of the prevailing political context.

A further issue relates to different traditions of interest mediation in different countries. The country sample for this study included countries with a long tradition of social partnership (i.e. co-operation and joint decision making between employers and unions in wage bargaining, training and other policies) such as Germany and Norway, and those with a less entrenched tradition of corporatist decision making such as Portugal and the United States. There is a broad challenge of how to ensure that decisions made at the peak level of national skills councils are transferred and translated to the membership base of intermediary associations to ensure that they are effectively implemented. However, this is more relevant in the case of countries without a strong tradition of social partnership.

The crucial factor is how the top level of associations communicate and interact with their members. If the top level of associations, which usually participates in the skills councils analysed in the country cases, is disconnected from its membership base, the political legitimacy of skills councils is put into question as it ultimately depends on their responsiveness to the needs of individuals and employers in the labour market. If stakeholders are not effective representatives of societal needs and demands, corporatist decision-making bodies can easily deteriorate into privileged points of access for special interest groups to capture public institutions. Vice versa, in order to be legitimate forums for decision making, actors that participate in corporatist skills councils need to be able and willing to effectively implement joint decisions (Streeck and Schmitter, 1985[3]).

The final challenge related to engaging stakeholders that emerged in a number of case studies is how to ensure that governance structures involving stakeholders are built on a permanent, sustainable basis. As laid out in the introduction of this report, involving stakeholders in decision making requires the building of mutual trust between governmental and non-governmental actors, as well as between stakeholders representing usually opposed societal interests (e.g. business and labour). Building this trust takes time.

The long-term sustainability of governance structures may be threatened for different reasons, for example because of the scarcity of fiscal resources (as in post-austerity Portugal) or because policy makers have decided to establish these structures for limited periods of time (as in Germany). Furthermore, the composition of governance bodies, as well as their mandate and mission, may change over time, which negatively affects the long-term foundation for meaningful stakeholder engagement.

Building integrated information systems

The goal of building integrated information systems in the area of skills policy holds multiple challenges, but there are also a number of opportunities for improving and strengthening governance structures. Once established, integrated information systems can provide policy makers with more detailed data on educational outcomes and trajectories, in particular the effects of policies and programmes. This kind of information is crucial to assess whether existing policies effectively address a particular problem, or whether they need to be amended. Information systems that are actively used and accessible to practitioners such as the Early Warning Indicator System (EWIS) in the US state of Massachusetts (Chapter 7) can further strengthen the governance of skills systems by providing actors with immediate feedback. However, in order to be a reliable source for decision making, data need to be of high quality and very accurate.

The establishment of information systems can also facilitate collaboration between stakeholders. In a world where information about the education system and the labour market involves a high degree of uncertainty, effective collaboration between policy makers and stakeholders may be blocked by competing problem definitions. Rather than devising solutions to these problems, stakeholders engage in conflicts about the nature and extent of the underlying problem. In the German case, for instance, employers and unions have long disagreed about the actual number of youth in need of a training place in the apprenticeship system (Busemeyer, 2009[4]). As this case study has shown, the German Alliance for Initial and Further Training, established in 2014, represented an important space and opportunity for actors to develop an agreement about the data sources to be used and how they should be interpreted. Similarly, in the Norwegian case, the Future Skills Needs Committee that advises the national Skills Policy Council is instrumental in identifying future labour market needs, and relies on scientific analyses of current trends and multiple sources of data in combination with expert assessments from stakeholders from the corporatist system. The committee thereby tries to reconcile scientific analysis with stakeholders' (and therefore practitioners') own assessments and know-how to facilitate compromise in the policy reform process and prevent reform deadlocks. Another example for such an institution is the System for the Anticipation of Labour Market Needs (SANQ) in Portugal.

Building up integrated information systems in the area of skills policy can be challenging from a purely logistical and administrative perspective compared to other policy areas. This is because skills policies span multiple sectors of governmental activity, most obviously education and labour market policy, but also issues related to financing, taxation and economic policy making. Furthermore, governance challenges emerge mostly at the intersections of these subsystems rather than within them, for example when individuals move from general to vocational or higher education, when individuals transition from the education system to the labour market, or when skills investment policies need to be matched with financing and taxation issues.

Assembling data on educational transitions requires the tracking of educational and labour market careers over long periods of time as individuals proceed through different sectors of the skills system. In terms of data collection, this requires co-ordination and collaboration between different sectors and statistical agencies, i.e. education statistics, labour market and unemployment statistics as well as social security administration and, potentially, tax authorities. Many countries already collect statistics on these subsectors, but they are not harmonised and synchronised to be able to provide a comprehensive assessment of the skills system as a whole. Furthermore, even when the system infrastructure is up and running, participating educational institutions, such as schools, need the required resources (i.e. in terms of expertise) and time to reliably enter the data into the system.

The Estonian Education Information System (EHIS) (Chapter 2) has to a large extent achieved and implemented this goal. In Estonia, each citizen has an individual identification number that is always included in statistical information. This allows the tracking of the development of individuals across time, which most other OECD countries do not have. This example shows that the establishment of comprehensive information management systems requires a certain permissive and supportive culture among both the stakeholders involved in the governance of the system as well as the population at large. In other countries such as Germany, this kind of culture is less prevalent.

Across countries, the establishment of integrated information systems has the potential to strengthen the governance structures of skills system, but it is not the only solution to persisting challenges. As became clear in the US case study, information systems must be designed in a way that maximises their usefulness and therefore the likelihood that they will be actually used by practitioners, stakeholders and policy makers. In this regard, involving stakeholders is, again, crucial. The challenge for governments is to strike the right balance between what is feasible from a technological point of view and what is sensible and useful from the point of view of the actors directly involved in the system.

Aligning and co-ordinating financing arrangements

Across the country cases in this report, there was a central question of how to ensure that the establishment of new governance structures is accompanied with the necessary fiscal resources. The socio-economic context in which skills policies unfold clearly plays an important role in this regard. For instance, financial constraints may more be binding in the case of Portugal, which is still dealing with the aftermath of the debt crisis, compared to Germany or Norway, which benefit from easier economic circumstances. Thus, within public budgets the task for central governments is to mobilise and safeguard fiscal resources to be invested in skills policies against competing interests that may dominate in the short term. As mentioned above, skills policy is more likely to rise to the top of the government's agenda in times of crisis, even though resources are scarce and need to be concentrated on fighting immediate short-term problems. Hence, the challenge for governments is to effectively commit to long-term strategies that ensure sufficient fiscal resources to address long-term and more structural problems in skills policies.

A second question is how to mobilise additional sources of funding besides public money. This is less of an issue in countries with a long tradition of employer involvement in vocational education and training such as Germany and, to some extent, Norway. It is more of a challenge in countries that lack such a tradition, for example Portugal. In these cases, the state has to step in to provide subsidies that encourage employers to participate in training. However, there are also complexities associated with this strategy, as employers might become accustomed to these subsidies and therefore even less willing to contribute in the future.

At the level of individual citizens and households, skills policies should set incentives for employees and citizens to participate in training, particularly lifelong learning. The Korean case study is a good example of how the provision of an encompassing lifelong learning system in combination with financial support for lowering the costs of education can lead to a high level of participation in lifelong learning activities by citizens. Aligning financial incentives across the potential sources of funding – public budgets, employers, individual citizens and other private sector stakeholders – should aim to lower barriers of access to training and channel resources to the sectors of the skills system where labour market needs are likely to be greatest. Establishing integrated information management systems will support this process.

Policy recommendations

The following section develops and presents a number of recommendations for policy makers related to the four main challenges in strengthening the governance of skills systems identified at the beginning of this chapter. Each subsection presents one main recommendation aligned with the four challenges, as well as a number of more detailed recommendations related to the main recommendation.

Establish co-ordinating committees with a meaningful mandate and clear internal governance structures

In order to promote co-ordination and collaboration across levels of government and to implement a whole-of-government-approach to skills policy, it is advisable to establish committees (skills councils or similar co-ordinating committees or cross-departmental institutions) that span different levels and departments of government, as well as involve non-governmental stakeholders. The potential downside of establishing this kind of inter-governmental committee is a proliferation of decision-making bodies that could, in the worst case, weaken rather than strengthen the governance of skills policy. To prevent this from happening, some key factors should be considered.

Define a clear mandate

Skills councils should have a clearly defined mandate. This may be either broad (e.g. devising a national skills strategy) or more limited (e.g. coping with a particular problem such as the integration of refugees into the training system), but it should be clearly defined to provide stakeholders with a clear orientation. Furthermore, the mandate should be defined so that potential overlap with existing institutions and decision-making structures is minimised. In cases where overlap is unavoidable, the mandate should clearly define the relationship and mutual accountability between newly established and existing institutions. These issues may appear self-evident; however, the case studies in this report include a number of examples where there are conflicts between old and new institutions about the proper division of labour.

Defining a clear mandate for newly established councils and committees may be more challenging in countries with a strong tradition of corporatism and social partnership as there are already a number of existing bodies with respective mandates. In these country contexts it is particularly important to highlight the added value of additional committees to the overall governance of the system so that stakeholders are effectively motivated to commit resources. In countries with a more pluralist and liberal tradition of interest mediation, competing mandates of existing committees are less of an issue; however, in comparison to corporatist countries, newly established committees might face more obstacles in filling their mandates with substance (see next point).

Define mandate with real substance

The mandate for skills councils and inter-departmental committees should have real substance, which means that they need a certain degree of autonomy and leeway in setting their agenda, as well as policy-making authority. On the part of the central government, delegating some decision-making responsibility to skills councils involves a certain willingness to trust the involved stakeholders, both governmental and non-governmental. If stakeholders realise that their participation in skills councils has an impact, they are more likely to commit and contribute constructively. In contrast, if setting up new skills councils does not provide added value as the established institutions are reluctant to concede any of their control, they are more likely to deteriorate into mere "talking shops" with little impact on strengthening the governance of skills systems.

Ensure strong internal governance structures

In order to work effectively, skills councils and similar committees need clear and strong internal governance structures. Decision-making processes within the skills council need to be agreed on, ideally with the goal of maximising the commitment and involvement of stakeholders. Important issues include who sets the agenda (the central government or the committee as joint decision-making body) and how decisions are made (by consensus or majority).

The case studies indicate that a division of labour between the top political level and a working level is effective. Less frequent meetings of the top level (e.g. heads of ministries and peak level associations) set the strategic priorities for the work of skills councils and provide an effective means to enhance the visibility of skills policy in the media. At the working level, experts and advisors should meet regularly to implement the top level's strategic priorities. These regular meetings also facilitate the development of a joint problem-solving perspective. Having two levels of decision making may also help to mitigate conflicts, with political level conflicts delegated to the working level for further discussion. Vice versa, if there is disagreement at the working level, political leaders ultimately decide on how these should be solved.

Promote the involvement and commitment of non-governmental stakeholders, while managing the risk of undue influence from special interests

The case studies have shown that skills councils and similar committees typically involve a number of non-governmental stakeholders, but there are significant differences regarding the relationship between governmental and non-governmental actors, with some councils more dominated by state actors, and others more equally balanced in the spirit of corporatist decision-making. A crucial insight from the case studies is that stakeholder involvement is essential to strengthen the governance of skills policies, for the reasons mentioned above. However, stakeholder involvement needs to be meaningful for stakeholders to commit and contribute, and governance structures need to be designed to prevent special interest groups from capturing public institutions and gaining privileged access. To achieve this delicate balance, the following recommendations are made.

Promote meaningful stakeholder involvement

Governance structures should be designed to allow stakeholders to participate and contribute in a meaningful way. The primary purpose of stakeholder engagement should not be to legitimise decisions and policies that were de facto decided beforehand. This kind of perfunctory involvement does not set strong incentives for stakeholders to commit themselves and provide resources. It also makes it difficult for intermediary associations such as employers' associations and unions to mobilise individual members (employers, workers) to participate in the production of collective goods, such as skills.

To achieve meaningful stakeholder involvement, stakeholders should be given the opportunity to have an input in the process of agenda-setting in joint skills councils. Although policy makers define the mandate (see previous point) and the overall strategic framework of skills councils and inter-departmental committees and agencies, these governance structures should be sufficiently open to allow for and even promote bottom-up initiatives, giving stakeholders the autonomy and ultimately the resources to try out innovative policy ideas. The German Alliance for Initial and Further Training, for instance, allows involved stakeholders to develop and experiment with practical solutions to concrete problems in labour market placement services.

Limit the overall number of stakeholders involved

Meaningful stakeholder involvement implies that not all potential stakeholders can and need to be involved. As discussed above, the identification of relevant (and less relevant) stakeholders is an important part of the process of designing effective governance structures. The exact number of stakeholders to be involved depends on the country context, i.e. the size and diversity of the labour market and the economy as a whole, political institutions (centralised vs. decentralised), and existing relationships between business and government. However, it is important to understand that maximising effective stakeholder involvement is not the same as maximising the number of stakeholders.

Simply maximising the number of stakeholders could, in the extreme, lead to a weakening of stakeholder engagement as there would be very little leeway for individual stakeholders to have a measurable impact on the policy process. In such an extremely pluralist setting, the influence of stakeholders would be commensurate to their economic power, leading to a de facto concentration of political influence in the hands of the economically powerful. To a certain extent it is legitimate that economic power correlates with political influence. However, as the economic theory of collective action argues (Olson, 1965[5]), special interest groups (i.e. small groups with clearly defined economic interests) have more economic and political clout in a pluralist setting than groups representing diffuse, collective interests. Hence, governance structures should be established to ensure that stakeholders representing economically less influential individuals and groups are also given a seat at the table. Typically, these stakeholders would be labour unions, but representatives from small and medium-sized enterprises, parental groups or other non-governmental civil society organisations could also be included.

Putting an upper limit on the number of stakeholders to be involved also ensures that joint skills councils can develop into forums where real deliberations take place, rather than a simply superficial exchange of positions. A smaller number of stakeholders also promotes the development of mutual trust between the involved actors, which is an important precondition for effective and legitimate decision making in these councils. Finally, it is important to note that limiting the number of stakeholders at the top also promotes organisational development at lower levels. For instance, if unions, employers or local governments are only allowed to send one or two delegates each to the top level of decision making in skills councils, they are pressed to organise, mobilise and interrogate their individual members and lower-level member associations. This is likely to be more effective in co-ordinating the different viewpoints and positions of individual members and lower-level associations in a certain part of the economy, rather than giving each actor a direct seat the table at the top level.

Prevent gridlock and manage the risk of undue influence by special interests

When delegating substantial decision-making authority to stakeholders, governments need to ensure that this does not lead either to gridlock – i.e. when stakeholders mutually block each other and therefore the whole process – or capture by special interests – i.e. when stakeholders "hijack" joint decision-making bodies to promote their own particularistic interests and positions rather than collective concerns. Both are prevented when and if the government effectively retains the ultimate political supremacy over the whole process. In a sense, governmental actors therefore need to remain "first among equals" among the stakeholders involved in joint decision-making bodies, walking a thin line between granting autonomy to non-governmental stakeholders on the one hand, while retaining the political capacity and authority to take over the whole process should problems develop on the other.

Retaining ultimate control over the process allows governments to cast a "shadow of hierarchy" (Scharpf, 1997[6]) on negotiation partners, which may be more or less constraining. For instance, the government could delegate certain tasks (defining a clear mandate, see above) such as reforming occupational standards in a particular economic sector to stakeholders, providing them with effective decision-making powers on the condition that they achieve a consensual solution. If, however, individual actors block joint decision making to maximise their own particularistic goals, the government should be able to step in to prevent the process from being unduly influenced by special interests.

Pursuing such a "neo-corporatist" approach requires a certain degree of self-restraint on the part of government, as well as a certain understanding on the part of stakeholders that participating in joint decision-making bodies is not akin to transactional bargaining, but ultimately aimed at developing instruments and strategies for collective problem solving.

Allow stakeholder engagement to develop over time

Building trust among non-governmental stakeholders, as well as between public and private actors, takes time. Countries with a long tradition of social partnership such as Germany and Norway find it easier to mobilise the commitment of private actors and stakeholders to strengthen the governance of skills policy. However, even in these countries, new committees such as the Skills Policy Council in Norway and the Alliance for Initial and Further Training in Germany need time to develop their organisational identity. In countries without a long tradition of social partnership, this process is likely to take even longer. However, as the case study of Portugal has shown, it is not impossible to establish working corporatist institutions if the government stays committed to providing the necessary resources over several years (see also below).

The success of new governance bodies such as skills councils are often the result of engaged stakeholders that are used to systems of social partnership and stakeholder involvement. Building on previous experience, they actively try to shape the council's and committee's mandate. This kind of stakeholder activism might be lacking (or less pronounced) in countries that do not have the same strong tradition of corporatism. Such problems are visible regarding expanding the Norwegian system of corporatism to regional skills policy (i.e. vertical co-operation), where most local authorities have to be actively convinced to put skills policy on their agenda. Ultimately, countries with a shorter history of social partner bargaining and corporatism have to be prepared to provide substantially more time and resources to allow for the success of similar policy measures.

Support the establishment of information management systems, but ensure that they provide usable and relevant information to stakeholders and policy makers

The case studies on Estonia and the United States focused explicitly on the role of comprehensive education information management systems in strengthening the governance of skills policy. However, information and data management systems also play a crucial role in establishing a common knowledge base among stakeholders in the other case studies. Overall, governments should invest more in building capacities in information and knowledge management, but they must pay particular attention to the usefulness of the collected data for all concerned. This can be ensured by involving stakeholders (i.e. the users of the data to be collected) in the design of the systems.

Involve stakeholders in the design of integrated information systems

The engagement of stakeholders throughout the whole policy cycle helps to mobilise and commit societal resources, which strengthens the overall governance of skills policy. In this spirit, stakeholders should also be involved in designing and updating integrated information systems that aim to inform governance decisions. Stakeholders, both governmental and non-governmental, can help to identify the different kinds and types of data needed from their perspective to better inform governance decisions.

Involving stakeholders in the design and upgrading of information systems increases the likelihood that these systems will be actively used by the stakeholders in the system. However, it is important to avoid a situation where actors (from students, parents and teachers to workers and firms) perceive information management systems as systems of control that outside actors might use to monitor and constrain their actions.

Use information management systems to inform rather than automate governance decisions

Integrated information systems have great potential to improve governance decisions by reducing uncertainties, for example regarding the effects of policy choices on labour market outcomes. However, opposition to the introduction of integrated information systems is more likely to occur when the public as well as the actors directly involved in the skills system perceive them (rightly or wrongly) as premeditating or even "automating" decisions that should be taken by stakeholders themselves.

Therefore, making use of information management systems to inform joint decisions by stakeholders is a more effective and legitimate strategy to strengthen the governance of skills systems than using these systems to circumvent collective decision making. This is largely because collective decision making usually involves a significant degree of redistributive bargaining that cannot be "outsourced" to automated systems. Furthermore, interactions between stakeholders can and do contribute to the development of a joint problem-solving perspective, at least in the long term. This requires continuous interaction between the actors involved, which again cannot be automated. However, using information management systems to establish and further develop a joint and shared knowledge base is useful in supporting interactions between stakeholders as it contributes to reducing contentious distributive conflicts.

Even when data are available, policy makers and end users on the ground need to be able to effectively use these data. The case studies of Estonia and of Massachusetts in the United States have shown that data are often available, but that their usage is much lower than hoped for by the government. Easy access to data, which might include visualisations, is important to get decision makers and practitioners to actually make use of the data. User-friendliness on both sides – for those who enter the data and for those who analyse and use the data – is critical for making the establishment of information management systems a sustainable success.

Make use of different kinds of data

Opposition to the broad introduction of information management systems may also occur because most of the data collected in these systems are quantitative in nature, i.e. based on the large-n measurements of, for example, competencies, educational attainment and labour market outcomes. Practitioners with considerable work experience in the field may regard quantitative data on student achievement as poor proxies for their own professional (qualitative) assessment of a certain student. Hence, information management systems that rely solely on quantitative sources of data may easily be perceived as undermining professional standards, as well as the status of professionals themselves.

Information management systems should be built so that they are able to collect and process data from different sources, including qualitative assessments from professionals. This is ultimately not a matter of technology, but a question of governance, i.e. which data sources will be used to achieve particular performance goals.

Invest and commit the diversified resources needed to strengthen skills policies

Strengthening the governance of skills policy takes time and commitment on the part of governments. The case studies have revealed that this can be challenging at times, depending on the country context. These challenges can be tackled when following a number of recommendations.

Provide adequate resources by setting long-term budgetary goals

As mentioned above, a significant challenge in the domain of skills policy and budgetary priorities is that governments are more likely to prioritise skills policies in times of economic crisis and fiscal austerity, i.e. when there is an acute need to counter short-term problems such as (youth) unemployment.

Even though skills policy can effectively contribute to solving these issues, its effectiveness is likely to be dampened in times of fiscal austerity as there are fewer resources available for skills investments. At the same time, the individuals and groups who benefit from skills policies during times of crisis are likely those who would fare better under better economic conditions anyway. The pro-cyclical approach to skills policy also implies that skills policy is less likely to be at the top of the government's agenda when economic conditions improve. This is unfortunate because structural long-term problems (e.g. bleak employment prospects for disadvantaged youth or a lack of further training opportunities for the long-term unemployed) are likely to persist. In principle, governments are more likely to be able to mobilise fiscal resources for skills policy in good economic times when the political incentives to do so are weaker.

Hence, the first recommendation to weaken the pro-cyclical approach to skills policy is to set budgetary priorities according to long-term strategic goals that are jointly decided in collective decision-making bodies such as the skills councils and inter-departmental committees mentioned above. These strategic goals should be focused on structural long-term challenges in the system and supported by the data collection in integrated information systems. Funding for skills policy could and should include a cyclical component to allow policy makers to respond to short-term crises, but the bulk of funding should be devoted to solving structural issues.

Furthermore, setting up new governance structures and committees needs to be supported by the provision of adequate fiscal resources. The establishment of comprehensive information management systems in particular is costly and requires significant and long-term commitment on the part of government. Similarly, setting up advisory boards such as skills councils should be accompanied with the provision of personnel and financial resources to allow these committees to work effectively.

Finally, the government can provide resources in terms of dedicated staff and personnel who are tasked with organising and facilitating collaboration and co-operation across levels of government, but also between the public and private sectors. For instance, in the Korean case study of lifelong learning in Suwon City, dedicated lifelong learning educators perform important bridging functions between the stakeholders involved by facilitating access, designing lifelong learning programmes and taking care of budgetary aspects.

Tap into multiple sources of funding while keeping equity concerns in mind

To some extent, the constraints of public financing can be mitigated if governments tap into multiple sources of funding. Skills investments create concrete benefits for different sectors and stakeholders, i.e. the public sector, businesses and individual households. Each of these sectors can therefore be expected to contribute to its financing. Countries differ widely regarding the exact division of labour between these different sources, as the case studies in this report have confirmed.

Broadly speaking, funding strategies that are concentrated on one funding source are more likely to lead to negative side effects than a more balanced approach. For instance, a strong reliance on public sources of funding might be suited to prevent inequalities in the distribution of funding, but this approach might lead to particularly binding funding constraints as public budgets are increasingly under pressure. Vice versa, focusing mostly on contributions from individuals and private householders (e.g. via tuition fees) could aggravate equity concerns related to accessing education and, in the worst case, overload private households with student debt. Finally, putting too much pressure on employers to commit and contribute resources to skills development could trigger counter-productive reactions as employers might pull out of collective training schemes.

Hence, a balanced approach to making use of multiple sources of funding seems advisable. This approach allows for individual contributions when and if skills investments lead to tangible and significant benefits (i.e. wage increases) at the individual level. When mobilising funding from private households, particular attention should be paid to equity concerns to prevent credit or other funding constraints. A balanced approach to funding also requires employers (businesses) to contribute to the financing of skills development, for example by paying for work-related on-the-job training, by investing in apprenticeship training, or by contributing to the financing of out-of-firm training workshops in particular regions or sectors of the economy. Furthermore, as the Korean case study has shown, costs for training facilities can be reduced if existing facilities (schools, libraries, cafés, etc.) are used as places of learning.

Finally, a balanced approach to funding skills development requires the public sector to commit adequate and commensurate resources (see previous point), but more importantly, to counteract potential inequalities in the distribution of funding across individuals, regions and sectors. This does not necessarily imply a full equalisation in the distribution of funding, which is neither achievable, nor – in the extreme – advisable. Rather, the contribution of the public sector to funding skills policy should strive to improve the most significant and obvious imbalances in the provision of fiscal resources, which are often related to and driven by differences in socio-economic background conditions.

A concrete example of how this could be achieved is to develop funding formulas for schools and other educational institutions that do not simply provide a fixed amount of funding per student, but that weight funding according to the socio-economic profile of the student body. Another example would be to provide subsidies for education, training and lifelong learning opportunities targeted at those most in need of such opportunities.

Most countries already have these kind of subsidy regimes, but they are mostly focused on initial education and training and neglect the growing sector of lifelong learning and further education. The Korean case study in this report provides a good example of how a balanced approach to funding lifelong learning that includes both individual and public contributions can help overcome barriers to accessing this type of learning. Regarding further training in the labour market, public funding could effectively compensate for inherent biases, such as employers focusing skills investments on highly-skilled workers, or resource-rich individuals being more likely to have the necessary resources to be able to invest further in their education.

References

Busemeyer, M. (2009), *Wandel trotz Reformstau: Die Politik der beruflichen Bildung seit 1970 (Change Despite a Backlog of Reforms: the Policy of Vocational Training Since 1970)*, Campus, Frankfurt a.M., New York. [4]

OECD (2019), *OECD Skills Strategy 2019: Skills to Shape a Better Future*, OECD Publishing, Paris, https://dx.doi.org/10.1787/9789264313835-en. [1]

Olson, M. (1965), *The Logic of Collective Action: Public Goods and the Theory of Groups*, Harvard University Press, Cambridge, MA. [5]

Scharpf, F. (1997), *Games Real Actors Play: Actor-centered Institutionalism in Policy Research*, Weastview, Boulder, CO. [6]

Schmitter, P. (1979), "Still the Century of Corporatism?", in Schmitter, P. and G. Lehmbruch (eds.), *Trends Toward Corporatist Intermediation*, Sage, Beverly Hills, London. [2]

Streeck, W. and P. Schmitter (1985), "Community, market, state – and associations? The prospective contribution of interest governance to social order", in Streeck, W. and P. Schmitter (eds.), *Private Interest Government: Beyond Market and State*, Sage, London, Beverly Hills, New Delhi. [3]

Annex A. Self-assessment tool

This annex contains a self-assessment tool that may be used by policy makers, stakeholders and other interested parties to provide an overall assessment regarding the potential of a particular country to strengthen the governance of its skills policy regime. The tool contains a number of "yes/no" questions which are framed in a manner that a positive (yes) response indicates agreement with the policy recommendations developed and presented in this report. The questions are grouped according to the four main challenges identified in the introductory chapter of this report and applied in the various case studies. This is followed by recommendations regarding these challenges developed in the concluding chapter of this report. The individual questions are further grouped under broader questions on a particular aspect and more detailed specifics of that aspect.

Some questions refer to the macro (systems) level in a particular country, whereas others are better answered at the level of a subsystem (e.g. a particular sector of the education system). This tool should be understood as an instrument supporting critical self-reflection: a higher number of positive (yes) responses signals a greater compliance with the recommendations presented in this report, and negative (no) responses may support a process of self-assessment and learning by means of critically engaging with the recommendations put forward.

Table A A.1. Self-assessment tool

Promoting co-ordination, co-operation and collaboration across the whole of government

Recommendations

Establish co-ordinating committees with a meaningful mandate and clear internal governance structures

- Define a clear mandate
- Define mandate with real substance
- Establish strong internal governance structures

Questions for self-assessment

			Yes	No
1.	**Is a comprehensive "map" of the skills system available?**			
	a	Is there centralised information on all available degrees and certificates, educational careers and progressions as well as entrance qualifications and requirements to different sectors of the skill system?	☐	☐
	b	Is the "map" open and publicly available? Is it accessible and transparent?	☐	☐
	c	Do actors involved in governance decisions know about it and is it used as a point of reference?	☐	☐
	d	Does the map include information on the legal and political competencies of various actors to influence governance decisions?	☐	☐
2.	**Do policy makers engage in "building the right institutions" for effective skill formation?**			
	a	Are skills policies at the top of the national policy agenda?	☐	☐
	b	Are efforts undertaken to co-ordinate the role of different bureaucratic agencies and political stakeholders across levels of government?	☐	☐
	c	Is there "horizontal" co-ordination between stakeholders at the same level of governance, i.e. co-ordination between different ministries and/or subnational governments via inter-ministerial committees, working groups or agencies?	☐	☐

	d	Is there co-ordination between policy makers, bureaucratic actors and civil society stakeholders?	☐	☐
	e	Is it clearly defined and widely known to the involved actors who sets the goals in policy-making and who decides about the distribution of decision-making power?	☐	☐
	f	Are procedures in place that support the management of conflicts between actors?	☐	☐
3.	**If new councils, committees or institutions are set up in order to strengthen collaboration across the whole of government:**		☐	☐
	a	Is the mandate of newly established institutions clearly defined?	☐	☐
	b	Are relationships between newly established and previously existing institutions well-defined, i.e. is there little/no overlap between new and existing mandates?	☐	☐
	c	Does the mandate have substance, i.e. does it involve the delegation of substantial decision-making authority for a clearly defined matter/issue?	☐	☐
	d	Are the internal governance structures of newly established bodies and institutions clearly defined?	☐	☐
4.	**Are policies in place that improve monitoring and evaluation processes?**			
	a	Is there a comprehensive statistical reporting system that documents progress in skills policies in the system as a whole rather than merely parts of it?	☐	☐
	b	Does the monitoring system include both quantitative data as well as qualitative assessments from stakeholders?	☐	☐
	c	Are monitoring and evaluation processes accepted as a legitimate and important source of information and supported by those concerned, i.e. stakeholders, parents, employers, teachers, students?	☐	☐
	d	Are monitoring and evaluation processes flexible enough to take into account new developments and to adjust reporting procedures accordingly?	☐	☐
	e	Are there sufficient (fiscal) resources available to collect the required information and data?	☐	☐
	f	Are the outcomes of monitoring and evaluation processes systematically connected to decision processes in the governance of skill formation?	☐	☐

Engaging stakeholders throughout the policy cycle

Recommendations

Promote the involvement and commitment of non-governmental stakeholders, while managing the risk of undue influence from special interests

- Provide opportunities for meaningful stakeholder involvement
- Limit overall numbers of stakeholders involved
- Prevent gridlock and manage the risk of undue influence by special interests
- Allow stakeholder engagement to develop over time

Questions for self-assessment

			Yes	No
1.	**Are all relevant stakeholders in the skills system well identified?**			
	a	Is knowledge available about how stakeholders interact with each other and how they are involved in the policy-making process?	☐	☐
	b	Are any groups or stakeholders systematically excluded?	☐	☐
2.	**Are stakeholders from business and civil society systematically involved in governance decisions?**			
	a	Are procedures in place that level the playing field between powerful or otherwise privileged stakeholders and less powerful ones?	☐	☐
	b	Are procedures in place that prevent powerful or otherwise privileged stakeholders ("special interests") from capturing the political decision-making process?	☐	☐
	c	Do state actors retain the ultimate responsibility for governance decisions in order to ensure than decision-making processes are both legitimate and effective?	☐	☐
	d	Are the current structures adequate to overcome deadlock or diverging interests and to reach compromise in policy-making?	☐	☐
3.	**Do governance structures of stakeholder involvement allow for meaningful engagement between the government and stakeholders?**			
	a	Are stakeholders given a real say in setting the government's agenda in skills policy?	☐	☐
	b	Does stakeholder involvement lead to tangible effects on the design and implementation of policies?	☐	☐
4.	**Do political and bureaucratic actors engaged in building trust with societal stakeholders?**			
	a	Are stakeholders involved in advisory boards and decision-making bodies on a permanent and sustainable basis?	☐	☐
	b	Are these boards and bodies systematically connected to the formal decision-making process?	☐	☐

			Yes	No
	c	Are stakeholder engagement processes based on a widely accepted, transparent and clearly communicated set of engagement rules?	☐	☐
	d	Do political and bureaucratic actors actively engage in managing conflict between societal stakeholders in order to ensure that collective concerns are met?	☐	☐

Building integrated information systems

Recommendations

Support the establishment of information management systems, but make sure that they provide usable and relevant information to stakeholders and policy makers

- Involve stakeholders in the design of integrated information systems
- Use information management systems to inform rather than automate governance decisions
- Make use of different kinds of data

Questions for self-assessment

			Yes	No
1.		**Are information management systems established that help decision-makers to mobilise the necessary quantitative and qualitative data to support decision-making processes?**		
	a	Do information management systems provide data on educational and employment careers according to the "life-course perspective", i.e. including data on transitions between different sectors of the skills system and the world of work?	☐	☐
	b	Are sufficient fiscal resources and expertise available in order to establish and maintain complex information systems?	☐	☐
	c	Are information management systems regularly used by agencies, stakeholders and other actors in the system to facilitate the exchange of information and to support the creation of a common knowledge base?	☐	☐
2.		**Are procedures in place that aim at improving data processing, information dissemination and tailoring?**		
	a	Are both societal stakeholders as well as experts involved in the updating and tailoring of instruments, indicators and measurements?	☐	☐
	b	Are efforts to collect data from different agencies co-ordinated across these agencies in order to ensure comparability and accessibility?	☐	☐
	c	Do information management systems include input from the different data sources – both quantitative and qualitative?	☐	☐
	d	Is the output from information management systems made available to researchers for further analyses?	☐	☐
	e	Is the output from research taken into account in governance decisions?	☐	☐
3.		**Are procedures in place that aim at continuously enhancing management and evaluation processes connected to information systems?**		
	a	Is the output from information management systems systematically connected to decision-making processes in the governance of skills systems?	☐	☐
	b	Are information management systems supported by a commensurate culture of evaluation among policy makers, stakeholders and citizens?	☐	☐
	c	Are efforts undertaken to make the data generated by information management systems as accessible to the public as possible?	☐	☐
	d	Do evaluation process clearly define and set performance goals that should be achieved and are indicators available that measure progress towards achieving these goals?	☐	☐

Aligning and co-ordinating financing arrangements

Recommendations

Invest and commit the diversified resources needed to strengthen skills policies

- Provide adequate resources by setting long-term budgetary goals
- Tap into multiple sources of funding while keeping equity concerns in mind

Questions for self-assessment

			Yes	No
1.		**Are efforts undertaken to mobilise funding for skills policies?**		
	a	Is the goal of investing in skills and skill formation at the top (or close to the top) of the government's fiscal policy agenda?	☐	☐
	b	Are the sources of financing sufficiently diversified, including both public and private sources, in order to ensure the sustainability of funding in the long term?	☐	☐

2.	**Is the budget planning regarding fiscal resources connected to long-term strategic goals and challenges rather than driven by immediate crisis needs?**			
	a	Do policy makers regularly assess the financial needs of actors in the skills system, independent of current business cycles?	☐	☐
	b	Is the financing of skill formation connected to medium- and long-term goals in the financial planning of governments?	☐	☐
	c	Are the priorities in the distribution of fiscal resources co-ordinated with the input from information management and evaluation processes?	☐	☐
3.	**Do fiscal resources match the current needs in terms of financing in skills systems?**			
	a	Are financial needs of different actors and institutions properly identified and legitimised?	☐	☐
	b	Are fiscal incentives of actors in the system aligned in order to achieve the maximum yield in terms of resources?	☐	☐
	c	Do actors at different levels of government in charge of governance decisions in skills policies have the required competencies to make decisions about the distribution of fiscal resources?	☐	☐
	d	Are accountability mechanisms in place that ensure that actors are held responsible for aligning needs to resources in the long term?	☐	☐
4.	**Are equity concerns taken into account in decisions about the distribution of funding?**			
	a	Does socio-economic need (and background) play a role in decisions about the distribution of public funding?	☐	☐
	b	If funding comes from private sources, do funding schemes pay attention to individual differences in ability to pay?	☐	☐
		Total	☐	

www.ingramcontent.com/pod-product-compliance
Ingram Content Group UK Ltd.
Pitfield, Milton Keynes, MK11 3LW, UK
UKHW051502290926
15471UKWH00008B/1369